教师资格考试学习用书

英语学科知识与教学能力
(高中)

主　编　谢华之（特级教师）
副主编　杨　帆　龙忠喜

长江出版传媒
湖北人民出版社

鄂新登字 01 号
图书在版编目(CIP)数据

英语学科知识与教学能力(高中)/丛书主编雷万鹏；
本册主编谢华之.
武汉：湖北人民出版社,2013.7
(教师资格考试学习用书)
ISBN 978-7-216-07643-2

Ⅰ.英…
Ⅱ.①雷…②谢…
Ⅲ.英语课—教学法—高中
    中学教师—资格考试—自学参考资料
Ⅳ.G633.412

中国版本图书馆 CIP 数据核字(2013)第 076220 号

英语学科知识与教学能力 （高中）	丛书主编　雷万鹏 本册主编　谢华之
出版发行：长江出版传媒 　　　　　湖北人民出版社	地址：武汉市雄楚大道 268 号 邮编：430070
印刷：京山德兴印刷有限公司	经销：湖北省新华书店
开本：787 毫米×1092 毫米 1/16	印张：15
版次：2013 年 7 月第 1 版	印次：2013 年 7 月第 1 次印刷
字数：289 千字	定价：35.00 元
书号：ISBN 978-7-216-07643-2	

本社网址：http://www.hbpp.com.cn

编者的话

"教育大计,教师为本"。在我国教育从外延式扩张向内涵式发展转型的时代背景下,优良的师资队伍对教育发展具有至关重要的意义。

开展中小学和幼儿园教师资格考试改革试点,完善并严格实施教师职业准入制度,严把教师入口关,对于提升教师队伍整体素质,提高教师社会地位,吸引优秀人才从教,推动教育改革发展,具有重要意义。创新教师资格考试制度,是贯彻落实《国家中长期教育改革和发展规划纲要(2010—2020年)》的重要举措,是建设高素质专业化教师队伍的制度保障,是推进教育现代化的重要抓手。为此,教育部自2011年起,开始在湖北、浙江两省先期试行教师资格考试和定期注册制度,并于2012年将试点增加至河北、上海、浙江、湖北、广西、海南等省市区。改革后各省市区原有的教师资格考试纳入全国统一的考核系统中,由此逐步建立"国标、省考、县聘、校用"的教师准入和管理制度。

为帮助广大教师适应新形势,形成符合教师职业从业资格要求的知识、能力与素质,华中师范大学教育学院专家牵头,聘请有深厚理论素养和丰富实践经验的专家学者和一线骨干教师,依据教育部最新出台的考试大纲与考试标准,结合湖北、浙江等改革试点地区教师资格考试的经验,针对我国教师队伍建设的专业要求和广大参加考试人员的实际需要,策划编写了这套《教师资格考试学习用书》。

这套教材具体包括《教师资格考试(面试)》、《综合素质(幼儿园)》、《综合素质(小学)》、《综合素质(中学)》、《保教知识与能力》、《教育教学知识与能力(小学)》、《教育教学知识与能力(中学)》,初中及高中语文、数学、英语、物理、化学、生物、历史、地理、音乐、美术、思想品德(思想政治)、体育与健康、信息技术等学科知识与教学能力。该教材紧扣最新的教师资格考试大纲,对教师资格考试必备的理论知识进行系统编写。内容完备系统,涵盖所有知识点,具有权威性、科学性,能方便考生迅速理清头绪,准确把握考试脉络,有针对性地进行复习。同时在编写过程中,遵循相关认知特点,从最基本、最重要的考点入手,深入浅出地进行讲解,有利于加深考生的印象和理解,便于考生迅速掌握核心知识点。

这套丛书的编写主要有以下几个特点：

第一，编写团队专业化。 丛书涉及与教育相关的广阔领域，仅凭个人力量难以保证其编写质量。因此，丛书编写组精选了多位在各个领域有专门研究的教授和副教授，中学学科一线骨干教师组成结构合理、力量强大的编写团队。大家分工协作，共同完成本套丛书的编写工作。

第二，主要内容模块化。 丛书内容涉及面广，唯有把握其广度和深度，才能方便广大考生的备考和实际教育能力的提高。丛书编写组在反复研读大纲精神和讨论考试标准的基础上，将编写内容确定为若干模块。同时，在每一模块中精选内容，力图做到结构清晰、内容全面，减轻考生负担。

第三，基本训练实战化。 本套丛书每章后均配有适量的习题，习题的设计覆盖本章的重要知识点，书后亦附有一至多套仿真题。各习题和仿真题在题型上均与考试一致，且配有详细参考答案；题目考点紧扣大纲，难度适中，适合于考生巩固所学和进行热身训练，快速提高应试能力。

由于时间和知识水平所限，本书在编写过程中难免有不足之处，恳请社会各界人士和广大考生批评指正，以便我们继续努力，进一步修订。

编　者

前 言

2011年教师资格考试大纲发布后,经过第一次考试,广大教师考生急需相关教材和辅导用书。为了满足这种需求,湖北省教师培训中心根据教育部2011年决定,即把湖北、浙江两省作为开展教师资格考试改革的试点,经过试点改革取得经验后再全面推开改革的精神,组织编写了一套全新的《教师资格考试教辅用书》。本书无先例参照,对编者是极大挑战。因此,我们首先抱着尊重读者、科学务实的态度认真对待这项编写任务。

《英语学科知识与教学能力(高中)》是专为报考高中英语教师资格的考生编写的一本备考辅导资料,涵盖了教师资格考试大纲规定必考的五项基本内容:"英语学科知识与能力、英语学科教学知识与能力、英语学科教学设计能力、英语学科教学实施能力、英语学科教学评价知识与能力。"我们把这五项基本内容分列五章编写,每章设四个栏目:"大纲描述、考点解读、练习题型、参考答案。"其中"考点解读"针对必考的五项基本内容中的关键、难点、重点进行了条理性很强的答案式解析,避免了考生在繁复的论述中寻觅要点之苦。"练习题型"密切关注大纲要求、命题原则和题型特点,在有限的篇幅里尽量覆盖极具命题价值的考点,着重呈现前沿和实战内容,旨在引导考生在提高分析问题和解决问题的能力的同时优化应试技巧。在"参考答案"中,编者根据教师知识和经验以及备考经验,展现了科学合理的解题思路,以供考生用来验证备考效果;同时,练习题与参考答案相互呼应,给考生提供了大量的英语教学法、英语课程标准和英美概况等方面的知识。在第三章英语学科教学设计能力中,我们选用了三位优秀青年教师的教学设计为示例;在第四章英语学科教学实施能力中,我们选用了2011年湖北省高中英语优质课比赛一等奖第一名的孟红生老师的课堂实录为示例,为全书增加了鲜活的色彩,更重要的是让考生真实地感受到高中英语教学设计和教学实施的现实版。

严格说来,《英语学科知识与教学能力(高级中学)》仅仅是一本备考辅导资料而已,它是集名家之经典和编者之体验,还有些许原创,并精心编缀的读物,具有如下特点:

1. 针对性:

本书针对教师资格考试大纲规定的考试目标和考试模块内容与要求进行编写,能够满足考试准备的需求。

2. 实用性:

本书注重理论与实践相结合,理论部分着重解读考试目标中的重难点,条分缕析,便于记忆;实践部分按照题型示例设计了大量练习题,利于考生把考试目标要求的知识与能力落到实处,转化为应试竞争力,提高成功率。

在编写过程中,我们参阅了大量文献,以验证我们的见解,优化本书对教师资格考试大纲的解读。在此,我们对被参阅文献的作者表示敬佩和谢意。

本书由谢华之(湖北省英语特级教师、武汉市十大名师、武汉二中英语高级教师),杨帆(武汉市英语学科带头人、武汉二十六中英语高级教师、教研组长),龙忠喜(武汉市硚口区英语学科带头人、武汉十一中英语高级教师)合作编撰而成。谢华之编写"考点解读";龙忠喜编写"语言知识与能力"中的"单项选择题";杨帆编写"语言教学知识"中的"单项选择题、简答题","教学设计"中的"教学设计题"和"教学实施与评价"中的"教学情境分析题"。由于时间仓促,且囿于水平,这本辅导资料如有不妥之处,欢迎指正。

编 者

目录 Contents
英语学科知识与教学能力（高中）

模块一　英语学科知识与能力　/1
　　第一章　大纲描述　/1
　　第二章　考点解读　/1
　　第三章　题型训练　/7

模块二　英语学科教学知识与能力　/49
　　第一章　大纲描述　/49
　　第二章　考点解读　/49
　　第三章　题型训练　/61

模块三　英语学科教学设计能力　/92
　　第一章　大纲描述　/92
　　第二章　考点解读　/92
　　第三章　教案示例　/95
　　第四章　题型训练　/104

模块四　英语学科教学实施能力　/119
　　第一章　大纲描述　/119
　　第二章　考点解读　/119
　　第三章　课堂教学实录示例　/125
　　第四章　题型训练　/130

模块五　英语学科教学评价知识与能力　/133
　　第一章　大纲描述　/133
　　第二章　考点解读　/133

仿真试题一 /137

仿真试题二 /146

参考答案 /155

参考文献 /230

模块一　英语学科知识与能力

第一章　大纲描述

考试目标

具有扎实的英语语言基础知识和语言能力；具备从事高中英语教学所需要的英语语言能力；能理解有关英语国家的语言、历史和文化等相关知识。

考试要求

1. 掌握英语语言的基础知识，了解语言学研究中与语言教学相关的基本概念和知识，并能在课堂教学中加以运用。

2. 具有良好的英语语言运用能力，包括用英语进行书面表达、获取教学资源和信息、表达思想情感和与学生良好沟通的能力；能够筛选并改编适合高中学生英语水平的语言材料。

3. 能在语篇中理解英语国家的语言、历史和文学等相关的社会文化知识。

第二章　考点解读

第一节　基本概念和知识

一、语言的三要素

语言的三要素是语音、词汇、语法。语音是语言的物质外壳；词汇是语言的建筑材料，是词语的总和；语法是语言的建筑蓝图，是语言规则的总和；词汇和语法都是音义结合的。

二、语言与言语的区别

索绪尔在《普通语言学教程》中提出了语言与言语的区别：语言是人类最重要的交际工具，是音义结合的词汇和语法的体系。言语就是在特定的环境中为完成特定的交际任务对语言的使用。语言与言语的区别是语言学最重要的理论问题，它对外语教学法的影响是深远的，成为外语教学法的关键。

三、语言和言语的关系

1. 语言体系是言语的基础，言语行为要选择语言中的词汇和语法手段，组成话语。

2. 人的言语行为有两个方面：一方面是口头交际——说和听；另一方面是书面交际——写和读。人们在言语行为中创造话语，理解话语。言语行为产生可接受、可理解的话语；说、写是表达过程，听、读是理解过程。

3. 言语行为中产生的，存在于话语中的新的语言现象补充到语言体系中，使语言不断丰富和发展。

4. 在语言体系中，词汇和语法处于经常的相互作用之中。

四、语言学研究中与语言教学相关的基本概念和知识

（一）理想的外语教学

学校的语言教学可以让学生自觉地掌握词汇和语法，然后理解话语，让学生通过语言学习言语。但是，如果离开言语就不能真正领会语言。所以，语言教学要让词汇和语法在话语中反复出现，让学生在话语中体会语言现象的细微意义，于是，又应通过言语学习语言。在外语教学中，学生一方面学习外语体系，一方面掌握外语言语。理想的外语教学不单是让学生学习语言体系的知识，也不单是进行言语训练，而是要培养学生熟练掌握语言工具的能力，直接理解话语，创造话语的交际能力，以及分析各种语言现象的能力。在外语教学过程中，掌握语言体系和学会使用外语两者要同时进行、相互促进，而在大多数情况下，语言体系应服从于使用语言，语言服从于言语。

（二）有效的外语学习

1. 学习外语要在言语活动中自觉地逐步掌握语言体系，进而自觉地不断提高言语能力。换言之，言语学习应是学习活动的主要方面，但也不应贬低语言体系的学习。

2. 在听、说、读、写过程中自觉地逐步掌握语音、语义、词汇和语法。

五、外语能力

外语能力分为语言能力和言语能力两类，它们之间有区别，又有联系，培养的方法有所不同。

（一）外语语言能力分为语音能力、词汇能力和语法能力

1. 语音能力

主要包括能区分外语音位的能力；准确发外语语音的能力；区分和再现外语语调的能力；地道的外语口语能力。

2. 如何培养语音能力

(1)用语言的方法：分析语音的物理属性，模仿发音部位和方法，进行语音对比等。

（2）用言语的方法：大量地听地道的外语话语，在口语实践中发展语音能力；从模仿入手学好语音语调，模仿英音或美音均可，但二者必择其一，不要夹杂；熟练掌握一种语音后，可再熟悉其他地区的英语发音，以备教学之需；模仿时，先有意识地标出重音和调型，这样做就重点突出，反复模仿，反复找差距，如此精益求精，必然能学到地道的语音语调。

3．词汇能力

主要包括会读会拼写词汇的能力；辨别词形理解词义的能力；区别同义词、同形词、同音词的能力；辨识反义词的能力；在上下文中确定多义词词义的能力；辨别词和俗语的能力；辨别词的语法属性，正确运用词语搭配的能力。

4．如何发展词汇能力

（1）分清消极词汇和积极词汇。

学习消极词汇或接受性词汇（receptive vocabulary），只需要看或听到某词时，能说出词义；而学习积极词汇或表达性词汇（productive vocabulary），则需要达到"会读、会拼写、能说出词义；能知道该词的语法属性；能正确运用该词的搭配；能指出该词所表达的感情色彩"等要求。现行的高中英语课程标准所规定的词汇基本上都应该作为积极词汇来掌握，但事实上其中有相当一部分仍旧是消极词汇。一般说来，我们掌握的消极词汇数量远远大于已掌握的积极词汇数量。因此，我们就要把有限的时间用在学习最有用的词汇上。

（2）利用阅读，通过上下文猜词义和查英英词典、英汉双解词典发展词汇能力。

（3）利用构词法的规则由此及彼、举一反三地识记大量的同根词。

（4）在"四大原则"指导下扩大词汇量。

①趣味性原则：阅读材料应选用时代性、趣味性强的文本；②词性原则：以动词、名词、修饰词为先后次序的原则；③高频词原则：掌握那些使用广泛、复现率高的词汇，即高频词；④转化原则：化消极词汇为积极词汇的原则。

（5）利用眼、耳、口、手、脑同时体验英语词汇，按中心词建立词汇串（semantic map）以发展词汇能力。

5．高中英语教师必备的英语词汇

（1）教育部制定的《高中英语新课程标准》中的词汇表。

（2）教育部制定的研究生入学考试英语词汇表。

6．语法能力

主要包括分析词语的词汇特点的能力；分辨词类和句子成分的能力；用词造句的能力；辨认词语搭配关系的能力。

7．如何发展语法能力

（1）系统地读一本英语语法书，并做该语法书的配套练习，以达到熟悉英语语法规则的目的。

（2）除依靠英语语法分析外，更要在言语中把英语语法规则具体化，以达到学英语语法是为了学好英语，学语法是为了运用的目的。

（3）语言是约定俗成的，除了一般语法规则外，还需熟记善用惯用法。

（二）外语言语能力

它是同言语行为和话语有关的能力，如听、说、读、写、译的能力以及修辞能力。修辞能力主要是辨认语体、再现语体和观察语体特征的能力。而语体首先是社会交际需要的结果，由于交际范围和领域不同，就形成了不同的语体，如谈话语体、书面语体，又如科学语体、艺术语体、政论语体和事务语体；同时，语体又是使用全民语言材料特点的综合，离开了实际的语言材料，语体就会变得不可捉摸。语体是客观存在的，任何使用语言的人都受到它的制约。在外语教学中，语体理论可以指导编选教材和改进教学方法，更有效地提高学生的言语能力。

（三）外语思维和外语语感

为了熟练地使用外语，更好地完成交际任务，还需培养两种要求更高的外语言语能力：外语思维能力和外语语感。

1. 外语思维

外语思维即掌握外语的程度与母语一样，可随时随地、灵活地运用流利而又纯正的外语表达所思所想，形成本能的、条件反射式的思维方式。同时这种外语表达，不仅要符合外语的语言习惯，还需要尽量靠近以外语为母语的人的逻辑思维方式和一些约定俗成、文化习惯等。

2. 外语语感

外语语感指直觉感知外语的能力。具有外语语感的人往往不假思索，立即领悟外语话语的意义。语言体系的知识可帮助语感形成，但言语实践是培养语感的决定因素。

学生有了外语思维能力和外语语感，就能有效地使用外语进行交际。这样，听、说、读、写就不是建筑在对语言体系分析和汉语翻译的基础上，而是建筑在外语语感和外语思维的基础上。（王德春，1983）

第二节 英语语言运用能力

一、英语语言运用能力的多元性

英语语言运用能力包含知识（knowledge）、技能（skills）和能力（ability & capacity）等多种不同性质成分的能力（competence）。

（一）语言知识（knowledge）在语言运用中的作用

仅仅掌握语言知识对培养英语语言的运用能力是没有用的，但是，英语语言运用能力的培养必须掌握语言知识，同时，英语语言运用能力里也包含语言知识的成分。

(二)技能(skills)及其在英语语言运用中的作用

英语语言运用上的技能,简单的有辨音发音、辨识和书写字母、拼音拼词等;复杂一点的包括交际中由于纯熟程度达到自动化,甚至不用动脑筋的连续的语言解码和编码。随着纯熟程度的提高,人们在听说读写中英语自动化解码和编码的单元越来越长,大脑能越来越多地解放出来做高层次的英语自动化解码和编码工作。

(三)能力(capacity)及其在英语语言运用中的作用

能力不同于技能,它是动脑的能力,包括推理、判断、创造、想象、审美、欣赏、同情、憎恶等等的能力。它可分为认知能力(cognitive capacity)和感受能力(affective capacity),分属于思想和情感两个范畴。语言运用依赖于人的认知和感受能力。

二、英语语言运用能力的多层次性

英语语言运用能力是在多层次上同时运用的能力。运用语言必须遵守共同的规则,否则互相难于理解和交际。光靠语言系统的规则(即语音词汇、语法规则)是不能达到顺利交际的目的。语言运用必须在多层次上同时运作,同时要在这些层次上遵守相应的规则。

第一层次是语言形式系统,遵守语音、词汇、语法规则,即广义的语法规则;
第二层次是语法层次,遵守上下文或语篇的规则;
第三层次是情景层次,遵守时、地、人及社会文化背景等的交际情景的规则。

真正的语言运用能力是在语法、语篇和情景三个层次上协调一致,恰到好处的运作能力。英语语言运用能力不是各个成分、各个层次的混合,而是互相作用化合的一个整体。

第三节 英语国家语言、历史和文学等相关的社会文化知识

一、英语国家语言概况

(一)英语发展史

英语的起源可以追溯到公元前500年左右,在大不列颠岛(Great Britain)上史料记载的最早的语言是公元前500年左右的凯尔特语(Celtic)。公元前55年,罗马人入侵大不列颠,并一直占领了大约500多年,此时,拉丁语进入了该地区,并成为官方语言,凯尔特语的地位下降。约公元449年,居住于丹麦与德国北部的3个日耳曼人部族趁罗马帝国衰落时入侵大不列颠岛。他们分别是盎格鲁人(Angles,入侵日德兰半岛中部)、撒克逊人(Saxons,入侵日德兰半岛南部)和朱特人(Jutes,入侵日德兰半岛北部)。在语言上,他们用自己的语言取代了当时该地所使用的凯尔特语。这三个日耳曼部族方言随着社会发展,逐渐融合为一种新的语言,即盎格鲁—撒克逊语(Anglo-Saxon),这就形

成了后来英语的基础。到公元700年，人们把大不列颠岛上三部族混合形成的语言称为Englisc。到公元1000年，岛上整个国家被称作Englaland。这两个词后来就演变成English(英语)和England(英格兰或英国)，这就是English和England两个词的由来。

(二)把英语作为第一或第二语言的国家

目前除了英国以外，把英语作为第一语言(即母语，Native language)的国家有爱尔兰(Ireland)、美国(America)、澳大利亚(Australia)、新西兰(New Zealand)、圭亚那(Guyana)、巴哈马(The Bahamas)、巴巴多斯(Barbados)、百慕大(Bermuda)、牙买加(Jamaica)、圣克里斯多福及尼维斯(Saint Christopher and Nevis)、特立尼达和多巴哥(Trinidad and Tobago)。在加拿大(Canada)大部分人说英语。把英语作为官方语言的国家有尼日利亚、加纳、肯尼亚、乌干达、坦桑尼亚、赞比亚、津巴布韦、南非、新加坡、印度、菲律宾等国；作为第二语言的有丹麦、芬兰、瑞典、挪威、冰岛等国。英语逐渐发展成为一种世界语言，在外交上的地位也取代了法语，成为今天世界政治、经济、科技、文化交流中最重要的语言。(西北大学，2008)

二、英语国家的历史概况与英语教学

把英语国家的历史概况，尤其是英国、美国、澳大利亚、新西兰的重要历史人物、重大历史事件和重要历史文件等基本史实作为英语教学必备的文化背景知识。

三、英语国家的文学概况与英语教学

把英语国家的文学概况，尤其是英国和美国的文学名家、文学名著、英语诗歌、戏剧以及文学简史作为英语教学必备的文化背景知识。

四、社会文化背景知识在英语教学中的作用

(一)任何语言都根植于特定的文化背景之中，反映特定的文化内容

实际上，英语学习中，语言的学习与运用就是一种文化与另一种文化的交流与传播。静止孤立地学习某种语言，只能得到语言知识的皮毛，不可能获得语言能力，更不可能得体地运用该语言。所以，要学好和使用好英语，就要了解产生、使用这种语言的特定的社会文化背景和文化习俗，才能在实际应用中表达正确、符合习惯。否则，对英语文化背景知识缺乏了解，必然导致交际障碍、冲突和误解，即"语用失误"(Pragmatic Failure)。

(二)语言意义系统受不同的自然环境和文化传统的影响

在阅读材料中，有很多词其表层含义相近，但其派生意义、联想意义却迥然不同，这就是文化背景对词语意义的影响，它给词语涂上了一层社会文化色彩，使词语具有字面和引申双重意义。字面意义可借助词典得以知晓，而引申意义只有依据文化背景知识才能被准确理解。

第三章 题型训练

一、单项选择题(一)

1. The official confirmed that they were charged with illegally _____ public funds for private use.

    A. diverting　　　　B. distorting　　　　C. disrupting　　　　D. dissipating

2. It was beyond her expectation that her first album burned up the charts and her fame began to _____ quickly.

    A. accumulate　　　B. accelerate　　　　C. correlate　　　　D. escalate

3. Whoever doesn't pay the registration fee by the end of this month will be _____ to have withdrawn from the project.

    A. contemplated　　B. deemed　　　　　C. segregated　　　　D. anticipated

4. To our astonishment, she refuses to _____ to society's traditional image of a mother.

    A. adhere　　　　　B. intervene　　　　C. conform　　　　　D. contribute

5. In the book review the author _____ the economy's success to the current policy.

    A. devotes　　　　　B. grants　　　　　　C. ascribes　　　　　D. imparts

6. She again rejected the charges when her trial resumed on Tuesday, calling it an "_____ show".

    A. abrupt　　　　　B. absurd　　　　　　C. acute　　　　　　D. adjacent

7. Most of them are small businessmen, hard-working and honest, _____ with no special privileges from people on high.

    A. ensured　　　　　B. attributed　　　　C. clarified　　　　　D. endowed

8. When punishing an older child, give him some space for self-introspection as a way of learning to _____ his feelings and recognize his mistakes.

    A. rationalize　　　B. justify　　　　　　C. authorize　　　　D. identify

9. Through doing this task, the teacher will be able to _____ the extent to which the child understands what he is reading.

    A. alternate　　　　B. assert　　　　　　C. ascertain　　　　D. assault

10. The lawyers _____ primarily to small enterprises and individuals, the same group targeted by online legal websites.

    A. admit　　　　　B. cater　　　　　　　C. resort　　　　　　D. cling

11. He felt that his role in the company was becoming more _____, which upset him increasingly.

    A. ingenious   B. ambitious   C. crucial   D. ambiguous

12. In the new biography the author _____ the painter's quest to find himself, and his uncertainties about who he was.

    A. permeated   B. alleged   C. depicted   D. drafted

13. Unfortunately, the peace talks merely _____ the great gulf in understanding between two sides.

    A. highlight   B. emphasize   C. activate   D. upgrade

14. Michael Bixon believes that justice will _____ when you work with him—an attorney who believes in a bright future for each of his clients.

    A. speculate   B. prevail   C. ascend   D. precede

15. The economist draws a perfect _____ between an artificial boom and a circus coming to a small town for a couple weeks.

    A. distinction   B. analogy   C. conclusion   D. assumption

16. The newly-published book is an attempt to lay _____ the secrets of this very powerful political family.

    A. barren   B. bare   C. bald   D. nude

17. The _____ was spotted by a resident, who said the "welcome" sign was fixed in the incorrect position overnight.

    A. blunder   B. instruction   C. reproach   D. scandal

18. Under no illusions about her mother and younger sisters, Elizabeth begins to see Darcy's _____ honest character.

    A. intricately   B. eternally   C. subtly   D. inherently

19. The new president has produced a remarkable _____ summary within a few hundred words but with all the important points included.

    A. concise   B. notorious   C. precise   D. elaborate

20. There is another advantage that you can always use _____ glass if you need to block a street view.

    A. explicit   B. luxurious   C. monstrous   D. opaque

21. Security forces used tear gas in several locations to try to _____ demonstrators, witnesses said.

    A. disperse   B. embody   C. compile   D. compact

22. Her punishment accumulated; she continued to bear it, however, with a good deal of _____ courage.

    A. sophisticated   B. exceptional   C. impartial   D. superficial

23. The most _____ structure in this district is a newly finished observation tower seventy-two feet high.
    A. cognitive   B. rigorous   C. conspicuous   D. exclusive

24. The science teacher's explanations were so _____ that students had no problems doing their assignments.
    A. intelligible   B. obscure   C. complicated   D. transparent

25. The fundamental dilemma: how do we _____ liberty with security in this new world?
    A. consolidate   B. amend   C. reconcile   D. intensify

26. The former athlete had lived illegally in the United States for five years after his visitor's visa _____.
    A. abolished   B. ceased   C. expired   D. constrained

27. The oil companies were accused of _____ a shortage of gasoline to justify price increases.
    A. fabricating   B. contemplating   C. contriving   D. dominating

28. To be a qualified salesman, your _____ rule is to do everything you can to satisfy a customer.
    A. cordial   B. cardinal   C. arbitrary   D. diplomatic

29. Foreign teachers would like students to eagerly ask questions, _____ theories, or to debate any required reading material.
    A. envisage   B. commit   C. limit   D. submit

30. If you can _____ yourself from the gossip chain, you cut the majority of the drama out of your work days.
    A. induce   B. deduce   C. derive   D. detach

31. Curiously enough, the twins haven't been taught anything, but they have this sort of _____ reaction to music.
    A. extinct   B. permanent   C. surplus   D. instinctive

32. Watching their houses _____, their retirement accounts decline, they've changed their way of lives.
    A. deteriorate   B. perish   C. deflate   D. decrease

33. According to the dental x-ray film, a dentist may decide to _____ the tooth to prevent recurrent trouble.
    A. distract   B. extract   C. boycott   D. extort

34. We know that more is to be gained when great powers cooperate than when they _____.
    A. coincide   B. collapse   C. overlap   D. collide

35. Many economists have expressed concerns that the spending cuts could threaten an already _____ economic recovery.

   A. feeble   B. indignant   C. vulgar   D. negligible

36. Honestly, we are not _____; restaurant meals are a luxury and designer clothes are out.

   A. vulnerable   B. extravagant   C. elegant   D. massive

37. There is no denying that his death has left a _____ in the entertainment world that can never be filled.

   A. void   B. vacancy   C. symptom   D. wrench

38. The aim of this investigation was to find when and how people would _____ authority in the face of a clear moral imperative.

   A. defy   B. magnify   C. abuse   D. expel

39. Their commitments do not permit them to _____ themselves in current affairs as fully as they might wish.

   A. facilitate   B. fascinate   C. immerse   D. indulge

40. He provided for his miniature family well and, in the fashion of the time, loved his son _____ and with little physical contact.

   A. casually   B. sternly   C. naively   D. offensively

41. Her ability to _____ information from her interview subjects is a model for journalistic investigation.

   A. eject   B. entail   C. elicit   D. enhance

42. Today, the association has over 87,000 members and more than 330 local groups and 800 _____ clubs and societies.

   A. affiliated   B. alienated   C. allocated   D. affirmed

43. What delighted the young children most was to watch the butterflies _____ in the garden.

   A. flaring   B. vibrating   C. fluttering   D. flushing

44. She described the interview with her in an Italian magazine as a "complete _____".

   A. manufacture   B. speculation   C. fabrication   D. contemplation

45. Event chiefs said partygoers would be "_____" by the biggest-ever selection of music at Edinburgh's Hogmanay 2011.

   A. sparkled   B. blazed   C. glittered   D. dazzled

46. If we drive our fellow species to extinction, we will leave a far more _____ planet for our descendants than the world we inherited from our elders.

   A. desolate   B. specific   C. fantastic   D. desperate

47. Although some children spend too much time playing online games, the reasons are not _____ to completely forbid them to use the computer.

   A. sufficient   B. conscient   C. efficient   D. alternative

48. He also said it is unlikely that someone _____ of these charges would face jail time.

    A. convicted   B. convinced   C. retorted   D. testified

49. By _____ the attic, they were able to have two extra bedrooms for the regular guests of their family.

    A. confining   B. conceiving   C. conserving   D. converting

50. They are unarmed but have the right to _____ any suspected wrong-doer until the police arrive.

    A. contain   B. detain   C. bankrupt   D. sustain

51. As the _____ between the products of different enterprises has become smaller, the enterprise has concentrated more upon brand strategy.

    A. disposition   B. discrepancy   C. defect   D. deficit

52. After authorities _____ his plan to leap across the Grand Canyon he set up an attempt on the narrower Snake River Canyon.

    A. shattered   B. refuted   C. excluded   D. vetoed

53. There's a _____ in the fact that although we're living longer than ever before, people are more obsessed with health issues than they ever were.

    A. paradox   B. perplexity   C. dilemma   D. contradiction

54. McEnroe then caused a _____ the same year by reaching the Wimbledon semi-final from the qualifying competition.

    A. stimulus   B. surge   C. spectacle   D. sensation

55. Please do not be _____ by his offensive remarks since he is merely trying to attract attention.

    A. distracted   B. ruptured   C. irritated   D. intervened

56. Keep in mind that offering advice on each and every problem will _____ your child's feeling of being adult.

    A. undermine   B. mingle   C. provoke   D. baffle

57. The next-door neighbour knocked on the man's door to try to _____ him, then phoned the fire service.

    A. alert   B. invert   C. avert   D. rectify

58. He was ashamed. That feeling _____, and he was never comfortable in church after that incident.

    A. resided   B. dwelt   C. lingered   D. limped

59. Before 10 minutes had _____ on the third experiment, the conventional house built to the new standards had fallen apart.

    A. terminated   B. elapsed   C. overlapped   D. skipped

60. Premiums vary depending on the sum _____, your age and the state of your health.
    A. ensured   B. reassured   C. assured   D. insured
61. She turns 80 next year, but that hasn't stopped her _____ of obsessive, repetitive dot-drawing.
    A. equilibrium   B. partition   C. warrant   D. momentum
62. When I do leave, I will leave in place a strong young team that will continue to succeed for my _____.
    A. predecessor   B. forerunner   C. successor   D. offspring
63. In such a system, it is required by law that all of the branches of government are _____ to the president.
    A. subjective   B. subordinate   C. liable   D. solitary
64. Mother reached across the table for my hand, _____ it to her lips, and kissed it warmly.
    A. haunted   B. tugged   C. revolved   D. submerged
65. He raised his eyebrows and stuck his head forward and _____ it in a single nod, a gesture boys used then for O.K. when they were pleased.
    A. shrugged   B. twisted   C. maneuvered   D. jerked
66. With headlines dominated by the euro zone's troubles, already-fragile European consumer confidence has _____ to rock bottom.
    A. tumbled   B. tossed   C. peered   D. flipped
67. Sixteen of the youngsters on the mountain set off for help, but during the _____ three collapsed in the cold and rain.
    A. terrain   B. recession   C. degeneration   D. descent
68. Phones are such intimate devices that many people _____ being sent an advertisement without their consent.
    A. resent   B. discern   C. tease   D. tackle
69. With the dramatic advance in technology, workers are being made _____ by the closure of traditional manufacturing industries.
    A. trivial   B. redundant   C. migrant   D. indignant
70. Police said a _____ investigation showed the veteran fatally shot himself in the head.
    A. delicate   B. stationary   C. versatile   D. preliminary
71. "America is on the _____ of potential economic devastation," he says. "The day of infamy is close."
    A. porch   B. ferry   C. epoch   D. threshold
72. The _____ of the program was brought forward due to its unexpected topicality.
    A. transfer   B. transition   C. conversion   D. transmission

73. Fierce storm have been _____ rescue efforts and therefore little chance of finding more survivors.

   A. corrupting   B. discriminating   C. oppressing   D. hampering

74. To see the famous scenic spot properly viewers should set aside a few _____ days for a visit.

   A. persistent   B. conservative   C. conventional   D. consecutive

75. Hundreds of citizens _____ formed a chain around the old building to protect it from being pulled down.

   A. homogeneously   B. anonymously   C. spontaneously   D. consentaneously

76. I do not intend to reveal anything else, since all of the interesting surprises will be presented in the intense and inspiring _____.

   A. climax   B. summit   C. pitch   D. maximum

77. In July he issued a _____ ordering all unofficial armed groups in the country to disband.

   A. remedy   B. referee   C. intrigue   D. decree

78. The judges were _____ in their decision, scoring the fight 115-112, 116-111 and 115-113 in the Welshman's favour.

   A. unanimous   B. instantaneous   C. simultaneous   D. gorgeous

79. Things might be different if a trusted outsider were available to _____ between Mr. Mugabe and the opposition.

   A. mediate   B. ventilate   C. propagate   D. postulate

80. Generally speaking, the marketing department has always played a _____ role to the sales department.

   A. reciprocal   B. overwhelming   C. legitimate   D. subsidiary

81. There are more and more people doing extra jobs outside their regular jobs to _____ their incomes.

   A. implement   B. complement   C. supplement   D. compliment

82. Apparently, consumption of alcohol _____ your ability to drive a car or operate machinery.

   A. incorporate   B. simulate   C. impairs   D. synthesizes

83. Science is not conducted by consensus, nor by how many scientific societies support a _____.

   A. hypothesis   B. intuition   C. sentiment   D. incentive

84. The key to successful investing is to understand that critical difference between _____ and reality.

   A. conception   B. perception   C. innovation   D. cognition

85. Overall, the business climate is characterized by sound legislation and a _____ approach to economic activity.
    A. literal   B. literary   C. liberal   D. linear
86. People all over the world were wild with joy when hearing the news of the collapse of the Fascist _____ at the end of the war.
    A. prestige   B. regime   C. administration   D. legislation
87. A portable device, consisting of a microphone attached to a loudspeaker, is used especially to _____ the voice.
    A. identify   B. amplify   C. foster   D. magnify
88. The general manager has been accused of failing to _____ an overall vision in the company's expansion plan.
    A. assimilate   B. articulate   C. circulate   D. insulate
89. Getting a grip on complex education issues can be a _____ task for many journalists.
    A. feminine   B. formidable   C. foul   D. furious
90. For leaders and managers looking at making lasting impact, Gandhi surely presents some ideas to _____.
    A. menace   B. manifest   C. perplex   D. ponder
91. They assert that _____ everyone has some capacity for creativity and innovative thinking.
    A. virtually   B. graciously   C. hysterically   D. initiatively
92. My cousin is a devoted walker, even in Los Angeles, where a _____ is a rare sight.
    A. warrant   B. descendant   C. pedestrian   D. tenant
93. Our great motherland has _____ a course of 5,000 years and made a great contribution to world civilisation.
    A. transcended   B. traversed   C. nourished   D. overtaken
94. Over time, however, the advanced technology is sure to be _____ and adopted by other countries.
    A. designated   B. diffused   C. deviated   D. dispatched
95. If you give your baby juice, you are supposed to _____ it well with cooled, boiled water.
    A. dilute   B. diminish   C. buffer   D. commute
96. With a violent drunkard for a husband, he thought that _____ woman must be leading a life of terror.
    A. exclusive   B. wretched   C. wrenched   D. gloomy
97. Many employers are _____ about whether older workers are at ease using Internet tools.
    A. suspicious   B. dubious   C. chronic   D. susceptible

98. The renowned scholar was taking part in an international _____ on population when his wife gave birth.

   A. federation   B. exposition   C. symposium   D. penalty

99. The more they _____ into his background, the more inflamed their suspicions would become.

   A. hover   B. probe   C. violate   D. grope

100. I thought her _____ complaints were going to prove too much for me. I could't stand them any more.

   A. prospective   B. prevalent   C. provocative   D. perpetual

二、单项选择题（二）

1. I was appointed as a volcanologist working for the Hawaiian Volcano Observatory (HVO) twenty years ago. What actually happened according to this statement?

   A. I directed HVO.   B. I was employed by HVO.
   C. I was rewarded by HVO.   D. I helped HVO come into being.

2. Having collected and evaluated the information, I help other scientists to predict where lava from the volcano will flow next and how fast. What actually happens according to this statement?

   A. I am responsible for prediction of volcano.
   B. Other scientists are less intelligent than me.
   C. I am expert at analyzing the relevant data.
   D. Other scientists lack predicting ability.

3. Our work has saved many lives because people in the path of the lava can be warned to leave their houses. What actually happened according to this statement?

   A. We accurately predicted the eruption.
   B. People were saved because lava changed its path.
   C. We saved people's lives by moving their houses.
   D. People were indifferent to our warning.

4. However, the eruption itself is really exciting to watch and I shall never forget my first sight of one. What actually happened according to this statement?

   A. I appreciated the eruption.   B. The eruption did lots of damage.
   C. I was terrified by the eruption.   D. The eruption happened regularly.

5. Two other scientists and I were driven up the mountain and dropped as close as possible to the crater. What actually happened according to this statement?

   A. We were not skilled at driving.   B. We were eager to know more.
   C. We were afraid to drive.   D. We were left alone there.

6. Today, I am just as enthusiastic about my job as the day I first started. What actually happened according to this statement?

    A. I have been devoted to my job.   B. My job cost me my health.

    C. I lost heart at the beginning.   D. My job was started with ease.

7. Having studied volcanoes now for many years, I am still amazed at their beauty as well as their potential to cause great damage. What can be learned from this statement?

    A. Volcanoes have become less violent.   B. I am overcome by fear of volcanoes.

    C. Volcanoes do more damage than ever.   D. I am curious about the attraction of volcanoes.

8. However, the attraction that arouses the greatest appreciation in the reserve is Tianchi or the Lake of Heaven. What can be learned from the statement?

    A. The reserve attracts tourists most.   B. Tianchi attracts tourists most.

    C. Tianchi belongs to the Lake of Heaven.   D. The reserve needs more tourists.

9. When you arrive you are rewarded not only with the sight of its clear waters, but also by the view of the other sixteen mountain peaks that surround Tianchi. What is implied in the statement?

    A. Tourists will be given some rewards.

    B. The clear waters and the mountain peaks are worth seeing.

    C. Tourists will have difficulty choosing what to see.

    D. The clear waters and the mountain peaks are expensive to visit.

10. The most well-known story concerns three young women from heaven. What can be learned from the statement?

    A. Three young women are concerned about the story.

    B. The story talks about three young women.

    C. Three young women enjoy the story.

    D. The story saddens three young women.

11. Having swallowed the fruit, the girl became pregnant and later gave birth to a handsome boy. What actually happened according to this statement?

    A. The fruit made the girl pregnant.   B. The fruit became the husband.

    C. The girl married the fruit.   D. The girl enjoyed eating fruits.

12. It is said that this boy, who had a great gift for languages and persuasion, is the father of the Manchu people. What actually happened according to this statement?

    A. The boy was skilled at persuading.

    B. The boy was fluent in foreign languages.

    C. Manchu people like exchanging gifts.

    D. Manchu people are persuaded easily.

13. Together, individuals can make a difference. We do not have to put up with pollution. What can be learned from the statement?
    A. Everyone should fight pollution.
    B. Something should be done to change individuals.
    C. Individuals can cause pollution.
    D. Individuals must be clean and tidy.

14. There are many people who have a commitment like yours, but they do not believe they have the power to do anything to improve our environment. What actually happens to many people according to this statement?
    A. They have confidence in improving our environment.
    B. They are willing to improve our environment.
    C. They lack enthusiasm for improving our environment.
    D. They are not willing to improve our environment.

15. Its 3-D cinemas and giant movie screens provide brand new experiences of the earth and beyond.
    A. The viewers do not have completely new experiences.
    B. The viewers have completely new experiences.
    C. The 3-D cinemas and giant movie screens are famous.
    D. The 3-D cinemas and giant movie screens are not famous.

16. They predict that any warming will be mild with few bad environmental consequences. What do they think of warming?
    A. Warming can be avoided.
    B. Warming cannot be avoided.
    C. Warming will do little harm to environment.
    D. Warming will do great harm to environment.

17. Dr. Foster thinks that the trend which increases the temperature by 5 degrees would be a catastrophe. What can be learned from the statement?
    A. The trend would be beneficial.   B. Dr. Foster welcomes the trend.
    C. The trend would be terrible.   D. Dr. Foster ignores the trend.

18. All scientists subscribe to the view that the increase in the earth's temperature is due to the burning of fossil fuels, natural gas and oil to produce energy. What can be learned from the statement?
    A. All scientists support the view.   B. All scientists support warming.
    C. All scientists are opposed to the view.   D. All scientists are against warming.

19. I still think people should advocate improvements in the way we use energy today. What can be learned from the statement?

    A. People save energy as much as possible.

    B. I save more energy than others.

    C. People don't save energy as much as possible.

    D. I save less energy than others.

20. They managed to catch sight of some mountain goats and even a grizzly bear and an eagle. What can be learned from the statement?

    A. Seeing a grizzly bear and an eagle astonished them.

    B. They succeeded in saving some mountain goats.

    C. They didn't see any mountain goats.

    D. A grizzly bear and an eagle were caught by them.

21. You see, during adolescence I also smoked and became addicted to cigarettes. What actually happened to me during adolescence according to this statement?

    A. I was tired of smoking.   B. I was unable to stop smoking.

    C. I often gave up smoking.   D. Smoking did much harm to me.

22. When I was taken off the school football team because I was unfit, I knew it was time to quit smoking. What can be learned from the statement?

    A. I was unwilling to give up smoking.   B. The school football team absorbed me.

    C. I was determined to give up smoking.   D. The school football team punished me.

23. So when the drug leaves your body, you get withdrawal symptoms. What can be learned from the statement?

    A. You feel comfortable.   B. Your body is slim.

    C. You don't feel comfortable.   D. Your body isn't slim.

24. John Snow suspected that the second theory was correct but he needed evidence. What actually happened according to this statement?

    A. John Snow favored the second theory.

    B. John Snow didn't favor the second theory.

    C. John Snow collected enough evidence.

    D. John Snow didn't need evidence.

25. He doubted that she would make further investigations. What actually happened according to this statement?

    A. He believed she would make further investigations.

    B. He didn't believe she would make further investigations.

C. She would make further investigations.

D. She wouldn't make further investigations.

26. The poems may not make sense and even seem contradictory, but they are easy to learn and recite. What can be learned from the statement?

    A. It is hard to write the poems.　　　B. Learning the poems by heart is easy.

    C. It is important to understand the poems.　　D. Learning the poems by heart is hard.

27. List poems have a flexible line length and repeated phrases which give both a pattern and rhythm to the poem. What can be learned from the statement?

    A. List poems tend to be long.　　　B. Repeated phrases help a rhythm.

    C. List poems tend to be short.　　　D. Repeated phrases don't help a rhythm.

28. People began to concentrate less on religious themes and adopt a more humanistic attitude to life. What actually happened according to this statement?

    A. Realistic themes were ignored.　　B. Realistic themes replaced religious themes.

    C. Realistic themes were emphasized.　　D. Religious themes replaced realistic themes.

29. So when another outbreak hit London in 1854, he was ready to begin his enquiry. What would happen according to the statement?

    A. He would look into the outbreak.　　B. The outbreak would not be more severe.

    C. The outbreak would be more severe.　　D. He wouldn't look into the outbreak.

30. It is easy to write and, like the cinquain, can give a clear picture and create a special feeling using the minimum of words. What can be learned from the statement?

    A. The cinquain is long.　　　B. The cinquain is ancient.

    C. The cinquain is special.　　　D. The cinquain is short.

31. Following Jane's way of studying chimps, our group are all going to visit them in the forest. What can be learned from the statement?

    A. Our group used Jane's way to study chimps.

    B. Jane led us to observe chimps in the forest.

    C. Our group didn't use Jane's way to study chimps.

    D. Jane gave up observing chimps in the forest.

32. We realize that the bond between members of a chimp family is as strong as in a human family. What can be learned from the statement?

    A. Members of a chimp family love each other.

    B. Human family needs to be improved.

    C. Members of a chimp family don't love each other.

    D. Human family doesn't need to be improved.

33. It seemed that the water was to blame for the outbreak of cholera. What can be learned from the statement?

   A. The outbreak polluted the water.
   B. The water resulted in the outbreak.
   C. The outbreak didn't pollute the water.
   D. The water didn't lead to the outbreak.

34. She has argued that wild animals should be left in the wild and not used for entertainment or advertisements. What actually happens according to the statement?

   A. All wild animals live in the wild.
   B. All wild animals don't live in the wild.
   C. She supports using wild animals for ads.
   D. She doesn't support wild animals for medicine.

35. A woman had the pump water delivered to her house every day. What actually happens according to the statement?

   A. The woman asked someone to fetch water for her.
   B. The woman used the water to wash.
   C. The woman fetched the water every day.
   D. The woman didn't want anyone to transport water.

36. And then I think about small chimps in cages though they have done nothing wrong. What is implied in the statement?

   A. I hope to let wild animals live in the wild.
   B. I don't hope to let wild animals live in the wild.
   C. Small chimps in cages deserve to be punished.
   D. Small chimps in cages live better.

37. That was a generation when girls' education was always placed second to boys'. What actually happened according to the statement?

   A. Girls' education was important.
   B. Boys' education was important.
   C. Girls' education was a failure.
   D. Boys' education was a failure.

38. The water companies were instructed not to expose people to polluted water any more. What would actually happen according to the statement?

   A. People would continue to drink the polluted water.
   B. People would not drink the polluted water.
   C. The water companies would continue to provide polluted water.
   D. The water companies made money illegally.

39. By now I could not wait to find out more about her. What actually happened according to the statement?

    A. I was proud of her.
    B. I was eager to know more about her.
    C. I was not interested in her.
    D. I was not willing to find out more about her.

40. I discovered that Lin Qiaozhi had devoted her whole life to her patients and had chosen not to have a family of her own. What actually happened according to the statement?

    A. Lin Qiaozhi got married.　　　　　B. Her patients were to blame for her marriage.
    C. Lin Qiaozhi remained single all her life.　D. Her patients didn't allow her to marry.

41. Dr. Yuan is now circulating his knowledge in India, Vietnam and many other less developed countries to increase their rice harvests. What actually happens according to the statement?

    A. Dr. Yuan's knowledge benefits many less developed countries.
    B. Dr. Yuan's knowledge is only useful in less developed countries.
    C. Dr. Yuan's knowledge doesn't benefit less developed countries.
    D. Dr. Yuan's knowledge is not useful in developed countries.

42. Thanks to his research, the UN has more tools in the battle to rid the world of hunger. What can be learned from the statement?

    A. His research helps ease the problem of hunger.
    B. The UN raised money for his research.
    C. The problem of world hunger cannot be eased.
    D. The UN has kept the countries free from hunger.

43. He grew more and more popular as his charming character, the little tramp, became known throughout the world. What can be learned from the statement?

    A. He was a lawyer.　　B. He was a minister.　　C. He was an actor.　　D. He was an athlete.

44. This character was a social failure but was loved for his optimism and determination to overcome all difficulties. What can be learned from the statement?

    A. A social failure is welcomed by people.
    B. This character was respected for his qualities.
    C. A social failure isn't welcomed by people.
    D. This character wasn't respected for his qualities.

45. The acting is so convincing that it makes you believe that it is one of the best meals he has ever tasted! What can be learned from the statement?

    A. His acting is terrible.　　　　　　B. His acting is just so so.
    C. His acting is excellent.　　　　　　D. His acting is strange.

46. When we met yesterday, he moved very close to me as I introduced myself. I moved back a bit, but he came closer to ask a question and then shook my hand. What actually happened according to the statement?

   A. I was frightened by his behaviour.

   B. He was too rude to be trusted.

   C. I wanted to keep more physical distance from him.

   D. He fell in love with me.

47. Of course, body language can be misread, but many gestures and actions are universal. What can be learned from the statement?

   A. Some gestures express similar meanings in different cultures.

   B. All gestures and actions are common.

   C. Gestures and actions don't belong to body language.

   D. Gestures and actions cannot be misread.

48. I bought tickets for myself and my friends at the park's entrance, but tickets are also available online. What would happen according to the statement?

   A. I would buy tickets online.

   B. I would buy tickets online for my friends.

   C. I would visit the park with my friends.

   D. I would sell tickets online.

49. John Snow was able to announce with certainty that polluted water carried the virus. What can be learned from the statement?

   A. John Snow was confident about his announcement.

   B. John Snow was not confident about his announcement.

   C. The virus polluted the water.

   D. The polluted water brought in the virus.

50. He did not want to be attacked by the Christian Church, so he only published it as he lay dying in 1543. What was implied in the statement?

   A. He was cautious.   B. He was unselfish.

   C. He was intelligent.   D. He was careless.

51. If time permits, a science fiction will be chosen. What does the statement mean?

   A. It takes a long time to read a science fiction.

   B. If it is agreed, a science fiction can be chosen.

   C. Choosing a science fiction or not depends on whether time is enough.

   D. A science fiction can be read in your free time.

52. It was claimed the crime had been solved. Though, is this how it looks? What does the statement imply?

    A. The fact of the crime has really been found out.

    B. Many want to know the fact of the crime.

    C. The real criminal is still free now.

    D. The real criminal is in prison.

53. I'm going to give it to you straight that I won't go abroad at all. What does the statement mean?

    A. I frankly tell you that I don't want to go abroad.

    B. I'll stay home and send it to you without any delay.

    C. It is hard to go abroad straightly.

    D. I would stay with you rather than go abroad.

54. It's really shocking when you get down to investigating into the cause. What does the statement mean?

    A. It will be shocking when you give up the business.

    B. You will find the truth astonishing.

    C. It is surprising that you are so curious about the cause.

    D. You will not find the truth shocking.

55. The lawyer makes up her mind not to let the suspect off. What actually happens according to the statement?

    A. The lawyer decides to lock the possible criminal in the room.

    B. The lawyer determines to get the suspect to admit his crime.

    C. The lawyer will tell others about the suspect.

    D. The lawyer will not allow the suspect to do anything.

56. What has been found is consistent with what has been supposed. What actually happened according to the statement?

    A. What people thought has been proved.

    B. What people thought hasn't been proved.

    C. People always want to find out the secret.

    D. People don't always want to find out the secret.

57. The police are sparing no effort to persuade the jury. What is actually happening according to the statement?

    A. The police are not prepared to persuade the jury.

    B. The police succeed in persuading the jury.

    C. The police are doing their best to convince the jury.

    D. The police fail to convince the jury.

58. That's all about the case, would you cut it out, already? What does the statement imply?

    A. Have you clearly understood the case?

    B. You'd better never mention this case again.

    C. You'd better make the case shorter to make it better understood.

    D. Have you detailed the case?

59. You may think anybody is the killer but him. What does the statement imply?

    A. He is likely to be a killer.   B. He is certainly not the killer.

    C. It is not impossible that he is the killer.   D. He must be a killer.

60. I'm with you on the mystery happening in the store. What does the statement imply?

    A. When the mystery happened we stayed together.

    B. I happened to be with you in the store.

    C. I will solve the mystery with you.

    D. I entirely agree with you.

61. She can concentrate on her studies for ages. What actually happens according to this statement?

    A. She can be absorbed in her studies for a long time.

    B. She is concerned about her studies for a while.

    C. She forgets time when focusing on her studies.

    D. She has lost interest in studies for a short time.

62. I set about researching the habits of snakes to find the easiest way to trap them. What actually happened according to this statement?

    A. I began to raise snakes in an easy way.

    B. Knowing the habits of snakes makes it easy to catch them.

    C. I began to find out more about how to raise snakes.

    D. I had known a lot about the habits of snakes.

63. Rarely have I seen a situation which made me so upset. What actually happened according to this statement?

    A. The situation made me sad.   B. The situation was encouraging.

    C. The situation made me cheerful.   D. The situation was worsening.

64. Nothing in the world is difficult for one who sets his mind to it. What does the statement mean?

    A. Failure is the mother of success.

    B. Everything is difficult if one works hard on it.

    C. Nothing is difficult if one takes it for granted.

    D. Nothing is hard if one puts all his heart to it.

65. He listened so carefully that not a single word did he miss. What actually happened according to this statement?

   A. He missed a single word.　　　B. He heard every word.
   C. He was unwilling to listen.　　D. He didn't hear any word.

66. Xie Lei told me that she feels much more at home in England now, and what had seemed very strange before now appears quite normal. What does the statement imply?

   A. Xie Lei has returned home.　　　B. Xie Lei used to be abnormal.
   C. Xie Lei is used to life in England.　　D. Xie Lei is not used to life in Britain.

67. Had he followed my advice, he wasn't in trouble. What does the statement mean?

   A. He saved the trouble.　　　B. He didn't fail to take my advice.
   C. He has got out of trouble by himself.　　D. He is in trouble.

68. The last thing that he needs is more work. What does the statement mean?

   A. He is in desperate need of more work.　　B. What he needs is nothing but more work.
   C. What he needs is nothing but exercise.　　D. He doesn't need more work at all.

69. Nothing is ever too much trouble for her. What actually happens according to this statement?

   A. She is always ready to help.　　B. She is always ready to make trouble.
   C. She is ready to struggle against others.　　D. She is ready to trouble others.

70. It is two weeks since he stayed at our hotel. What does the statement mean?

   A. He has stayed at our hotel for two weeks.

   B. He stayed at our hotel for two weeks.

   C. He left our hotel two weeks ago.

   D. He will stay at our hotel for a longer time.

71. It is likely that his sorrow will wear off. What does the statement mean?

   A. It is likely that his sorrow will be temporary.

   B. It is possible that his sorrow will gradually come to an end.

   C. It seems that his sorrow will deserve no more attention.

   D. It is unlikely that his sorrow will come to an end.

72. I haven't the slightest idea what he had in mind. What actually happens according to this statement?

   A. I know nothing about what was on his mind.

   B. I know very well what he made up his mind to do.

   C. I know little about what he did.

   D. I don't know very well what he would do.

73. We were just too delighted to hear that Mary had been invited to the party. What actually happened according to this statement?

   A. We felt embarrassed about the news. B. We were really glad to hear the news.
   C. We were disappointed with the news. D. We were concerned about the news.

74. His parents have managed to talk him out of playing computer games. What has actually happened according to this statement?

   A. He has stopped playing computer games.
   B. He has succeeded in designing computer games.
   C. He has got accustomed to playing computer games.
   D. He has failed in designing computer games.

75. The criteria are so strict that it is difficult to get new ideas accepted unless they are truly novel. What actually happens according to the statement?

   A. New ideas are difficult to accept.
   B. The criteria are unfavorable for new ideas.
   C. Really new ideas are likely to accept.
   D. The criteria are favorable for novels.

76. Leave the beaten track occasionally and dive into the woods. What does the statement imply?

   A. Traveling in the woods benefits us.
   B. Driving carefully can avoid accidents.
   C. Thinking differently leads to success.
   D. Exploring something different will open up your mind.

77. California also has the distinction of being the most multicultural state in the USA, having attracted people from all over the world. What does the statement imply?

   A. California is known for its multiculture.
   B. California is known for are tourists.
   C. The USA has the most tourists in the world.
   D. The USA is famous for California.

78. In China, employed females now account for some 44 percent of the total number of employees. What can be learned from the statement?

   A. There are more women employed than the men in China.
   B. There are more men employed than women in China.
   C. Chinese females are not hard-working.
   D. Chinese females work less hard than men.

79. In the 16th century, after the arrival of the Europeans, the native people suffered greatly. What actually happened according to the statement?

   A. The settlers lived in harmony with the native people.

   B. The settlers didn't live in harmony with the native people.

   C. The native people welcomed the Europeans.

   D. The native people attacked the Europeans.

80. Under no circumstances will she quit his dream of being a hairdresser. What is implied in the statement?

   A. She will give up her idea of becoming a hairdresser.

   B. She thinks nothing of the career as a hairdresser.

   C. She will try to pursue a career as hairdresser.

   D. She thinks she can't realize her dream.

81. Jane has a preference for bananas rather than apples. What actually happens according to the statement?

   A. Jane eats more bananas.
   B. Apples taste better than bananas.
   C. Jane eats more apples.
   D. Bananas taste better than apples.

82. In the early 1800s, Russian hunters, who had originally gone to Alaska, began settling in California. What actually happened according to the statement?

   A. Russian hunters settled in California earlier than in Alaska.

   B. Russian hunters settled in Alaska earlier than in California.

   C. California was more suitable for settlement than Alaska.

   D. Alaska was more suitable for settlement than California.

83. They participate in some voluntary activities, which they find pleasurable and rewarding. What actually happens according to the statement?

   A. Voluntary activities bring them much money.

   B. They think it costs money to do volunteer activities.

   C. Voluntary activities enrich their life but bring no good.

   D. They think it worthwhile to do volunteer activities.

84. New Zealanders' interests are extensive, ranging from hiking to bungee jumping. What actually happens according to the statement?

   A. New Zealanders have a wide range of interests.

   B. New Zealanders prefer hiking to bungee jumping.

   C. New Zealanders prefer bungee jumping to hiking.

   D. New Zealanders have limited outdoor activities.

85. In many ways my disability has helped me grow stronger psychologically and become more independent. What actually happens according to the statement?

   A. I feel sorry for my disability.

   B. I think highly of my disability.

   C. Disability prevents me living a normal life.

   D. Disability doesn't prevent me living a normal life.

86. Every time I returned after an absence, I felt stupid because I was behind the others. What actually happened according to the statement?

   A. I was made fun of by others.　　B. I made a fool of myself in class.

   C. I regretted missing some lessons.　　D. I was slower in mind than my classmates.

87. So sometimes some children in my primary school would laugh, when I got out of breath after running a short way or had to stop and rest halfway up the stairs. What actually happened according to the statement?

   A. I was good at running.　　B. I was very weak.

   C. I was jealous of other children.　　D. I had a particular way of doing sports.

88. Even after all that, no one could give my disease a name and it is difficult to know what the future holds. What actually happens according to the statement?

   A. I had a common disease.　　B. My disease gave me a new future.

   C. I ignored my disease.　　D. My disease was unusual.

89. In addition, sometimes I am very clumsy and drop things or bump into furniture. What actually happened according to the statement?

   A. I had a violent temper.　　B. I enjoyed hiding in furniture.

   C. I walked steadily.　　D. I didn't walk steadily.

90. Unfortunately, the doctors don't know how to make me better, but I am very outgoing and have learned to adapt to my disability. What does the statement imply?

   A. I didn't take my disability seriously.　　B. The doctor was good at comforting me.

   C. I was not optimistic with my disability.　　D. The doctor was not good at comforting me.

91. However, when she first saw the robot, she felt alarmed. What actually happened according to the statement?

   A. She was scared by the robot.　　B. The robot appealed to her.

   C. She was satisfied with the robot.　　D. The robot threatened her.

92. Also she felt her home wasn't elegant enough for someone like Larry who wanted to improve his social position. What actually happened according to the statement?

   A. She thought little of Larry.　　B. She didn't love Larry.

   C. She was not content with her home.　　D. She and Larry were in a bad mood.

93. Claire thought it was ridiculous to be offered sympathy by a robot. What actually happened according to the statement?

    A. Claire was a robot, too. B. The robot behaved like a man.
    C. Claire disliked the robot. D. The robot looked down on Claire.

94. She looked at his fingers with wonder as they turned each page and suddenly reached for his hand. What actually happened according to the statement?

    A. The robot shook hands with her. B. She felt the robots' hands.
    C. She read very quickly. D. The robot read very quickly.

95. By the amused and surprised look on her face, Claire knew that Gladys thought she was having an affair. What actually happened according to the statement?

    A. Gladys thought Claire was not loyal to her husband.
    B. Claire thought Gladys was not loyal to her husband.
    C. Gladys supported Claire's behaviour.
    D. Claire supported Gladys' behaviour.

96. He died as a result of an HIV infection that he had got from a blood transfusion nine years earlier. What actually happened according to the statement?

    A. He died soon after a blood transfusion.
    B. He died when getting a blood transfusion.
    C. A blood transfusion caused his HIV infection.
    D. A blood transfusion was not blame for his HIV infection.

97. There his parents bought a candy store which they ran for the next 40 or so years. What actually happened according to the statement?

    A. They liked running in the store. B. They didn't like running in the store.
    C. They owned a candy store. D. They didn't own a candy store.

98. As we drew closer, I could see a whale being attacked by a pack of about six other killers. What actually happened according to the statement?

    A. We took delight in attacking a whale.
    B. Six other killers worked as a team.
    C. We didn't take delight in attacking a whale.
    D. Six other killers didn't work as a team.

99. Seeing such extraordinary beauty, I think every cell in my body woke up. What actually happened according to the statement?

    A. The beauty disappointed me. B. The beauty frightened me.
    C. The beauty impressed me. D. The beauty harmed me.

100. More importantly, I am now a more autonomous learner. What actually happens according to the statement?
   A. I enjoy learning.   B. I am a lazy learner.
   C. I hate learning.   D. I am a slow learner.

三、阅读理解

Passage 1

I used to look at my closet and see clothes. These days, whenever I cast my eyes upon the stacks of shoes and hangers of shirts, sweaters and jackets, I see water.

It takes 569 gallons to manufacture a T-shirt, from its start in the cotton fields to its appearance on store shelves. A pair of running shoes? 1,247 gallons.

Until last fall, I'd been oblivious to my "water footprint", which is defined as the total volume of freshwater that is used to produce goods and services, according to the Water Footprint Network. The Dutch nonprofit has been working to raise awareness of freshwater scarcity since 2008, but it was through the "Green Blue Book" by Thomas M. Kostigen that I was able to see how my own actions factored in.

I've installed gray-water systems to reuse the wastewater from my laundry, machine and bathtub and reroute it to my landscape - systems that save, on average, 50 gallons of water per day. I've set up rain barrels and infiltration pits to collect thousands of gallons of storm water cascading from my roof. I've even entered the last bastion of greendom—installing a composting toilet.

Suffice to say, I've been feeling pretty satisfied with myself for all the drinking water I've saved with these big-ticket projects.

Now I realize that my daily consumption choices could have an even larger effect-not only on the local water supply but also globally: 1.1 billion people have no access to freshwater, and, in the future, those who do have access will have less of it.

To see how much virtual water 1 was using, I logged on to the "Green Blue Book" website and used its water footprint calculator, entering my daily consumption habits. Tallying up the water footprint of my breakfast, lunch, dinner and snacks, as well as my daily dose of over-the-counter uppers and downers — coffee, wine and beer — I'm using 512 gallons of virtual water each day just to feed myself.

In a word: alarming.

Even more alarming was how much hidden water I was using to get dressed. I'm hardly a clotheshorse, but the few new items I buy once again trumped the amount of water flowing from my faucets each day. If I'm serious about saving water, I realized I could make some simple lifestyle shifts. Looking more closely at the areas in my life that use the most virtual water, it was food and clothes, specifically meat, coffee and oddly, blue jeans and leather jackets.

Being a motorcyclist, I own an unusually large amount of leather-boots and jackets in particular. All of it is enormously water intensive. It takes 7,996 gallons to make a leather jacket, leather being a byproduct of beef. It takes 2,866 gallons of water to make a single pair of blue jeans, because they're made from water-hogging cotton.

Crunching the numbers for the amount of clothes I buy every year, it looks a lot like my friends swimming pool. My entire closet is borderline Olympic.

Gulp.

My late resolution is to buy some items used. Underwear and socks are, of course, exempt from this strategy, but I have no problem shopping less and also shopping at Goodwill. In fact, I'd been doing that for the past year to save money. My clothes' outrageous water footprint just reinforced it for me.

More conscious living and substitution, rather than sacrifice, are the prevailing ideas with the water footprint. It's one I'm trying, and that's had an unusual upside. I had a hamburger recently, and I enjoyed it a lot since it is now an occasional treat rather than a weekly habit.

(One gallon = 3.8 litres)

1. Which of the following reasons can best explain the authors feeling of self-satisfaction?
    A. He made contribution to drinking water conservation in his own way.
    B. Money spent on upgrading his household facilities was worthwhile.
    C. His house was equipped with advanced water-saving facilities.
    D. He could have made even greater contribution by changing his lifestyle.
2. According to the context, "...how my own actions factored in..." means _____.
    A. how I could contribute to water conservation
    B. what efforts I should make to save fresh water
    C. what behaviour could be counted as freshwater-saving
    D. how much of what I did contributed to freshwater shortage
3. "My entire closet is borderline Olympic" is an example of _____.
    A. exaggeration　　　B. analogy　　　C. understatement　　　D. euphemism

Passage 2

In her novel of "Reunion, American Style", Rona Jaffe suggests that a class reunion "is more than a sentimental journey. It is also a way of answering the question that lies at the back of nearly all our minds. Did they do better than I?"

Jaffe's observation may be misplaced but not completely lost. According to a study conducted by social psychologist Jack Sparacino, the overwhelming majority who attend reunions aren't there invidiously to compare their recent accomplishments with those of their former classmates. Instead, they hope, primarily, to relive their earlier successes.

Certainly, a few return to show their former classmates how well they have done; others enjoy observing the changes that have occurred in their classmates (not always in themselves, of course). But the majorities who attend their class reunions do so to relive the good times they remember having when they were younger. In his study, Sparacino found that, as high school students, attendees had been more popular, more often regarded as attractive, and more involved in extracurricular activities than those classmates who chose not to attend. For those who turned up at their reunions, then, the old times were also the good times!

It would appear that Americans have a special fondness for reunions, judging by their prevalence. Major league baseball players, fraternity members, veterans groups, high school and college graduates, and former Boy Scouts all hold reunions on a regular basis. In addition, family reunions frequently attract blood relatives from faraway places who spend considerable money and time to reunite.

Actually, in their affection for reuniting with friends, family or colleagues, Americans are probably no different from any other people, except that Americans have created a mind-boggling number and variety of institutionalized forms of gatherings to facilitate the satisfaction of this desire. Indeed, reunions have increasingly become formal events that are organized on a regular basis and, in the process, they have also become big business.

Shell Norris of Class Reunion, Inc., says that Chicago alone has 1,500 high school reunions each year. A conservative estimate on the national level would be 10,000 annually. At one time, all high school reunions were organized by volunteers, usually female homemakers. In the last few years, however, as more and more women have entered the labour force, alumni reunions are increasingly being planned by specialized companies rather than by part-time volunteers.

The first college reunion was held by the alumni of Yale University in 1792. Graduates of Pennsylvania, Princeton, Stanford, and Brown followed suit. And by the end of the 19th century, most 4-year institutions were holding alumni reunions.

The variety of college reunions is impressive. At Princeton, alumni parade through the town wearing their class uniforms and singing their alma mater. At Marietta College, they gather for a dinner-dance on a steamship cruising the Ohio River.

Clearly, the thought of cruising on a steamship or marching through the streets is usually not, by itself, sufficient reason for large numbers of alumni to return to campus. Alumni who decide to attend their reunions share a common identity based on the years they spent together as undergraduates. For this reason, universities that somehow establish a common bond — for example, because they are relatively small or especially prestigious—tend to draw substantial numbers of their alumni to reunions. In an effort to enhance this common identity, larger colleges and universities frequently build their class reunions on participation in smaller units, such as departments or schools. Or they encourage "affinity reunions" for groups of former cheerleaders, editors, fraternity members, musicians, members of military organizations on campus, and the like.

　　Of course, not every alumnus is fond of his or her alma mater. Students who graduated during the late 1960s may be especially reluctant to get involved in alumni events. They were part of the generation that conducted sit-ins and teach-ins directed at university administrators, protested military recruitment on campus and marched against "establishment politics." If this generation has a common identity, it may fall outside of their university ties—or even be hostile to them. Even as they enter their middle years, alumni who continue to hold unpleasant memories of college during this period may not wish to attend class reunions.

4. According to the passage, Sparacinos study _____.

　　A. provided strong evidence for Jaffe's statement.

　　B. showed that attendees tended to excel in high school study.

　　C. found that interest in reunions was linked with school experience.

　　D. found evidence for attendees intense desire for showing off success.

5. Which of the following is NOT mentioned as a distinct feature of U.S. class reunions?

　　A. U.S. class reunions are usually occasions to show off one's recent success.

　　B. Reunions are regular and formal events organized by professional agencies.

　　C. Class reunions have become a profitable business.

　　D. Class reunions have brought about a variety of activities.

6. What is the passage mainly about?

　　A. Reasons for popularity and (non) attendance for alumni reunions.

　　B. A historical perspective for alumni reunions in the United States.

　　C. Alumni reunions and American university traditions.

　　D. Alumni reunion and its social and economic implications.

Passage 3

　　Warning: reading too much Cinderella to your daughter may damage her emotional health in later life.

A paper to be delivered at the international congress of cognitive psychotherapy in Gothenburg next month suggests a link between the attitudes of women abused by their partners and early exposure to the wrong sort of fairytales.

It says girls who identified with Cinderella, Rapunzel and Beauty in Beauty and the Beast were more likely to stay in destructive relationships as adults.

The theory was developed by Susan Darker-Smith, a psychotherapist and masters student at the University of Derby. She interviewed 67 female abuse survivors and found that 61 put up with serial abuse because they believed they could change their partner with patience, compassion and love.

Hardly any of the women in a control group, who had not experienced abuse, thought they could change a partner in this way. The same view was taken by male survivors who had been abused as children. These women and men said they would leave a relationship rather than put up with abuse from a partner.

Ms Darker-Smith looked further into the differences between the groups and found the abused women were much more likely to identify with Cinderella and other submissive female characters in fairytales, who were later rescued by a strong prince or hero. Although most girls heard the stories, damage appeared to be done to those who adopted the submissive characters as role models.

"They believe if their love is strong enough they can change their partners' behaviour," she said yesterday. "Overexposure in childhood to stories that emphasise the transformational qualities of love may make women believe they can change their partners."

For example, they might never have understood the obvious flaw in the story of Rapunzel, who remained locked in a high tower until rescued by a knight on a white horse, who broke the door down. The question, said Ms Darker-Smith, is why she did not break the door down herself.

She acknowledged that the size of her interview sample was not large enough to draw definitive conclusions. But her study is being treated seriously enough for discussion at the congress by the world's most influential therapists.

Ms Darker-Smith's advice to parents was to carry on reading to their children, but choose a variety of role model, including Pocahontas, the adventurous native American heroine. Thomas the Tank Engine and Paddington Bear were also suitably unsubmissive.

Older girls could usefully identify with the bright independence of Hermione in the Harry Potter series and the sparky Sabrina the Teenage Witch.

Ms Darker-Smith said younger generations exposed to television and other entertainment media might react differently and be less submissive than those weaned solely on literature.

Margaret Smith, who runs the Prevention of Domestic Abuse Centre at Derby, said, "It is an excellent study for others to research further. We learn about ourselves and how we relate to others through stories in childhood." If we hold these beliefs deeply enough, and have submissive personalities as adults, it can be difficult to break away from destructive relationships.

The theory was regarded more sceptically by Kim Reynolds, professor of children's literature at Newcastle University. "We have heard these arguments about fairytales since the 1970s, particularly from feminist critics," she said. "It is far too simplistic to say that girls who grow up reading fairytales with submissive characters will themselves become submissive."

7. The passage is especially intended for _____.
   A. parents with young daughters
   B. girls who like reading fairy stories
   C. girls who think they can change their partners
   D. parents with grown-up daughters

8. Cinderella, Rapunzel and Beauty in Beauty and the Beast are similar in that they _____.
   A. all married some princes
   B. all changed their partners with love
   C. were all abused by their partners
   D. all put up with abuse

9. Which of the following statements is true of the women in a control group?
   A. They don't believe in fairy tales.
   B. They don't believe in the transformational qualities of love.
   C. They have also experienced abuse.
   D. They survived abuse.

Passage 4

When Paul was a boy growing up in Utah, he happened to live near an old copper smelter, and the sulfur dioxide that poured out of the refinery had made a desolate wasteland out of what used to be a beautiful forest. Paul vowed that some day he would bring back the life to this land.

Many years later Paul was in the area, and he went to the smelter office. He asked if they had any plans to bring the trees back. The answer was "No." He asked them if they would let him try to bring the trees back. Again, the answer was "No." They didn't want him on their land. After praying about the matter, Paul realized he needed to become more knowledgeable before anyone would listen to him, so he went to college to study botany.

At the college he met a professor who was an expert in Utah's ecology. Unfortunately, Paul was told that the wasteland he wanted to bring back was beyond hope. He was told that his goal was foolish because even if he planted trees, and even if they grew, the wind would only blow the seeds forty feet per year, and that's all you'd get because there weren't any birds or squirrels to spread the seeds, and the seeds from those trees would need another thirty years before they started producing seeds of their own. Therefore, it would take approximately twenty thousand years to revegetate that six-square-mile piece of earth. His teachers told him it would be a waste of his life to try to do it. It just could not be done.

So he tried to go on with his life. He got a job operating heavy equipment, got married, and had some kids. However, as a good Christian, he knew that "faith by itself, if not accompanied by action, is dead" (James 2:17). So, he kept studying about the subject, and prayed for guidance on the matter. Then one night he felt led to take action by faith alone. He would do what he could, and trust God to do the rest. This was an important turning point.

Samuel Johnson wrote, "It is common to overlook what is near by keeping the eye fixed on something remote. In the same manner, present opportunities are neglected and attainable good is slighted by minds busied in extensive ranges." Paul stopped busying his mind in extensive ranges and looked at what opportunities for attainable good were right in front of him. Who among us hasn't wondered what God wants us to do in our life here on earth? Under the cover of darkness, Paul sneaked out into the wasteland with a backpack of seedlings and started planting. For seven hours he planted seedlings.

He did it again a week later. And every week, he made his secret journey into the wasteland and planted trees and shrubs and grass. But most of it died. Like so many of our hopes and dreams. However, Paul had faith, and kept planting.

For fifteen years he did this. Freezing winds and blistering heat, landslides and floods and fires destroyed his work time and time again. But he kept planting. One night he found a highway crew had come and taken tons of dirt for a road grade, and all the plants he painstakingly planted in that area were gone. I don't know about you, but this sounds like the way things have gone in my life. Time for some major prayers. Then Paul kept planting.

Week after week, year after year he kept at it, against the opinion of the authorities, against the trespassing laws, against the devastation of road crews, against the wind and rain and heat... even against plain common sense. He just kept planting.

Slowly, very slowly, things began to take root. Then gophers appeared. Then rabbits. Then porcupines. The copper smelter eventually gave him permission, and later, as times were changing and there was political pressure to clean up the environment, the company actually hired Paul to do what he was already doing. They even provided him with machinery and crews to work with. Progress accelerated.

Now the place is fourteen thousand acres of trees, grass, bushes, as well as all kinds of wildlife. Paul has now received almost every environmental award Utah has. He says, "I thought that if I got this started, when I was dead and gone people would come and see it. I never thought I'd live to see it myself!"

It took him until his hair turned white, but he managed to keep that impossible vow he made to himself as a child.

10. When Paul was a boy, _____.
   A. he decided never to leave his hometown
   B. the economy of Utah depended wholly on the copper smelter
   C. no laws were made to protect the environment against pollution
   D. he determined to stop the copper smelter polluting the area

11. The underlined phrase "the plain common sense" probable means that _____.
   A. it was impossible for trees to grow on the wasteland
   B. his normal work and life would be greatly affected
   C. no one would like to join him in the efforts
   D. he had to keep everything he did secret

12. The message of the passage is that _____.
   A. action speaks louder than words   B. perseverance will work wonders
   C. God helps those who help themselves D. many hands make light work

Passage 5

Electronic health records (EHRs) have received a lot of attention since the Obama administration committed $19 billion in stimulus funds earlier this year to encourage hospitals and health care facilities to digitize patient data and make better use of information technology. The healthcare industry as a whole, however, has been slow to adopt information technology and integrate computer systems, raising the question of whether the push to digitize will result in information that empowers doctors to make better-informed decisions or a morass of disconnected data.

The University of Pittsburgh Medical Center (UPMC) knows firsthand how difficult it is to achieve the former, and how easily an EHR plan can fall into the latter. UPMC has spent five years and more than $1 billion on information technology systems to get ahead of the EHR issue. While that is more than five times as much as recent estimates say it should cost a hospital system, UPMC is a mammoth network consisting of 20 hospitals as well as 400 doctors' offices, outpatient sites and long-term care facilities employing about 50,000 people.

UPMC's early attempts to create a universal EHR system, such as its ambulatory electronic medical records rolled out between 2000 and 2005, were met with resistance as doctors, staff and other users either avoided using the new technology altogether or clung to individual, disconnected software and systems that UPMC's IT department had implemented over the years.

Although UPMC began digitizing some of its records in 1996, the turning point in its efforts came in 2004 with the rollout of its eRecord system across the entire health care network. eRecord now contains more than 3.6 million electronic patient records, including images and CT scans, clinical laboratory information, radiology data, and a picture archival and communication system that digitizes images and makes them available on PCs. The EHR system has 29,000 users, including more than 5,000 physicians employed by or affiliated with UPMC.

If UPMC makes EHR systems look easy, don't be fooled, cautions UPMC chief medical information officer Dan Martich, who says the health care network's IT systems require a "huge, on going effort" to ensure that those systems can communicate with one another. One of the main reasons is that UPMC, like many other health care organizations, use a number of different vendors for its medical and IT systems, leaving the integration largely up to the IT staff.

Since doctors typically do not want to change the way they work for the sake of a computer system, the success of an EHR program is dictated not only by the presence of the technology but also by how well the doctors are trained on, and use, the technology. Physicians need to see the benefits of using EHR systems both persistently and consistently, says Louis Baverso, chief information officer at UPMC's Magee-Women's Hospital. But these benefits might not be obvious at first, he says, adding, "What doctors see in the beginning is that they're losing their ability to work with paper documents, which has been so valuable to them up until now."

Given the lack of EHR adoption throughout the health care world, there are a lot of opportunities to get this right (or wrong). Less than 10 percent of U.S. hospitals have adopted electronic medical records even in the most basic way, according to a study authored by Ashish Jha, associate professor of health policy and management at Harvard School of Public Health. Only 1.5 percent have adopted a comprehensive system of electronic records that includes physicians' notes and orders and decision support systems that alert doctors of potential drug interactions or other problems that might result from their intended orders.

Cost is the primary factor stalling EHR systems, followed by resistance from physicians unwilling to adopt new technologies and a lack of staff with adequate IT expertise, according to Jha. He indicated that a hospital could spend from $20 million to $200 million to implement an electronic record system over several years, depending on the size of the hospital. A typical doctor's office would cost an estimated $50,000 to outfit with an EHR system.

13. In America, it is slow to adopt information technology because _____.

   A. the funds invested by the government is not enough in the past

   B. EHRs have received less attention of the public in the past

   C. whether it will be useful to doctors or not is doubtful

   D. UPMC knows how difficult it is to digitize the hospital

14. The University of Pittsburgh Medical Center (UPMC) _____.

   A. is the first medical center to adopt information technology

   B. satisfies the requirement of the government on information technology

   C. spends less money on information technology than it is estimated

   D. attempts to create a universal EHR system, but meets some difficulties

15. The most important reason of most hospitals being reluctant to adopt EHR system is that _____.

   A. the cost is too high for the hospital to afford

   B. physicians are unwilling to adopt it

   C. there is a lack of staff with adequate IT expertise

   D. doctor worry about its negative influence on patients

Passage 6

AARON SORKIN: I don't know if there is such a thing as a typical New York Times reporter, but if there is, then you ain't it.

DAVID CARR: No, I'm not.

SORKIN: You're from the Twin Cities?

CARR: Yes. I grew up outside Minneapolis, in Hopkins, Minnesota.

SORKIN: Did you go to college there?

CARR: Yeah. I went to two undistinguished land-grant universities in the seven short years it took me to graduate.

SORKIN: What did you major in?

CARR: Um ... Frisbee and smoking doobies ... But I did double major in journalism and psychology at the University of Minnesota. I began working at a great little weekly that no longer exists called the Twin Cities Reader. My first story was about a friend of my father's, an older white guy who had been beaten up by some cops when he intervened on the arrest of two black males who seemed fairly subdued. So I said to my dad, "Boy, somebody should do a story about that." And my dad said, "I thought that's what you were doing—that you were a journalist." So that became my first story.

SORKIN: Well, you rose pretty fast, because you eventually became the editor of the Twin Cities Reader.

CARR: There were a few detours along the way, and I ended up sort of washing out of journalism for a while, but I did wind up becoming the editor.

SORKIN: I don't know if this is the period when you washed out of journalism, but you wrote a book a few years ago / The Night of the Gun, 2008 / in which you refer to something that you and I both have in common, which is that we are recovering cocaine addicts.

CARR: That's correct.

SORKIN: I don't want to dwell on that, but it's worth mentioning because it's an uncommon route that you took to the Times. How much time do you have now?

CARR: I'm five years sober. I had 13 years, and that was off of being sort of poly-addicted. I was a low-bottom crackhead, sobered up for 13 years, and then decided to try to be a nice, suburban alcoholic and see how that would go. That lasted ... Well, it ended in handcuffs, so it didn't go great. But I have about five-and-a-half years back now.

SORKIN: Congratulations. I reached 10 years in April and started thinking ... You know, I go to meetings, and there are these old-timers, and I'm not sure how many years you need to be considered an old-timer, but that's my new goal.

CARR: I think it begins with double-digits recovery. I think you're officially now long in the tooth.

SORKIN: [laughs] Awesome. I've been waiting for that.

CARR: But, you know, I hit double digits, and it sort of got away from me—and there's no insurance that you're going to get another swing at bat. I've got a lot of friends who never made it back, so I'm just happy to be one of the lucky ones. When I did my book tour, a lot of people asked me about why their brother is dead or their mother is dead and I'm still here. I'd say, "You know what? I really don't know. Couldn't say." You quickly learn that it doesn't matter where you are or what level of accomplishment you're sitting on top of. If you can't stay off the juice or the drugs, then you'll end up on the wrong side of the grass just as quickly as the homeless guy down the street.

16. What does Sorkin works for?
   A. The University of Minnesota.   B. Two undistinguished land-grant universities.
   C. Twin Cities Reader.   D. New York Times.

17. He wrote his first story when he _____.
   A. worked at the Twin Cities Reader   B. washed out of journalism
   C. was in prison   D. was a homeless guy down the street

18. The underlined sentence "How much time do you have now?" can be replaced by "How long have you been successful in _____".

   A. becoming a journalist   B. quitting drug addiction
   C. writing a book The Night of the Gun   D. double-digits recovery

Passage 7

Gabrielle Melchionda broke into tears when firefighters accidentally flooded the headquarters of Mad Gab's, the beauty company she had founded two decades ago, even though she knew that insurance would replace the desks, computers, and shelves of lip balm she had lost. To her surprise, however, the real pain came in the months that followed, when she continued to owe salaries and rent while her sales slowed to a trickle.

"The critical piece that was missing was business-interruption insurance," said Ms. Melchionda, who had property and liability insurance but had never got around to adding a policy that replaces income lost after accidents.

Business owners have plenty of stories like Ms. Melchionda's, of policies that didn't cover enough damage or covered the wrong risk. Some of these complaints can be attributed to tight-fisted insurance companies or misinformed agents, but the fault often lies with entrepreneurs who gloss over their insurance decisions.

"Generally speaking, small-business owners are not completely aware of the coverage they have or the coverage they need," said Steven Spiro, an independent insurance agent, explaining that many small-business owners buy insurance simply to comply with the requirements of an office lease.

Buying insurance can be intimidating, and it's difficult to know who is trying to take advantage of you and who is giving honest advice. That's why you should start by asking other entrepreneurs in your industry what kinds of insurance they carry and who they bought it from. There are three types of vendors who can help you pick insurance: independent agents, captive agents, and risk consultants.

Independent agents, also known as brokers, offer the greatest choice because they typically represent many carriers. They are paid on commission by the insurance company, between 10 percent and 20 percent of the annual premium depending on the policy. Beware: because some carriers pay a higher commission than others, brokers may be tempted to play favorites.

Captive agents represent one insurance company that pays them a salary and commands their loyalty. Some companies such as Allstate only deal with their own agents; that means you can only buy their policies through one of their agents.

Both independent and captive agents receive bonuses at the end of the year based on their ratio of policies sold to damages paid. That means it's in their interest to sell you as much insurance as possible and minimize your claims as much as possible.

Understand, also, that most agents focus solely on insurance. "Sometimes there are solutions to your problem that might be better treated without insurance," said Arthur Flitner, a small-business expert at the Insurance Institute of America. In some cases, for example, it makes more financial sense to self-insure against certain property risks by setting up a rainy-day fund, or to minimize lawsuit risks by enforcing strict employment policies.

That's when a risk consultant can help. Because they're costly — you'll usually pay a few thousand dollars for a basic project — it makes sense to hire a risk expert only if you have an unusually risky operation, or run a business with more than, say, $25 million in revenue(收入) or more than 100 employees.

After you've found some trustworthy vendors, it's time to shop for bids. Go to as many brokers and agents as you like, but keep in mind that insurance companies won't bid on the same account through different brokers.

19. The passage mainly focuses on how to _____.

   A. buy the most suitable insurance for your own business

   B. pick an agent for you own business

   C. pick a policy when you buy the insurance

   D. deal with the insurance company

20. Buying insurance sometimes is frightening in that _____.

   A. you should ask other people in your industry for the advice

   B. it is not easy to distinguish the honest advice and the lie

   C. there are different types of agents for you to choose from

   D. you do not know where to buy insurance for your company

21. If you have an unusually risky operation you should _____.

   A. find a trustworthy vendor   B. seek help from insurance company

   C. hire a risk expert   D. weigh the risk of your company by yourself

Passage 8

In recent years, teams of workers dispatched by Google have been working hard to make digital copies of books. So far, Google has scanned more than 10 million titles from libraries in America and Europe — including half a million volumes held by the Bodleian in Oxford. The exact method it uses is unclear; the company does not allow outsiders to observe the process.

Why is Google undertaking such a venture? Why is it even interested in all those out-of-print library books, most of which have been gathering dust on forgotten shelves for decades? The company claims its motives are essentially public-spirited. Its overall mission, after all, is to "organise the world's information", so it would be odd if that information did not include books.

The company likes to present itself as having lofty aspirations. "This really isn't about making money. We are doing this for the good of society." As Santiago de la Mora, head of Google Books for Europe, puts it: "By making it possible to search the millions of books that exist today, we hope to expand the frontiers of human knowledge."

Dan Clancy, the chief architect of Google Books, does seem genuine in his conviction that this is primarily a philanthropic(慈善的) exercise. "Google's core business is search and find, so obviously what helps improve Google's search engine is good for Google," he says. "But we have never built a spreadsheet(电子数据表) outlining the financial benefits of this, and I have never had to justify the amount I am spending to the company's founders."

It is easy, talking to Clancy and his colleagues, to be swept along by their missionary passion.

But Google's book-scanning project is proving controversial. Several opponents have recently emerged, ranging from rival tech giants such as Microsoft and Amazon to small bodies representing authors and publishers across the world. In broad terms, these opponents have levelled two sets of criticisms at Google.

First, they have questioned whether the primary responsibility for digitally archiving the world's books should be allowed to fall to a commercial company. In a recent essay in the New York Review of Books. Robert Darnton, the head of Harvard University's library, argued that because such books are a common resource — the possession of us all — only public, not-for-profit bodies should be given the power to control them.

The second related criticism is that Google's scanning of books is actually illegal. This allegation has led to Google becoming mired in(陷入) a legal battle whose scope and complexity makes the Jarndyce and Jarndyce case in Charles Dickens' Bleak House look straightforward.

At its centre, however, is one simple issue: that of copyright. The inconvenient fact about most books, to which Google has arguably paid insufficient attention, is that they are protected by copyright. Copyright laws differ from country to country, but in general protection extends for the duration of an author's life and for a substantial period afterwards, thus allowing the author's heirs to benefit. (In Britain and America, this post-death period is 70 years.) This means, of course, that almost all of the books published in the 20th century are still under copyright—and the last century saw more books published than in all previous centuries combined. Of the roughly 40 million books in US libraries, for example, an estimated 32 million are in copyright. Of these, some 27 million are out of print.

Outside the US, Google has made sure only to scan books that are out of copyright and thus in the "public domain" (works such as the Bodleian's first edition of Middlemarch, which anyone can read for free on Google Books Search).

But, within the US, the company has scanned both in-copyright and out-of-copyright works. In its defence, Google points out that it displays only small segments of books that are in copyright—arguing that such displays are "fair use". But critics allege that by making electronic copies of these books without first seeking the permission of copyright holders, Google has committed piracy.

22. Google claims its plan for the world's biggest online library is _____.
    A. to save out-of-print books in libraries   B. to serve the interest of the general public
    C. to encourage reading around the world   D. to promote its core business of searching

23. Opponents of Google Books believe that digitally archiving the world's books should be controlled by _____.
    A. the world's tech giants   B. the world's leading libraries
    C. non-profit organisations   D. multinational companies

24. Google defends its scanning in-copyright books by saying that _____.
    A. making electronic copies of books is not a violation of copyright
    B. the online display of in-copyright books is not for commercial use
    C. it is willing to compensate the copyright holders
    D. it displays only a small part of their content

Passage 9

When I was a graduate student in biochemistry at Tufts University School of Medicine, I read an abridged version of Montaigne's Essays. My friend Margaret Rea (a.k.a. Marci Trindle) and I spent hours wandering around Boston discussing the meaning and implications of the essays. Michel de Montaigne lived in the 16th century near Bordeaux, France. He did his writing in the southwest tower of his chateau, where he surrounded himself with a library of more than 1,000 books, a remarkable collection for that time. Montaigne posed the question, "What do I know?" By extension, he asks us all: Why do you believe what you think you know? My latest attempt to answer Montaigne can be found in Everyday Practice of Science: Where Intuition and Passion Meet Objectivity and Logic, originally published in January 2009 and soon to be out in paperback from the Oxford University Press.

Scientists tend to be glib about answering Montaigne's question. After all, the success of technology testifies to the truth of our work. But the situation is more complicated.

In the idealized version of how science is done, facts about the world are waiting to be observed and collected by objective researchers who use the scientific method to carry out their work. But in the everyday practice of science, discovery frequently follows an ambiguous and convoluted route. We aim to be objective, but we cannot escape the context of our unique life experiences. Prior knowledge and interests influence what we experience, what we think our experiences mean, and the subsequent actions we take. Opportunities for misinterpretation, error, and self-deception abound.

Consequently, discovery claims should be thought of as protoscience. Similar to newly staked mining claims, they are full of potential. But it takes communal scrutiny and acceptance to transform a discovery claim into a full-fledged discovery. This is the credibility process, through which the individual researcher's me, here, now becomes the community's anyone, anywhere, anytime. Objective knowledge is the goal, not the starting point.

Once a discovery claim becomes public, the discoverer receives intellectual credit. But, unlike with mining claims, the community takes control of what happens next. Within the complex social structure of the scientific community, researchers make discoveries; editors and reviewers act as gatekeepers by controlling the publication process; other scientists use the new finding to suit their own purposes; and finally, the public (including other scientists) receives the new discovery and possibly accompanying technology. As a discovery claim works its way through the community, a dialectic of interaction and confrontation between shared and competing beliefs about the science and the technology involved transforms an individual's discovery claim into the community's credible discovery.

Two paradoxes infuse this credibility process. First, scientific work tends to focus on some aspect of prevailing knowledge that is viewed as incomplete or incorrect. Little reward accompanies duplication and confirmation of what is already known and believed. The goal is new-search, not re-search. Not surprisingly, newly published discovery claims and credible discoveries that appear to be important and convincing will always be open to challenge and potential modification or refutation by future researchers. Second, novelty itself frequently provokes disbelief. Nobel Laureate and physiologist Albert Szent-Györgyi once described discovery as "seeing what everybody has seen and thinking what nobody has thought." But thinking what nobody else has thought and telling others what they have missed may not change their views. Sometimes years are required for truly novel discovery claims to be accepted and appreciated.

In the end, credibility "happens" to a discovery claim — a process that corresponds to what philosopher Annette Baier has described as the commons of the mind. "We reason together, challenge, revise, and complete each other's reasoning and each other's conceptions of reason," she wrote in a book with that title. In the case of science, it is the commons of the mind where we find the answer to Montaigne's question: Why do you believe what you think you know?

25. According to the first paragraph, the process of discovery is characterized by its _____.

    A. uncertainty and complexity   B. misconception and deceptiveness

    C. logicality and objectivity   D. systematicness and regularity

26. Albert Szent-Györgyi would most likely agree that _____.

    A. scientific claims will survive challenges

    B. discoveries today inspire future research

    C. efforts to make discoveries are justified

    D. scientific work calls for a critical mind

27. Which of the following would be the best title of the test?

    A. Novelty as an Engine of Scientific Development.

    B. Collective Scrutiny in Scientific Discovery.

    C. Evolution of Credibility in Doing Science.

    D. Challenge to Credibility at the Gate to Science.

Passage 10

Last year, I was accepted into the E.O./M.I.T. Entrepreneurial Masters Program. The first session focused on employees, culture and communication. Our goal was to take the systems we learned in class and implement them in our respective companies over the next 12 months. I've recently returned from the program's second annual session where we evaluated our performance.

The first thing I did when I returned a year ago was to hold a team retreat at which we agreed upon seven core values on which the company would operate (they emphasized customer service, teamwork, integrity, etc.). We posted these core values on the wall, and we agreed to adhere to them on a daily basis. In addition, we created awards to honor team members who consistently demonstrate these values.

There is a box located in our team room area for members to nominate someone for representing a core value during a given week. Our intern, David, collects the nominations and announces them to the entire company every Friday during our team meeting. At the end of the quarter, the person who has the most nominations for each core value gets a financial bonus, and his or her name goes up on the wall for the quarter. In addition, we have an overall award given to the team member who receives the most nominations across the board. The awards have given us extra incentive to help each other and to show our appreciation for superior service. But it also did something else. It made it more obvious who is and who isn't a good fit for the company.

When I scheduled our quarterly one-on-ones, I asked everyone fill out a simple form and rate each team member — on a scale of 1 to 10 — on how they align with our new core values. The ratings were done anonymously. I trusted that each person would rate people honestly, but I knew that if one person gave another straight for every core value, I would have to omit that s core from the tally (and have a separate conversation to figure out the underlying problem). I also had each person rate his or her own performance.

The good news is that people evaluated each other fairly. However, while most of the team scored extremely high on each value, not everyone passed. In fact, one employee — despite a self-rating of 10 for teamwork, and despite receiving high marks in other categories — received very low teamwork scores.

I recognized the problem immediately. This was an employee who complained frequently without offering solutions. It became clear to me that this person was not a good "fit" with the rest of the team. I tallied all of the feedback and reviewed the scores with each person individually. As a result of our new evaluation process, I ended up losing two team members (the good news is that they realized it themselves). But we brought on new members who fit better, and I think this is something I will keep doing on a quarterly basis.

When I went back to E.O./M.I.T. this year, I found classmates who were concerned about the morale in their offices. I also found that while many of the other chief executives had gathered management together to create their lists of core values, not all of those lists had made their way into the hands of the employees. It seemed there was a disconnect between creating the core values and actually living them. Others, however, did a great job integrating the values into every aspect of their organizations.

I think this is one of the great take aways from my class. While I am proud of how my team bonded through this exercise, I know that there were other areas where we didn't succeed as well. I look forward to connecting with my fellow classmates throughout the coming year to learn better approaches for our business and for my own personal journey.

28. The seven core values are put forward based on _____.

  A. the writer's concept   B. the systems learn in the program

  C. the decisions of team meeting   D. numbers of awards

29. What can be leaned about the quarterly one-on-ones?

　　A. It is carried out every week.

　　B. The highest score is 70 in theory.

　　C. A score of straight 1 for a value is useless.

　　D. The writer worries about the fairness of ratings.

30. The writer of this passage aims to recommend an approach to _____.

　　A. figuring out employees who stand out in the team

　　B. firing some employees unfit for the company

　　C. distinguishing between nominations and rating

　　D. strengthening employees' teamwork spirit

模块二　英语学科教学知识与能力

第一章　大纲描述

考试目标

掌握外语教学基本理论、英语教学专业知识与国家英语课程标准内容等学科教学知识，并能用以指导高中英语教学。

考试要求

1. 了解外语教学基本理论，理解语言观、语言学习观、语言教学观等对高中英语教学的指导作用。
2. 理解国家颁布的英语学科课程标准的目标内容（语言技能、语言知识、情感态度、学习策略和文化知识），以及课程标准的其他相关知识，并能在教学设计和实施中运用。
3. 掌握英语语言知识（语音、词汇、语法、语篇等）的教学基本原则、讲解和训练方法。
4. 掌握英语语言技能（听、说、读、写）教学的基本原则和训练方法。
5. 能结合中外社会文化语境，设计并实施英语知识和技能的教学与训练。

第二章　考点解读

一、外语教学基本理论

主要包括：语言学和文学的一般原理、所学外语的语言理论、外语习得理论、外语教学和翻译理论、教育心理学理论、认知理论、互动理论、社会文化理论、任务型教学思想、外语教师发展理论。

二、外语教学基本观念

（一）语言观

语言观是人们对整个语言体系的基本看法，系统的语言观包括对语言的起源、语言的性质、语言的功能、语言的发展以及对语言的运用等问题的认识。人们的语言观千差万别。在当代,相当多的语言学家认同的语言观是:语言是一种特殊的社会现象,是人类的思维工具和最重要的交际工具,是一种音义结合的符号系统。

(二)语言学习观

英语教师对英语学习的本质及其过程各有不同的理解和解释,这就是英语教师的语言学习观。

我国中学英语教师的语言学习观主要表现以下三种:

1. 基于"接受"的学习观(或称"接受观")

具有这种学习观的教师把英语学习看成一个被动"接受"语言知识和技能的过程,同时认为学生所接受的语言知识和技能主要源于教材,因此他们认为学生需要记住教材上记载的所有知识和方法,而不重视学生自身的学习动机,已有的知识、经验和对知识的创造,只强调与"注意"和"记忆"有关的策略,因为他们相信"熟能生巧",相信随着学生记住的教材上的语言知识和技能越多,它们就能自动地生成语言。

"接受观"的主要理论基础是行为主义学习论,该理论的核心思想是:言语行为是"可操作的"(及可通过外部"刺激"和主体"反应"得到"巩固"),因此是可以通过各种"强化"手段获得的。

持"接受观"的教师在课堂教学中最明显的特征就是:过分强调对语言形式的重复操练(如反复朗读、背诵、模仿和记忆,同时对语言输入和学生的自主性进行高度控制,要求学生的话语绝对准确等)。这种机械性的学习可能产生的积极影响是:学生能够较清楚地了解和记住各种语言形式知识(如词语和各种语法项目);但难以避免的消极影响是使学生成为被动的记忆者,影响学生个人对语言的假设和检验。

2. 基于"体验"的学习观(或称"体验观")

具有这种学习观的教师通常把英语学习看成一个主动"尝试"和"体验"语言的过程,认为学生是"中心",语言的学习与发展是学生利用自己已有的知识、技能、策略和经验重构个人知识的结果,而教师只是学习机会和条件的提供者,强调的学习策略大多与语言的"理解"和"产生"有关,因为他们相信,正是学生在语言"理解"和语言"产生"时需要经历的这一系列心理体验(如"注意"、"理解"、"计划"、"监察"和"修正"等),特别是学生有关语言"错误"的体验,才使他们能有效地获得系统的英语语言知识和能力。

体验观的理论基础是认知论和建构主义理论。认知论的核心思想是:引起语言行为的是人的内心活动,语言学习是一种人的认识和创造的过程;建构主义理论进一步认为:导致人的语言认知结构变化的是认知结构和外部环境刺激之间"同化"和"顺化"的关系:主体的认识结构因受到同化的刺激而发生整体性变化,即个人知识的"建构"涉及人的信念、意图及其他心理建构因素。

持"体验观"的教师在课堂教学中有两个明显的特征:其一,在选择学习内容时考虑学生的主观因素(如学生已有的知识、经验、兴趣、需要等);其二,在设计学习活动时往往会注意扩展语言输入,重视语义逻辑,积极为学生的个人选择提供理解语言的机会,培养学生监察语言的意识和能力等。这种教学的积极意义是:大量的语言尝试可能使学生获得内化语言的机会,但可能因为缺乏与他人充分的交流而影响其语言运用能力的发展。

3. 基于"协商"的学习观(或称"协商观")

具有这种学习观的教师把英语学习看成一个在特定社会环境中用语言进行"协商"的过程,认为学生的语言学习和发展都是与外部交流环境"协商"的结果,教师除了应该为学生提供合作与交流的机会,还应该成为"协商"的引导者和促进者,使学生能够在与其他交流者的"合作"和与整个环境的"互动"中,实现有意义的协商与共享,从而修正和发展自己对原有的知识、技能、策略和经验的理解。

协商观主要以社会建构主义理论为基础,该理论的核心思想是:认知结构的发展是个人将外部的、存在于主体间的东西内化为个人特有的东西,即学生根据自己的知识背景,在有教师和同伴合作与帮助下主动建构个人意义。

持"协商观"的教师在课堂教学中有两个明显特征:首先是对课堂环境的积极建设,包括组织小组活动,培养合作与交流的课堂气氛与习惯,使学生在与环境(特别是与其他学生)的协商中互动、互助、互补;其次是根据学生的需要给予引导和支持,而非指令性要求,以便更充分地发挥学生的自主性和挑战学生潜能,但也可能因学生的差异性而无法实现统一的学习目标。

中国英语学习者的英语学习观念有七个主要构成成分:自信心、词汇、信赖权威依赖母语、敢于冒险、语言天赋、综合性方法、学习动机。

(三)语言教学观

语言教学观是教师对语言教学本质的看法,如教师对知识、语言、学习、课堂,特别是教与学的密切关系等一系列问题的综合看法。

我国中学英语教师通常有三种教学观:

1. 知识传授观

持这种教学观的英语教师把教学看成"传授"英语语言文化知识的简单过程,认为教师通过对各种知识的介绍、呈现、示范、解释、拓展、分析、归纳,就能让学生理解、记住、掌握,甚至运用这些知识。

这种教学观的理论基础是实证主义的知识观和行为主义的学习论,将知识仅仅看成可以传递的客观实体,忽略学生在"知"的过程中对知识的主体作用;不关注学生已有的知识结构和学生理解、掌握知识的具体过程,采用以"记忆"为主要心理特征的模仿性、重复性、巩固性操练活动,来取代学生个体的知识建构过程。

知识传授观认为教学活动的主要性质是"传授",在这种教学中,"知识"是整个教学活动的核心,因为教师是"知识"的传授者,学生是"知识"的接受者,人们关心的是教师传授的"知识"是否清楚、准确,学生接受的"知识"是否正确、全面,对教师和学生的发展不太关心,他们较多关心的是学生知识性考试的成绩及其所决定的教师工作价值。

2. 目标管理观

持这种教学观的英语教师把教学看成一个可以管理的系统工程,以课程"目标"为中心,根据学生英语语言学习的需要来设计和实现对课程内容、过程、学习方式和评估的一系列课程要素的科学管理,如对"课程"的宏观计划和对"任务"的微观设计,包括开发课程主题,选择课程的语言和文化内容,确定学习任务的具体目标、内容、过程和策略方式,决定引导学生思考和检测学习效果的具体方案等。

这种教学观的理论基础是建构主义的认识论对"知识"和"学习"的解释,以及教育学关于课程理论的发展。语言知识的发展是学生内在"建构"的结果,学生是学习的主体,教师作为学习的管理者,通过课程为学生提供学习的机会和条件,比如教师根据学生内在的知识结构(包括其建构语言知识所需要的各种语言与非语言知识、技能、策略和经验),尽可能为学生提供体验、理解和使用语言的机会和有利条件。新课程标准对中学英语教师这种教学观的形成起了很大的推动作用。

目标管理观认为教学活动的主要性质是"管理",教师是整个教学活动的核心:教师既是"知识"的管理者(对知识的选择与检测);也是"学生"的管理者(对学习任务的设计和管理)。教师可能忽略不同经验背景和个性特点学生的发展,但必然关心自己作为教师的专业技能发展,特别是教学设计和课堂管理的专业技术和经验。

3. 学习促进观

持这种教学观的英语教师把教学看成一个教师为促进学习而进行协商和决策的过程。由于每个学生所需要语言学习的机会和条件可能不尽相同,教师为学生提供的统一课程(即共同学习的机会和条件)难以满足每个学生的实际需要,教师必须在特定的课堂环境中与瞬息万变的课堂因素进行协商,尽可能为学生创造健康、和谐、生态的课堂环境与人文关系,促进学生个体之间的交流、协商、合作、激励,甚至碰撞,让他们根据个人的需要去寻找或发掘更多属于自己的学习机会和条件。

这种教学观的理论基础是解释主义的知识观和社会建构主义的学习论,它强调知识建构的"个人性"和个体认知的"差异性"(知识是个体基于个人经验和所处环境的个人理解与解释),更强调个体之间的社会交流、合作与协商,强调个人将外部的,"存在于主体间的东西"内化为个人经验的能力。

学习促进观认为教学活动的主要性质是"促进","学生"才是教学活动的核心,因为学生需要在教师的支持下自己去获得知识,学会管理自己(学会学习和学会选择个人发展方式)。在与学生"互动性协商"的过程中,教师不但可能促进学生的发展,也可能更大限度地挑战自己的课堂决策潜能,从而发展自己,并在对学生更深入、更细致的人文关怀中获得对教师职业更多的理解。(韩刚,2011)

三、英语课程标准的目标内容

国家教育部颁布的英语课程标准的目标内容包括：语言技能、语言知识、情感态度、学习策略和文化意识。

（一）语言技能

英语课程标准指出：语言技能是构成语言交际能力的重要组成部分。语言技能包括听、说、读、写以及这四种技能的综合运用能力。听和读是理解的技能，说和写是表达的技能。这四种技能在语言学习和交际中相辅相成、相互促进；听、说、读、写既是学习的内容，又是学习的手段。因此，高中英语教学应通过大量的专项和综合性语言实践活动，引导学生形成综合语言运用能力，为真实语言交际打基础。

英语课程标准对语言技能中的听、说、读、写四种技能提出九个级别的目标要求，高中英语教师应重点熟悉、理解并掌握六、七、八级目标要求（详见《英语课程标准》第二部分课程目标之一，语言技能）。

（二）语言知识

英语课程标准指出，英语语言基础知识包括：语音、词汇、语法、功能和话题五个方面的内容。知识是语言能力的有机组成部分，是发展语言技能的重要基础。因此，高中英语教学应创设大量的语境，引导学生积累丰厚英语语言知识，为发展英语技能夯实基础。

英语课程标准对语言知识中的语音、词汇、语法、功能和话题提出二级、五级、八级的目标要求，高中英语教师应重点熟悉、理解并掌握八级目标要求（详见《英语课程标准》第二部分内容标准之二，语言知识）。

（三）情感态度

英语课程标准指出：情感态度指兴趣、动机、自信、意志和合作精神等影响学生学习过程和学习效果的相关因素以及在学习过程中逐渐形成的祖国意识和国际视野。保持积极的学习态度是英语学习成功的关键。高中英语教师应在教学中，不断激发并强化学生的学习兴趣，并引导他们逐渐将兴趣转化为稳定的学习动机，以使他们树立自信心，锻炼克服困难的意志，认识自己学习的优势与不足，乐于与他人合作，养成和谐和健康向上的品格，并能通过英语课程，增强祖国意识，拓展国际视野。

英语课程标准对情感态度提出二级、五级、八级的目标要求，高中英语教师应重点熟悉、理解并掌握八级目标要求（详见《英语课程标准》第二部分内容标准之三，情感态度）。

（四）学习策略

英语课程标准指出：学习策略指学生为了有效地学习和发展而采取的各种行动和步骤。英语学习的策略包括：认知策略（指学生为了完成具体的学习任务而采取的步骤和方法）；调控策略（指学生对学习进行计划、实施、反思、评价与调整的策略）；交际策略（是学生为了争取更多的交际机会，维持交际以及提高交际效果而采取的各种策略）；资源策略（是学生合理并有效利用多种媒体进行学习并运用英语的策略）。

英语课程标准对学习策略提出二级、五级、八级的目标要求,高中英语教师应重点熟悉、理解并掌握八级目标要求(详见《英语课程标准》第二部分内容标准之四,学习策略)。

(五)文化意识

英语课程标准指出:语言有丰富的文化内涵。在外语教学中,文化是指所学语言国家的历史、地理、风土人情、传统习俗、生活方式、文学艺术、行为规范、价值观念等。接触和了解英语国家文化有益于对英语的理解和使用,有益于培养世界意识。在高中英语教学阶段,要通过扩大学生接触异国文化的范围,帮助学生拓展视野,使他们提高对中外文化异同的敏感性和鉴别能力,进而提高跨文化交际能力。

英语课程标准对文化意识提出二级、五级、八级的目标要求,高中英语教师应重点熟悉、理解并掌握八级目标要求(详见《英语课程标准》第二部分内容标准之五,文化意识)。

四、英语语言知识(语音、词汇、语法、语篇等)的教学基本原则,讲解和训练方法

(一)英语语音的教学原则和训练方法

1.英语语音教学应遵循的原则

(1)主动性原则。鼓励学生"不怕丑、多开口"。

(2)实践性原则。加强实践,认真模仿。

(3)规范性原则。掌握发音要领,突破发音难点,力求发音准确清晰。

(4)有效性原则。在英语语流中练习语音。

(5)全面优化原则。注重语音、重音、语调、节奏的相互联系,彼此渗透的综合性训练。

2.英语语音训练方法:在进行适当的语音理论知识教学的情况下,应做到以下几点:

(1)合理运用演示法、对比法、手势法、辨音法、口形定位法、模仿法、录音法等进行英语语音训练。

(2)把语音教学与听力、朗读教学相结合,注意发音与语境和内容的联系,注意语音在语流中的变化,注意连贯话语中发音技巧,使语音教学在交际活动中变得妙趣横生。

(3)努力剔除母语语音习惯对英语语音系统的干扰。

(4)重视语音的交际性功能的养成训练:重视句子重音、句子连读、失去爆破、语调、朗读或口语节奏的感知和模仿。

(二)英语词汇的教学原则与方法

1.英语词汇的教学原则

(1)主动性原则。鼓励学生主动并饶有兴趣地记忆运用词语。

(2)词语的音形义相结合的教学原则。

(3)联想性原则。利用中心词的音、形、义或话题进行联想扩展以加大词汇的习得范围。

(4)"词不离句,句不离文"的原则。

(5)学用结合的教学原则。

(6)巩固性原则。适度复现,克服遗忘。

2.英语词汇的教学方法

(1)结合语境进行词汇教学:词不离句,句不离文。十分得体地把词语放在特定的语境中去感知、体验、理解、记忆、复习和巩固,有益于学生扩大词汇量,更有益于学生逐渐养成英语思维的习惯。

(2)通过让学生用已知词语来解释生词词义进行词汇教学。

(3)引导学生围绕话题联想并习用相关词汇。

(4)利用教材中的主要阅读语篇和课外英语读物加深对词汇的含义和用法的理解与记忆,增加对生词的兴趣和专注力,以提高学生的英语词汇能力。

(5)联想归纳法:心理学研究表明:把相关内容集中或联系起来记忆,效果更佳。对已学的词汇按照构词法、词汇意义、短语搭配等进行联想归纳,不仅可以巩固和扩大词汇量,而且可以使英语词汇网络化和系统化,这样就能有效地改变学生的认知方式,进而有力支撑英语表达。英语词汇教学是英语教学的重点、难点,其教学方法难以数语概全,随着英语教学研究的发展,更新更有效的方法会令英语词汇教学大有改观。

(三)英语语法的教学原则与方法

1.英语语法的教学原则

英语语法教学应与交际法语言课程相结合,坚持实践性、针对性、区别性、渐进性等原则;注意交际法与传统法并用,适当集中、突出重点等具体教学要求,摆正语法教学在整个英语教学中的位置。

2.英语语法的教学方法

(1)要把传统的教师灌注式的语法教学变为师生、生生互动式的学用语法教学。

(2)语法教学与听、说、读、写训练紧密结合,在语言环境中开展语法教学活动。

(3)语法教学与话题、功能的教学结合,与语篇教学和实际运用结合,开展任务型语法学习活动。

(4)采用自然语法(Natural Grammar)教学思想,通过词汇教学语法。

(5)采用归纳法,启发学生观察、发现、体验、感悟、分析、综合、逐步理解和掌握英语语法。

(6)为适应善于理性分析的学生的需求,可适时地运用演绎法进行英语语法教学。

(7)实施三维语法教学(Grammar 3D),既要让学生明白语法结构变化规则,即形式(form),又要弄清该结构在语境中的意义(meaning),更要善于使用(use)。

(四)英语语篇的教学原则与方法

1.英语语篇的教学原则

(1)主动性原则。鼓励学生主动参与英语语篇教学活动。

(2)趣味性原则。与学生一起挖掘发现语篇的新奇点,以激发师生共同探讨研究的兴趣。

(3)整体性原则。把语篇作为一个整体来进行教学。

(4)整合性原则。把与该语篇相关的信息有选择性地适度整合使用,拓宽见识,加深理解。

(5)有效性原则。有效提高阅读速度、阅读能力和优化阅读技巧。

(6)发展性原则。通过语篇教学,为学生今后学习和终身学习打下坚实基础。

2.英语语篇的教学方法

(1)整体教学法:主要抓主旨大意(main idea),分析标题(title)和寻找主题句(topic sentence)进行语篇教学,让学生从整体上理解全文的结构和内容,同时也引导学生发散思维,收放自如。

(2)线索教学法:针对记叙文,主要抓5W+H(Who,When,Where,What,Why,How)。

(3)速记教学法:用Note-making进行语篇教学,引导学生抓具有逻辑关联的细节,深入理解全文内容。

(4)社会文化背景知识介绍法:针对反映英语国家历史、地理、风土人情、社会热点等的语篇,可利用背景知识教学,把语篇的情景语境与社会文化语境有机结合,提高学生的文化素养,提升语篇教学的境界。

(5)段落提问教学法:将整体教学法细化到段落中。

(6)讨论教学法:关键在于设疑并正确引导,让学生各抒己见,增强对语篇理解表达的真实感和开放性,还可充分调动学生的参与性、主动性与创造性。

(7)意译法(Paraphrase):让学生用已知的英语表达形式去意译语篇中的复杂的句子或新的语言形式,从而理解其内涵。

(8)翻译法和结构分析法:适度使用可在翻译这门艺术中体现学生的认知水平和综合素养;对于结构复杂,难度大的表达形式应适当翻译,更有助于学生感悟汉语和英语的韵味和语言的内在魅力。

五、英语语言技能(听、说、读、写)教学的基本原则和训练方法

(一)英语语言技能教学的基本原则

听、说、读、写,四会并举,阶段侧重,循序渐进,统筹兼顾,协调发展。

(二)英语语言技能的训练方法

1.明确听力训练的教学目标

(1)理解所听语言材料的主旨和要义。

(2)获取事实性的具体信息。

(3)对所听内容作出简单推断。

(4)理解说话者的意图、观点和态度。

2. 听力训练方法

(1)听力材料的选择应循序渐进,标准是英语材料的真实性。

(2)泛听和精听相结合。

(3)兼顾分析性(细节把握)和综合性(整体理解)的听力训练。

(4)分散训练和集中训练相结合。

(5)充分认识并解决听力理解困难的主客观因素,尤其要提高学生的心理素质,克服非智力因素的干扰。

(6)听、说有机结合。

3. 明确听说训练的教学目标

(1)语音训练:语音准确,会听会说。

(2)语调训练:注意升降调变化、句读重音、停顿、语气、速度等说话技巧。

(3)语流训练:说话流畅,有条理,前后连贯,层次清楚。

(4)语意训练:表意清楚,生动朴实,简洁流畅。

(5)语体训练:注意语言的得体性。

(6)语态训练:适当的体态、表情、手势帮助语言表达,达到理想的交际效果。

4. 听、说训练方法

(1)直观性听说训练法:观察图画、实物、自然景色、场景,听说结合训练。

(2)模仿性听说训练法:模仿教师或音像制品的语音、语调、语气,或听语言材料后复述,追求惟妙惟肖的效果。

(3)实践性听说训练法:按教材中的人物分角色对话;或采访;或辩论;或主持;或按真实的交际话题作专门训练。

(4)持续性听说训练法:指导学生听适量的难度适中的英语广播节目,鼓励学生课内外用英语交流。

5. 阅读教学的原则

(1)整体性原则。

(2)细节理解和整体理解相结合的原则。

(3)精读与泛读相结合的原则。

(4)听、说、读、写统筹兼顾的原则。

6. 阅读训练的教学目标

(1)理解语篇的主旨和要义。

(2)理解文中具体信息。

(3)根据上下文推断生词词义。

(4)作出恰当判断和推理。

(5)理解语篇的基本结构。

(6)理解作者的意图、观点、态度。

(7)能欣赏浅显的文学作品。

(8)除教材外,高中生课外阅读量应达到36万词以上。

7. 阅读训练方法

(1)利用有效的阅读材料来提高学生的阅读兴趣,丰富学生的阅读活动,拓展学生的阅读视野。教师为学生选择阅读材料时请注意:文章的难易度的适中性,文章内容的广泛性和文章的趣味性。

(2)师生共同归纳提炼并掌握阅读技巧。

技巧一:进行正确的预测阅读。学生在阅读过程中主动利用文理脉络预测下文可能出现的信息,从而积极地与作者进行心理沟通,直入文章主题,透彻理解文章和作者的意图。

技巧二:依据上下文准确猜测生词词义,提高在语境中悟意的能力,这是阅读能力高低的一种标志。

技巧三:针对不同文体特征,进行有效阅读方法训练。

技巧四:养成良好的阅读习惯。

其一要养成默读习惯,使注意力集中在文字符号上,纠正唇读、心读、喉读等做法,以免分散精力,影响阅读速度。

其二要克服指读、回视、重读等不良习惯,避免理解只停留在部分词句所造成支离破碎的信息摄取。

其三尽量减少眼停次数,扩大视力范围,在单位时间捕捉到更多的语言信息,进行连贯性的阅读理解。

(3)注意精读和泛读在社会文化背景知识和语言特色上的互补性和延展性。

(4)注意把获取信息式阅读与学习语言式阅读结合起来,跟踪研究学生进行阅读和语言习得的心理过程与学习方法,从而调适教师的教学策略。

8. 写作训练的教学目标

(1)能用文字及图表提供的信息进行简单描述。

(2)能写出常见体裁的短文,如报告或信函。

(3)能描述人物或事件,并表达自己的见解。

(4)能填写有关个人情况的表格,如申请表、求职表。

(5)能做简单的书面翻译。

9. 写作训练方法

英语写作要求学生有扎实的语言基本功,具备一定的审题能力、想象能力、表达能力、评价能力等。教师只有在平时教学中有意识地系统训练学生的英语写作能力,才能较好应对书面交际的随时之需。

(1)重视写作的整体训练,尤其在准备和写作阶段,把写和听、说、读结合训练。

(2)在英语写作教学中融合有关语言要素的训练,有效提高学生的词语运用能力和运用句型规范地道的呈现能力。

(3)在英语写作教学中融合篇章结构训练,更好地培养学生的逻辑思维能力,训练其写作的条理性和连贯性。侧重训练学生按时空线索、因果线索、转折或顺承线索、对比线索、顺序线索等,以及难度、感兴趣的程度、重要程度等不同的逻辑方法来安排组织信息,增强学生运用有序思维来写作的技巧。

(4)重视范文引路的英语写作训练,加强模仿、增加积累、借鉴写作技巧和章法,从而优化写作能力。

(5)写作修改阶段,将教师批改与学生自查、生生互查相结合,关注对内容、篇章结构和书写形式等不足的改进。

六、语境与高中英语教学

(一)语境

1. 语境的含义

语境(context)原意是文章或言谈中某一句的上句或下句,或许是上段或下段。后来这一含义得以拓展,Malinowski 1923年指出:语境指使用语言时所处的实际环境,包括语言内外的环境;Firth则认为:语境不仅指一句话的上下文,即由语言因素构成的上下文,而且也包括各种社会环境,即由语言与社会环境因素构成的情景的上下文。简言之,语境就是具体语言形式出现的环境。

2. 语境的分类

语境有广义与狭义之分。

(1)广义语境又称社会文化语境,是指语言形式赖以生存的社会文化形态,它涉及人类的衣食住行、风俗习惯和价值观念等各个方面。任何语言都有着深刻的社会文化内涵,这便是语言的文化功能。作为一种社会文化现象,语言被人们用来在社会文化语境中进行交际。

(2)狭义语境是指语言形式出现的具体语境,又称情景,即词语的搭配、句式的选择、语段语篇的内部结构等。有的语言学家认为:情景语境是由"场景"、"方式"和"交际者"三个部分组成;有的语言学家又进一步地把情景语境细分为八个因素:场景、角色、功能、意念、语体、重音和语调、语法和词汇,以及语言辅助手段。

社会文化语境与情景语境相辅相成,人们在用语言交际时必须遵循约定俗成的社会交际规则,同时又必须根据情景语境中的各个因素关系作相应调整。

(二)结合语境实施英语教学的重要意义

交际功能是语言的最本质的功能。学习英语的最根本的目的就是:用英语和话语规则在真实的社会情景中即席地进行言语交际活动。只有在具体的语境中呈现和练习语言形式,才能培养学生的"三种能力"。

1. 判断语言形式是否得体的能力;
2. 结合语境理解语言形式和意义的能力;
3. 在特定的语言环境中使用适当语言的能力。

更令人关注的是:在全面生动、真实可信的语境中操练语言是学生自主学习的策略之一,能调动学生的非智力因素,提高教学质量。

(三)如何结合语境设计并实施英语教学

1. 结合语境进行词汇教学

在高中英语词汇教学中,只有通过不同语境进行词语之间的比较分析,才能使学生真正理解该词,区分出同义词内在的一些细微差异,从而达到理解并准确使用词汇的目的。因此,教师在词汇教学中,要调动一切手段(如直观法、体态语、多媒体、检测试题的上下文设置等),提供足够的语境,使学生养成在语境中掌握词的观念意义和用法的良好习惯。

更重要的是:言语行为不仅总是发生在特定的语境中,而且总是发生在特定的文化语境中,因此,利用文化语境可以帮助学生了解词汇的文化意义(如汉语中的"力大如牛"在英语中表达为"as strong as a horse")。这样才能领悟和掌握英语的精神实质。

2. 结合语境进行语音教学

高中英语的语音教学重要的是把语音语调、重音节奏与语篇情景联系起来,让学生在语境中把握轻重缓急,高低起伏,以便更深地了解作品的思想和情感内涵。

3. 结合语境进行语篇教学

现行的高中英语教材是以背景与话题为主线编写的,每篇课文都体现了不同的语境。在教学中,教师应精心钻研教材,寻找、挖掘和活化篇章本身的语境。同时调动恰当的教学手段,创设真实的英语氛围,让学生受到语境的感染和暗示,从而情不自禁地融入语境,选择适当的语言形式进行思想情感和信息的交流,把教材上固化的文字符号转化成声情并茂的语言交际活动。

4. 结合语境进行语法教学

高中语法教学应坚持"先语境,后语法"的原则和顺序,只有在听或读完整的语篇中呈现语法结构,引导学生注意、发现并根据上下文理解、领悟语法结构的表意功能,才能准确把握"语法形式、意义和运用"三者关系的平衡,从而有效地帮助他们学习语法。

5. 创设良好的课堂语境,促进英语教学

高中英语教师应善于利用现代化的教学设施,因"课"制宜地呈现文化背景知识和真实的情景,把语篇转化为具有地道的英语文化味的现场语境,这样有利于提高语言输入的质量。与此同时,教师应把握好输入的度,控制在学生可理解——略高于学生现有的英语水平上,使他们更多地获取可理解的输入,更坚实更快地提高英语水平。

第三章 题型训练

语言教学知识与能力练习题(一)

一、单项选择题

1. The Jazz Age of the 1920s characterized by frivolity and carelessness is brought vividly to life in_____.
   A. The Great Gatsby   B. The Sun Also Rises
   C. The Grapes of Wrath   D. Tales of the Jazz Age

2. The characteristics of the listening process include spontaneity, visual clues, _____, listener's response, and speaker's adjustment.
   A. context   B. body language   C. intonation   D. gestures

3. English colonial expansion began with the colonization of _____ in 1583.
   A. Canada   B. Australia   C. India   D. Newfoundland

4. Robinson Crusoe is written by _____.
   A. Daniel Defoe   B. Henry Fielding
   C. Samuel Richardson   D. Jonathan Swift

5. When teaching _____, we should pay attention to the distinction between pronunciation and phonetics.
   A. spelling   B. writing   C. pronunciation D. intonation

6. _____ was not a Puritan himself but his view of man and human history originated to a great extent in Naturalism.
   A. Shakespeare   B. George Dickens   C. Charlotte Bronte D. Hawthorne

7. The Grand Canyon in north-western _____ is one of nature's most impressive sights.
   A. Utah   B. Arizona   C. Nevada   D. Idaho

8. The Tories were the forerunners of _____, which still bears the nickname today.
   A. the Labour Party   B. the Liberal Party
   C. the Social Democratic Party   D. the Conservative Party

9. The deductive method of teaching grammar lies in _____.
   A. ethic devotion, professional qualities   B. explaining, imitating and practising
   C. reasoning, analysing and comparing   D. listening, reading and writing

10. Which of the following activities is the most suitable for group work?

   A. Guessing games.　　　　　　　B. Story telling.

   C. Information gap .　　　　　　D. Drama performance.

11. If the air stream meets with no obstruction when a sound is pronounced, it is a(n) _____.

   A. voiced consonant　　　　　　B. voiceless consonant

   C. vowel　　　　　　　　　　　D. explosive

12. In the 18th century, there appeared _____ in England, which owed a great deal to the invention of machines.

   A. the Industrial Revolution　　　B. the Bourgeois Revolution

   C. the Wars of the Roses　　　　D. the Religious Reformation

13. In the Direct Method, teachers encourage learners to _____ rules of grammar through active use of the target language in the classroom.

   A. apply　　　　B. analyze　　　　C. induce　　　　D. paraphrase

14. "That government of the people, by the people, for the people, ... " were the words by _____.

   A. Thomas Jefferson　　　　　　B. Abraham Lincoln

   C. Andrew Johnson　　　　　　　D. Theodore Roosevelt

15. Britain's leading customers and suppliers are _____, Germany and the United States.

   A. Japan　　　　B. Belgium　　　C. the Netherlands　　D. France

二、简答题

1. Is this the research center that you visited last year?

   Is this research center what you visited last year?

2. Jim had a big time at the party last night.

   Don't worry; he is in the big time now.

3. According to the newspapers, Bush will come to China tomorrow.

   You may do it today or tomorrow according as the situation requires.

4. He added color to my performance.

   The boy's torn clothes gave color to his story of a fight.

5. She was afraid of hurting my feelings.

   She was afraid to wake her husband up.

6. He is alone.

   He is lonely.

7. Is the old man still alive?

   Is the old man still living?

8. At the age of sixteen, he began to learn to drive a car.

   By the age of sixteen, he had learned to drive a car.

9. The bad weather added to our difficulties.

   Add two to seven, and you will get nine.

10. They have agreed to our plan.

    They have agreed with my opinion.

11. I believe in him.

    I believe him.

12. All of them have seen the film except Wu Dong.

    All of them have seen the film besides Wu Dong.

13. We're sure you'll be well-known as an artist.

    We're sure you'll be well-known for your contribution to art.

14. The doors of the palace were made of beaten gold.

    Wine is made from grapes.

15. She opened the door wide.

    English is widely used in the world.

三、简要回答下列问题

1. 你采用的教学方法有哪些？请对其中一种举例说明。
2. 你是如何根据教学内容选择教学策略的？请举例说明。
3. 为什么说教学模式等于学习模式？
4. 从语言学习的角度看，自主学习者需要具备哪些特征？
5. 你选择教学方法和教学策略的原则有哪些？请加以概要描述。
6. 备课中的"备学生"的含义是什么？
7. 怎么将探究式教学策略运用到词汇教学？
8. 你怎样理解教师的指导作用？
9. 当学生遇到较复杂的学习任务时，教师应该怎么办？
10. 你认为任务型教学的实施步骤包括哪些？
11. 语言的主要功能是什么？
12. 交际能力由几个部分组成？
13. 阅读技能训练的活动有哪些？
14. 课外学习活动主要形式有哪些？
15. 用英语释义能够促进学生应用语言知识，请举例说明。

语言教学知识与能力练习题(二)

一、单项选择题

1. When designing speaking tasks, we must follow the principles of "_____, even participation, high motivation, and right language level".
   A. chorus   B. repetition
   C. maximum foreign talk   D. accuracy

2. The modern _____ technique was frequently and skillfully exploited by Faulkner to emphasize the reactions and inner musings of the narrator.
   A. stream-of-consciousness   B. flashback
   C. narrative and argumentative   D. mosaic

3. By means of "_____", Whitman believed he has turned the poem into an open field, an area of vital possibility, where the reader can allow his own imagination to play.
   A. balanced structure   B. free verse   C. fixed verse   D. regular rhythm

4. In 1954 _____ was awarded the Nobel Prize for "his powerful style-forming mastery of the art" of creating modern fiction.
   A. Ernest Hemingway   B. Sherwood Anderson
   C. Stephen Crane   D. Henry James

5. In English teaching classrooms very often writing is seen as _____, and it is believed to be pseudo writing.
   A. writing for communication   B. writing for real needs
   C. writing as language learning   D. communicative writing

6. To motivate students, it is _____ that we adopt a communicative approach to writing.
   A. a good idea   B. a waste time   C. of no use   D. of no significance

7. Pronunciation covers more than just phonetic symbols and rules. It also includes _____, and all these are not isolated from each other.
   A. letters, phonetic transcripts, and sounds   B. sounds, letters, and words
   C. sounds, words, and grammar   D. stress, intonation, and rhythm

8. The first immigrants in American history came from _____.
   A. England and Germany   B. England and Ireland
   C. England and the Netherlands   D. England and Spain

9. The United States went to war with _____ in 1812, the last war fought between these two countries.

   A. Britain   B. France   C. Spain   D. Mexico

10. One of the reasons why the deductive method of teaching grammar is criticized is that _____ in the method.

    A. grammar is taught in an isolated way   B. much attention is paid to meaning
    C. the practice is often meaningful   D. students do not benefit from the method

11. One of the reasons why the deductive method of teaching _____ is criticized is that the practice is often mechanical in the method.

    A. writing   B. listening   C. grammar   D. reading

12. What is the teacher doing by saying "Now you are going to do this in pairs"?

    A. Demonstrating.   B. Setting up tasks.
    C. Controlling discipline.   D. Getting feedback.

13. In teaching reading, if the teacher teaches the background knowledge first so that the students can be equipped with such knowledge and will be able to guess meaning from the printed page, we believe that this teacher is following _____ in his teaching.

    A. the top-down model   B. the bottom-up model
    C. the interactive model   D. all of the above

14. The American black population consists of _____ of the total population.

    A. 1/10   B. 1/5   C. 1/9   D. 1/6

15. To _____, it is advocated that we adopt a communicative approach to writing.

    A. motivate students   B. demotivate students
    C. free students from too much work   D. keep students busy

二、简答题

1. Tell us the cause of the fire.

   Tell us your reason for changing the plan.

2. The policeman went close.

   The policeman followed the strange man closely.

3. Have you finished your work?

   Have you completed your project?

4. Compare this car with that one, and you will find the differences between them.

   This song compares our country to a big family.

5. Reporters are then sent to cover the events.

   He interviewed five people in the morning.

6. Today is her birthday, so we're going to celebrate it.

   He congratulated me warmly on my excellent exam results.

7. The big fire destroyed the house.

   The big fire damaged the house.

8. The boy is getting better day by day.

   I have to do the work day after day.

9. What will you do with the old cell phone?

   How will you deal with the old cell phone?

10. Who invented the telephone?

    Columbus discovered America in 1492.

11. This coat doesn't suit you.

    This coat doesn't fit you.

12. The two girl students talked for the first time at the beginning of the term.

    I knew we would be good friends the first time I met her.

13. They stared at him.

    They glared at him.

14. After they had read the text, the students went on to do the exercises.

    The students went on talking and laughing all the way.

15. That proved to be my undoing, for I soon got back to my old bad habit of dozing off in front of the screen.

    From the moment of his birth the customs into which he is born shape his experience and behaviour.

三、简要回答下列问题

1. 英语课堂教学是动态的、发展的活动,教师通过组织教学这个环节去加以掌握。你通常的做法是什么?
2. 你是如何评价课堂学习任务的?请举例说明。
3. 产生教学策略的途径有哪些?请举例说明。
4. 就你认为最好的教学方法举一例说明。
5. 教师在教学设计中主要考虑到哪几个方面?
6. 自主计划阶段也是学习前的准备阶段,教师怎样帮助学生准备自主计划?
7. 在学生尚未接触到所学内容的情况下,怎样预测学习材料的内容?
8. 教师怎样指导学生进行词义猜测?
9. 具有人际沟通特点的学习任务有哪些?请举例说明。

10. 将"最近发展区"概念运用于教学中时,教师需要做什么?
11. 你平时采用的英语技能训练方法包括哪些?请对其中一项进行举例说明。
12. 怎样对待学生口语表达中流利性与准确性的关系?
13. 交际的形式包括什么?
14. 你怎样培养学生的语言应用能力?请举例说明。
15. 交际课堂环境下教师的角色是怎样的?

语言教学知识与能力练习题(三)

一、单项选择题

1. Thomas Hardy's most cheerful and idyllic work is _____.
   A. The Return of the Native B. Far from the Madding Crowd
   C. Under the Greenwood Tree D. The Woodlanders

2. There are many situations in which we use more than one language skill, so it is valuable to integrate the four skills, to improve the students' _____.
   A. communication B. pronunciation C. vocabulary D. grammar

3. Integration of the four skills is concerned with realistic communication, the implication of which is that we must teach English at the discourse level, that we must adjust the timetable, and _____.
   A. vocabulary and grammar B. practice method
   C. body language and pictures D. the textbook contents

4. All people involved in education, i.e. _____, teachers, parents, and students have some reasons to consider assessment necessary.
   A. friends B. businessmen C. administrators D. politician

5. As far as school assessment is concerned, we have teacher's assessment, continuous assessment, _____, and portfolios.
   A. students' self-assessment B. relative's assessment
   C. informal assessment D. formal assessment

6. Because no textbooks are written for any particular class, it is _____ for teachers to adapt materials.
   A. unnecessary B. necessary C. easy D. useless

7. Views on language and _____ both influence theories on how language should be taught.
   A. styles of life B. views on culture learning
   C. values of life D. views on language learning

8. The way a language teacher learned a language will influence the way he _____ to some extent.

   A. learns a language   B. learns his mother tongue
   C. teaches a language   D. obtains linguistic knowledge

9. One of the disadvantages of traditional pedagogy is focused on _____.

   A. form   B. functions   C. sentences   D. translation

10. The first mass movement of the English working class and the early sign of the awakening of the poor oppressed people is _____.

    A. The Enclosure Movement   B. The Protestant Reformation
    C. The Enlightenment Movement   D. The Chartist Movement

11. _____ is used by native speakers to express meanings in many subtle ways such as surprise, complaint, sarcasm, friendliness, threats, etc.

    A. Intonation   B. Stress   C. Rhythm   D. Speed

12. The most important play among Shakespeare's comedies is _____.

    A. A Midsummer Night's Dream   B. The Merchant of Venice
    C. As You Like It   D. Twelfth Night

13. The most perfect example of the verse drama after Greek style in English is Milton's _____.

    A. Paradise Lost   B. Paradise Regained
    C. Samson Agonistes   D. Areopagitica

14. The first American President from the Republic Party is _____.

    A. George Washington   B. Andrew Johnson
    C. Thomas Jefferson   D. Abraham Lincoln

15. What's the teacher doing by saying "Yes, but why..."?

    A. Giving prompt.   B. Praising students' work.
    C. Claiming the promise.   D. Meeting with students' approval.

二、简答题

1. The soldiers had the boy stand with his back to his father.
   The soldiers had the boy standing with his back to his father all night long.

2. I hear from my brother twice a month.
   I heard of her death last week.

3. I hurt my leg badly in the football match.
   A bullet injured his left eye.

4. He suffered from mountain sickness.
   The child has suffered from illness for two years.

5. The production cost of these trucks has increased by one third compared to last year.

   The population of India has increased to one billion.

6. There are 25,000 Inuit in all.

   I thought he was going to help us, but he didn't after all.

7. Tell the boy not to stand in the way.

   The article is well written in a way.

8. Look out! Don't knock into others.

   Look out! Don't knock down others.

9. He often comes late for school.

   I haven't heard from him lately.

10. It is possible to go to the moon now.

    It is probable to go to the moon now.

11. How much baggage does she have?

    How much luggage does she have?

12. He managed to finish the work in time.

    He tried to finish the work in time.

13. The department head met her on the street.

    The department head met with her in his office.

14. The students had a class meeting last Friday.

    Many reporters came to attend the press conference.

15. He happened to know the place.

    Didn't it occur to you to phone them about it?

三、简要回答下列问题

1. 你认为评价学生的语言技能的方法包括哪些?请举例说明。
2. 评价策略使用的手段有什么？请举例说明。
3. 你认为影响语音教学的因素有哪些？
4. 词汇展示教学中应采取什么策略？请举例说明。
5. 培养学生听说能力应遵循哪些原则？
6. 什么是任务型教学？它的主要特点是什么？
7. 什么是阅读整体教学？
8. 英语水平测试的目的是什么？
9. 怎样激发中学生学习英语的动力？
10. 授课中,英语教师一般从哪几个方面保证学生的安全感？
11. 基础教育阶段英语课程的总体目标是培养学生综合语言运用能力。综合语言运用能力由哪几个部分组成？这些部分之间的关系是什么？

12. 什么是模拟交际性操练？请举例说明。

13. 英语综合训练包括哪几个方面？

14. 能力倾向测试的目的是什么？

15. 什么是学习动机？

语言教学知识与能力练习题（四）

一、单项选择题

1. Best of all the Romantic well-known lyric pieces is Shelley's _____.
   A. "The Cloud" B. "To a Skylark"
   C. "Ode to a Nightingale" D. "Ode to the West Wind"

2. As far as teaching grammar is concerned, in the inductive method, the teacher induces the learners to realize grammar rules _____.
   A. without any explicit explanation B. by explaining in an explicit way
   C. with explicit explanation D. by telling them the rules

3. In April 1949 twelve nations established the NATO to coordinate the military actions of member nations against _____.
   A. Germany B. Japan C. the Soviet Union D. France

4. When teaching pronunciation, we should _____.
   A. make students feel anxious B. destroy students' confidence
   C. build-up students' confidence D. make students distracted

5. Pre-listening activities include predicting, setting the scene, listening for the gist, and _____.
   A. learning new sentence structures B. learning new words
   C. listening for specific information D. concluding

6. "Listen and act" is an activity in the _____ stage.
   A. pre-listening B. while-listening C. post-listening D. all of the above

7. What a good writer usually doesn't pay attention to in the pre-writing stage of the writing process is _____.
   A. the spelling B. the purpose C. the contents D. the audience

8. Writing exercises like completion, reproduction, compression, and transformation are mainly the type of exercises used in which writing task? _____.
   A. Controlled writing B. Guided writing
   C. Free writing D. Imaginative writing

9. Which type of grammar tends to teach you how the grammar is used by the people rather than how it should be used?

   A. Descriptive grammar.   B. Prescriptive grammar.
   C. Traditional grammar.   D. Modern grammar.

10. When students are given the structure in an authentic or near authentic context and are asked to work out the rule for themselves, what kind of method their teacher is using? _____.

    A. Deductive grammar teaching   B. Inductive grammar teaching
    C. Traditional grammar teaching   D. Modern grammar teaching

11. In which stage of the Presentation-Practice-Production approach will students have the chance to use the new language freely and incorporate it into their existing language? _____.

    A. Presentation Stage   B. Practice Stage
    C. Production Stage   D. Consolidation stage

12. Rolls-Royce is world-famous as _____.

    A. luxury automobiles   B. machine tools
    C. household appliances   D. high-quality engines

13. Which of the following techniques can best present the word "virtue"?

    A. Showing or drawing a picture.
    B. Giving a definition or an example.
    C. Demonstrating the meaning by acting or miming.
    D. Comparing it with a similar word in form.

14. What are the most important parts of a lesson plan?

    A. Textbooks and classroom aids.   B. Anticipation of problems.
    C. Objectives of the lesson.   D. Students and their backgrounds.

15. The longest river in Britain is _____.

    A. the Clyde   B. the Severn   C. the Mersey   D. the Thames

二、简答题

1. His father is an officer in the army.
   His father is an official in the government.

2. Why on earth did you tell a lie?
   We live on the earth.

3. We both see each other at the office every day.
   The six blind men couldn't agree with one another.

4. Tom persuaded his father to give up smoking at last.
   Tom advised his father to give up smoking, but he wouldn't listen.

5. We are preparing for the mid-term examination.

   We are prepared for the mid-term examination.

6. Einstein won the Nobel Prize for Physics in 1921.

   Carl Lewis has won four gold medals.

7. Please put the umbrella behind the door.

   She placed the table in the middle of the room.

8. He has lied since his childhood.

   He lay on the floor, reading a book.

9. Jane is a quiet girl.

   Jane is a silent girl.

10. All is silent.

    All are silent.

11. He raised those goats from new-born kids.

    She supports her old mother.

12. He referred to the map of the city when he first drove here.

    He referred me to the map when I first drove here.

13. The car is running along the road.

    Go along the street, and take the third turning on the right.

14. There isn't space in the classroom for thirty desks.

    Wuhan is a hot place in summer.

15. The dog is running after the hare now.

    When the policeman arrived, the thief had run away.

三、简要回答下列问题

1. 什么是直接法?
2. 什么是认知法?
3. 为什么英语教师反思能力及效果不容乐观?
4. 你认为有哪些训练方式可以促进学生对词汇的记忆?
5. 简答研究性学习方法的实质。
6. 你怎样看待课堂上老师和学生说话的时间分配?
7. 简要说明合作学习的基本理念。
8. 高中生英语阅读理解的障碍是什么?
9. 普通高中英语课程标准的基本理念是什么?
10. 中学英语教学中词汇教学的两大主要任务是什么?
11. 什么是学习策略?学习策略包括哪些内容?

12. 班级的大小会影响教学方法吗？举例说明。

13. 语言学习者有什么差别？

14. 教师如何鼓励学生自主学习？

15. 怎样激发中学生学习英语的动力？

语言教学知识与能力练习题（五）

一、单项选择题

1. Among the five subcategories of classroom management, that is people, language, environment, organization, tools and so on, which of the following elements can be classified under environment? _____.

    A. Textbook and exercise book

    B. Interaction between teacher and students

    C. Arrangement of desks and chairs

    D. Students and their response

2. What role does a teacher take to create an environment in which learning can take place?

    A. Instructor   B. Manager   C. Assessor   D. Guide

3. A question that views on language learning involve is "_____"

    A. Why do human beings have language?

    B. What are the psycholinguistic?

    C. How a language is different from another?

    D. How do people use language?

4. Among the factors affecting a lesson plan, which of the following is human factor?

    A. Personality of the teacher.   B. Class size.

    C. Course requirement.   D. Students' level.

5. British Recorded history began with _____.

    A. the Viking and Danish invasion   B. the Norman Conquest

    C. Roman invasion   D. the Anglo-Saxons invasion

6. The highest mountain in Britain is _____.

    A. Scafell   B. Ben Nevis   C. the Cotswolds   D. the Forth

7. For better classroom management, what should the teacher do while the students are doing activities?

    A. Participate in a group.   B. Prepare for the next procedure.

    C. Circulate to monitor, prompt and help.   D. Observe and discuss.

8. Which of the following expresses instrumental motivation?

   A. To survive in the target language country.   B. To be interested.

   C. To get promoted in one's position.   D. To communicate.

9. Which of the following activities can best motivate junior learners?

   A. Games.   B. Recitation.   C. Role-play of dialogues.   D. Reading.

10. Britain's General Election is held every _____ years and there are _____ members of Parliaments are elected.

    A. five; 600   B. five; 651   C. five; 650   D. four; 651

11. The Prime Minister is appointed by _____ and he or she always sits in _____ in Britain.

    A. the Archbishop of Canterbury; the House of Commons

    B. the Archbishop of Canterbury; the House of Lords

    C. the Queen; the House of Commons

    D. the Queen; the House of Lords

12. The ultimate authority for law-making resides in _____ in Britain.

    A. the Queen   B. the House of Commons

    C. the House of Lords   D. the Cabinet

13. To help students understand the structure of a text and sentence sequencing, we could use _____ for students to rearrange the sentences in the right order.

    A. cohesive devices   B. a coherent text

    C. scrambled sentences   D. sentences in order

14. The purpose of the outline is to enable the students to have a clear organization of ideas and a structure that can guide them _____.

    A. in the actual writing   B. in free writing

    C. in controlled writing   D. in exam writing

15. _____ tells you what you should use in order to produce accurate utterances.

    A. The descriptive grammar   B. The prescriptive grammar

    C. The traditional grammar   D. Modern grammar

二、简答题

   1. We are running out of our fuel.

      The fuel is running out.

   2. I am satisfied with your success.

      I am content with your success.

   3. The policeman is searching the thief.

      The policeman is searching for the thief.

4. He told us such a funny story.

   He told us so funny a story.

5. I saw him sometime in July.

   I'll stay here for some time.

6. He plants rice fastest in the village.

   They can only grow potatoes in the fields.

7. He spent 20 yuan on the pen.

   The work will take us two hours.

8. The young man stepped into the house.

   The young man walked into the house.

9. Our friendship is as firm as a rock.

   He is making steady progress.

10. Lincoln fought hard for freedom of all people.

    The Canadians struggled all through the years with us against the Japanese.

11. They supply the survivors with food.

    He provides his family with food and clothes.

12. Last night, before I went to bed, I thought of my parents.

    Think about what you have done!

13. The students walked through the gate with Mr White.

    The students walked across the street with Mr White.

14. We went on a pleasant trip to the nearest seaside during our vacation.

    He made a long journey from Beijing to London.

15. The new hat is for you. Please try it on.

    I'll try it out and see if it works.

三、简要回答下列问题

1. 教师使用的教学设备有哪些？如何正确使用教学设备？
2. 怎样理解教学既是一门科学，又是一门艺术。
3. 在外语教学中，文化指什么？
4. 你怎样理解新课标中提出的"面向全体学生，为学生全面发展和终身发展奠定基础"？
5. 形成性评价和终结性评价分别是对什么进行评价？
6. 在英语口语即口头交流活动中，需要哪些词汇？这些词汇有多少？
7. 学习方法指导内容包括哪些方面？

8. 教师如何处理好英语课堂上母语和英语的关系。
9. 研究性学习的内容包括哪些？
10. 根据词汇学习特点，词汇策略可以分为哪几类？请对其中一项加以说明。
11. 什么是语言的习得？习得和学习的区别是什么？
12. 什么是可理解的输入？
13. 什么是语法翻译教学法？
14. 什么是PPP教学法？请举例说明。
15. 什么是拆词记忆策略训练？

语言教学知识与能力练习题（六）

一、单项选择题

1. The grammar rules are often given first and explained to the students and then the students have to apply the rules to the given situations. This approach is called _____.
   A. deductive grammar teaching   B. inductive grammar teaching
   C. prescriptive grammar teaching   D. traditional grammar teaching

2. It is easier for students to remember new words if they are designed in _____ and if they are used again and again in _____ situations and contexts.
   A. context; the same   B. context; different
   C. concept; difficult   D. concept; the same

3. Which of the following activities is the most suitable for pair work?
   A. Guessing games.   B. Speech preparations.
   C. Dialogue reading.   D. Discussing a topic.

4. In the inductive method of teaching grammar, the teacher induces the learners to realise grammar rules _____.
   A. by telling them the rules   B. by explaining in an explicit way
   C. with explicit explanation   D. without any explicit explanation

5. In meaningful practice the focus is on the production, comprehension or exchange of _____.
   A. structures   B. sentences   C. form   D. meaning

6. In criminal trials by jury, _____ passes sentence and _____ decide the issue of guilt or innocence.
   A. the Lord Chancellor; the jury   B. the judge; the judge
   C. the jury; the jury   D. the judge; the jury

7. Which of the following activities would BEST help to prepare students for their real life speech in English?

   A. Doing a drill.

   B. Learning a piece of text or dialogue by heart.

   C. Reading aloud.

   D. Interviewing someone, or being interviewed.

8. It is believed that the way a language teacher learned a language will to some extent influence the way he or she _____.

   A. learns a language　　　　　　B. teaches a language

   C. learns his mother tongue　　　D. obtains linguistic knowledge

9. From the sentence "When he came into the room, the large crowd grew silent" the students may know that here "he" must be a man of power, e.g. a boss or a teacher. In this example, the students are making _____ when reading.

   A. an inference　　B. a reference　　C. perception　　D. production

10. The Declaration of Independence was drafted by _____.

    A. James Madison　　　　　　B. Thomes Jefferson

    C. Alexander Hamilton　　　　D. George Washington

11. The while-listening stage is _____ for the teacher to control, because this is where the students need to pay attention and process the information actively.

    A. the easiest　　　　　　　　　　B. as easy as the pre-listening stage

    C. as easy as the post-listening stage　D. the most difficult

12. One of the reasons why the deductive method is criticized is that _____ in the method.

    A. language is taught in a context　　B. much attention is paid to meaning

    C. the practice is often mechanical　　D. not enough explanation is provided

13. One of the reasons of providing the students with a variety of speaking activities is that the variety of activities helps _____.

    A. keep motivation high　　　　B. keep good relationship

    C. memorise the speech　　　　D. learn the dialogues by heart

14. _____ is written by Alan Poe.

    A. Twice-Told Tales　　　　　　B. The Fall of the House of Usher

    C. The House of the Seven Gables　D. The Scarlet Letter

15. As far as learning pronunciation is concerned, the realistic goals for the students are consistency, intelligibility, and _____.

    A. communicative efficiency　　B. accuracy

    C. correctness　　　　　　　　　D. fastness

二、简答题

1. He used to work hard.
   He is used to hard work.
2. This area is covered in vast forests.
   That's a huge ship.
3. The hills rise green and sheer above the broad river.
   All worktops should be wide enough to allow plenty of space for food preparation.
4. At the very beginning of this term, they took an exam.
   He is just the actor I want.
5. Xiao Wang has on a white shirt today.
   I like to put on my hat when I go out in winter.
6. Miss Liu is working on a new book.
   Mr.Zhang is working at a new invention.
7. He would sit by the seashore for hours.
   He used to get up late.
8. He hit him on the face.
   That man was beaten until he was black and blue.
9. We love peace but we are not afraid of war.
   Later, however, he decided to go.
10. They will go to America by sea.
    There is a small village by the sea.
11. He doesn't care about his clothes.
    Who will care for your children when you are away?
12. After destroying the village, the enemy carried off all the cattle.
    We were carried away by her songs.
13. The boys cheered their football team.
    We greeted our guests at the gate.
14. We must clear away such ideas among ourselves.
    She cleared up her desk before she moved to another school.
15. Your question came up at the meeting.
    When will her new book come out?

三、简要回答下列问题

1. 什么是词汇图记忆策略训练?

2.在英语教学中,既要有学生的个别活动,又要有学生的集体活动,协调这两种活动的原则是什么?

3.常见的教学策略分类方法是什么?

4.常见的给老师提供的反思的研究活动有哪些?

5.词汇教学是否应该成为英语教学的内容?

6.教学设计是一成不变的预设吗?

7.交际教学法的两个主要的指导原则是什么?请举例说明。

8.教学设计对青年教师有何益处?

9.阅读教学原则是什么?

10.小组活动的规则是什么?

11.教学设计的具体形式是什么?

12.一般情况下学习方式可以分哪几个类型?

13.什么是 PWP 教学模式?

14.在口语活动中教师应该做什么?

15.听力教学的原则是什么?

语言教学知识与能力练习题(七)

一、单项选择题

1. Natural language, spoken or written, uses referential word such as pronouns to refer to people or things already mentioned previously in the context. Therefore, the activity "understanding references" can be performed in the _____ stage when teaching reading.

   A. pre-reading   B. while-reading   C. post-reading   D. language-focus

2. When we are teaching pronunciation, stress and _____ should be taught from the very beginning.

   A. knowledge about sounds   B. phonetic rules
   C. phonetic transcripts   D. intonation

3. The typical organizational pattern for elementary and secondary schools in the United States is that of _____.

   A. classified schools   B. graded schools   C. vocational schools   D. public schools

4. Martin Luther King, Jr., a young black clergyman, became a national leader of the _____ Movement.

   A. Boycott   B. Integration   C. Segregation   D. Civil Rights

5. Activities such as "Listen and tick", "_____", "Listen and act", "Listen and draw", "Listen and fill" can be performed in the while-listening stage of teaching listening.
   A. Listen and repeat B. Listen and recite
   C. Listen and sequence D. Listen and read

6. The concept of present, past and future time, the expressions of certainty and possibility, the roles of agents, instruments with a sentence, and special relationships between people and objects are examples of language _____.
   A. functions B. notions C. structures D. behavior

7. Dickens and Thackeray, who are most famous for their novels, lived in the period of _____.
   A. Queen Elizabeth Ⅰ B. Henry Ⅷ
   C. Queen Victoria D. Charles Ⅱ

8. The Communicative Approach lays emphasis on learning to communicate through _____ in the target language.
   A. listening and note-taking B. interaction
   C. role play D. oral presentation

9. The Canadian population is chiefly characterized by _____.
   A. its linguistic duality B. its growth C. its size D. its French origins

10. The _____ of language sees language as a linguistic system made up of various subsystems: the sound system (phonology), the discrete units of meaning produced by sound combinations (morphology), and the system of combining units of meaning for communication (syntax).
    A. structural view B. functional view
    C. interactional view D. behaviorist view

11. Discovering missing information, discovering missing features, and following directions are examples of _____.
    A. mechanical practice B. drilling language
    C. functional communicative activities D. social interaction activities

12. The five main components of communicative competence include linguistic competence, pragmatic competence, discourse competence, strategic competence, and _____.
    A. accuracy B. fluency C. correctness D. grammaticality

13. In the traditional classroom, very often, too much attention has been paid to _____, with little or no attention paid to practising language skills.
    A. linguistic competence B. linguistic knowledge
    C. language use D. language functions

14. Pre-reading activities include predicting, setting the scene, _____ and scanning.

    A. skimming B. information transfer activities

    C. reading comprehension questions D. reproducing the text

15. The generative linguist is interested not only in describing language but also in _____ language.

    A. teaching B. explaining C. using D. understanding

二、简答题

1. Colds are common in winter.

    His ordinary supper consists of only bread and milk.

2. This book is intended for the general reader, not for the specialist.

    What's the normal temperature of the human body?

3. China is a great country with a long history.

    The whole nation was in deep sorrow at this news.

4. In our country, railways are state-owned.

    This is my native land. I'll defend it with my life!

5. The building cut off our view.

    She cut up the cake and gave each of us a piece.

6. I don't like damp weather.

    He is wet to the skin.

7. The lecturer illustrated his point with a blackboard.

    These figures clearly demonstrate the size of the economic problem facing the country.

8. He was in disgrace after his ungentlemanly behavior.

    His desertion to the enemy was a dishonor to his family.

9. I think it a shame to be so wasteful.

    It is a scandal for officials to take bribes.

10. Finally, turn off the lights and lock the door.

    At last the project has been completed and we can rest.

11. Mr. Wu always wears a blue coat in winter.

    Her mother is dressing her.

12. He works like a waiter.

    He works as a waiter.

13. The soldiers lived on wild plants.

    Writers live by their pens while fishermen live by fishing.

14. Once he makes up his mind, he'll never give it up.

    As soon as I get to Beijing, I'll write to you.

15. He got away from the fire.

　　I won't let him get away with that excuse.

三、简要回答下列问题

1. 词汇的教学方法有哪些？
2. 高中生英语阅读障碍有哪些？
3. 词汇学习的途径有哪些？
4. 任务教学的教学过程包括哪些内容？对其中一项进行说明。
5. 怎样理解教学中没有必不可少的媒体，只有效的媒体和对媒体的有效利用？
6. 参与"自主学习"教学模式的学生应具备哪些能力？
7. 为什么说听、说、读、写四项技能的培养必须全面，不可偏废？
8. 什么是基于"互动性反思"的课堂教学研究？
9. 阅读教学原则是什么？
10. 在教学实施过程中如何抓住即时信息？
11. 教学设计一般模式是什么？
12. 什么是自主学习？
13. 教师应怎样处理学生在运用语言过程中的错误？
14. 为什么要鼓励水平低的学生阅读简写本或简易读物作为泛读材料？
15. 根据阅读目的的不同，阅读可分为哪两种类型？

语言教学知识与能力练习题（八）

一、单项选择题

1. When we ask the students to do predicting tasks in listening, we should let students read or hear the listening comprehension questions _____.
   A. before they listen　　　　　　B. while they are listening
   C. after their listening　　　　　D. none of the above

2. According to the _____ there are a finite number of grammatical rules in the system and with knowledge of these rules an infinite number of sentences can be produced.
   A. Behaviourist theory　　　　　B. Cognitive theory
   C. structural view　　　　　　　D. functional view

3. Role-playing through cue dialogues, role-playing through situation and goals, and role-playing through debates or discussion are examples of _____.
   A. mechanical practice　　　　　B. drilling language
   C. pre-communicative activities　D. social interaction activities

4. In summer there are open-air theatres, including one in London's Regent's Park, where _____ are performed, and the Minack Theatre, which is an open cliffside near Land's End in Cornwall.

   A. Christopher Marlowe's plays   B. William Shakespeare's plays
   C. Ben Johnson's plays   D. George Bernard Shaw's plays

5. Role-play, _____, and writing can be done at the post-reading stage when we are teaching reading.

   A. retelling   B. skimming   C. scanning   D. predicting

6. The BBC World Service broadcasts international news worldwide, using English and _____ other languages.

   A. 37   B. 38   C. 39   D. 40

7. Explanation of phonetic rules should _____ at the beginning stage of teaching pronunciation.

   A. always be adopted   B. take place   C. be emphasized   D. be avoided

8. Widowers' House, a play written by George Bernard Shaw, is a grotesquely realistic exposure of _____.

   A. prostitution   B. slum landlordism   C. social life   D. social evil

9. Frost's first collection A boy's Will, whose lyrics trace a boy's development from self centered idealism to maturity, is marked by an intense but restrained emotion and the characteristic flavor of _____.

   A. England life   B. the Southern American life
   C. New England life   D. the Western American life

10. PPP and TBL are two approaches to language teaching. PPP stands for Presentation, Practice and Production and TBL stands for _____.

    A. Task Book Language   B. Text Book Learning
    C. Teacher-based Learning   D. Task-Based Learning

11. Most of Walt Whitman's poems in _____ sing of the "enmasse" and the self as well.

    A. Drum Taps   B. North of Bosten   C. The Cantos   D. Leaves of Grass

12. Receptive skills of language include _____.

    A. listening and reading   B. listening and speaking
    C. reading and writing   D. speaking and writing

13. At Christmas, the home is decorated with the following except _____.

    A. colorful paper chains   B. leaves of holly and mistletoe
    C. firecrackers   D. a young fir-tree

14. Easter is traditionally associated with the following except _____.
    A. the resurrection of Christ   B. the eating of Easter eggs
    C. the coming of spring   D. the custom of giving presents
15. Most pregnant working women receive their statutory maternity pay directly from their employer for a maximum of _____ weeks.
    A. 17   B. 15   C. 19   D. 18

二、简答题

1. All the girls finished the race except two who gave up half way.
   As neither of the two sides would give in, the agreement fell through.
2. The story was handed down from one generation to another.
   Please hand over this money to Xiao Zhou.
3. She works like a teacher.
   She works as a teacher.
4. Please do the experiment as Mr Li.
   The fish doesn't taste like it should.
5. There is a genuine painting by Picasso.
   The Nanking massacre is one of the real events.
6. This is a matter of everyday occurrence.
   She goes to school every day.
7. He is my elder brother.
   I have an older brother.
8. She lent some money to him.
   He borrowed some money from her.
9. She is a little girl.
   She is a small girl.
10. The farm grows various kinds of crops, such as wheat, corn, cotton and rice.
    A lot of people here, for example, Mr John, would rather have coffee.
11. I was astonished to see him in Tibet.
    I was surprised to see the great changes in my hometown.
12. The poor boy was shaking with cold.
    Her voice was trembling with anger.
13. He has risen in rank.
    The people's living standard has greatly been raised.
14. She burst into tears.
    She burst out crying.

15. Let's suppose he is right.

   Guess how much it is worth.

三、简要回答下列问题

1. 什么是形成性评价？
2. 交际教学法有什么优点？
3. 自主学习模式中，教师在教学设计过程主要考虑哪些因素？
4. 当一个学生正在进行一个像角色扮演或会话的说话活动时，即时插入的纠错是否合适？
5. 你选择教学策略的原则有哪些？请加以简要描述。
6. 教学设计的依据是什么？
7. 当学生遇到较复杂的学习任务时，教师应该怎么办？
8. 构建教学过程的具体步骤是什么？
9. 简答教学目标设计的重要性。
10. 教学设计不同于教案，它们在哪些方面有所区别？
11. 如何进行教学评价？
12. 简答教学设计的内容。
13. 交际课堂环境下教师的角色是怎样的？
14. 教学活动的九个环节是什么？
15. 英语"四位一体"复习法将高考英语总复习分为哪四个阶段？

语言教学知识与能力练习题（九）

一、单项选择题

1. When teaching pronunciation, we should _____.
   A. never use visual aids B. use explanation rather than demo
   C. use dictionaries to show the sounds D. bring variety to the classroom

2. Ireland is divided into two political parts: _____.
   A. Northern Ireland and Southern Ireland
   B. Southern Ireland and the Republic of Ireland
   C. Northern Ireland and Britain
   D. the Republic of Ireland and Northern Ireland

3. The Grand Canyon in north-western _____ is one of nature's most impressive sights.
   A. Utah   B. Arizona   C. Nevada   D. Idaho

4. The first immigrants in American history came from _____.
   A. England and the Netherlands   B. England and Ireland
   C. England and Germany   D. England and Spain

5. Examples of pronunciation perception practice include _____.
   A. using pictures   B. using minimal pairs and "Odd one out"
   C. brainstorming   D. using tongue twisters

6. Canada was divided Into Upper Canada (English speaking) and Lower Canada (French speaking) in _____ and they were united again in _____.
   A. 1775;1867   B. 1775;1791   C. 1840;1867   D. 1791;1840

7. Australia has always been a continent with few people mainly because _____.
   A. Australia is too far away from Europe
   B. Australia is the least mountainous and most level of the world's continents
   C. most of the continent is hot and dry
   D. Australia is separated from the rest of the world by seas

8. The Second Anti-English War broke out in _____ and ended in _____. The U.S. won the war.
   A. 1812;1815   B. 1813;1815   C. 1812;1814   D. 1813;1815

9. In Feb. _____ came President Nixon's historic visit to China.
   A. 1972   B. 1979   C. 1973   D. 1978

10. The English Civil War is also called _____.
    A. the Glorious Revolution   B. the Puritan Revolution
    C. the Catholic Revolution   D. the Bloody Revolution

11. "If Winter comes, can Spring be far behind!" is an epigrammatic line by _____.
    A. J.Keats   B. W.Blake   C. W.Wordsworth   D. P.B.Shelley

12. One of the problems in vocabulary learning is that students _____.
    A. use context for their vocabulary learning
    B. try hard to understand the words
    C. use a variety of vocabulary building strategies
    D. treat vocabulary items indiscriminately

13. The following states are among the first thirteen colonies except _____.
    A. Maryland   B. South Carolina   C. Colorado   D. Delaware

14. _____ was the first man who sailed around the earth.
    A. John Cabot   B. Magellan   C. Balboa   D. Cartier

15. Hester Prynne is the heroine in Hawthorne's novel _____.
   A. The Scarlet Letter
   B. the House of the Seven Gables
   C. MobyDick
   D. Daisy Miller

二、简答题

1. The girl walked between her father and mother.
   She is the tallest among her classmates.
2. But above all tell me quickly what I have to do.
   After all, your birthday is only two weeks away.
3. It could be a constructive thing.
   It is an unpleasant matter.
4. A great deal has been studied and this is the best way.
   A great deal of money has been spent on the project.
5. The building of a new car factory was agreed on last month.
   They have agreed to our plan.
6. Visitors are not permitted to take photos.
   His parents won't allow him to stay out late.
7. Though he believes it, yet he will not act.
   They said they would come; they did not, though.
8. We argued with them about this problem for a long time.
   He often quarrels about their housework with his wife.
9. Here is a sleeping baby.
   He was asleep with his head on his arms.
10. He will not tell the secret even though he knows it.
    He will not tell the secret though he knows it.
11. Germany began to attack the Soviet Union in 1941.
    The cavalry charged to the front.
12. Many people saw the strange thing happen at the time.
    Take the medicine three times a day and three pieces at a time.
13. As he was not feeling well, I decided to go there alone.
    Since everyone is here, let's start.
14. All of them have been there except Tom.
    All of them have been there besides Tom.
15. You're to hand in your papers by 10 o'clock.
    I was about to go out when someone knocked at the door.

三、简要回答下列问题

1. 交际语言教学的原则是什么？
2. 语言能力与语言交际能力有什么关系？
3. 语义变化（semantic change）是什么？
4. 什么是教学设计？
5. 探究式教学策略怎样运用到词汇教学？
6. 你怎样理解教师的指导作用？
7. 当学生遇到较复杂的学习任务时，教师应该怎么办？
8. 在进行教学设计时首先要分析学生的需要，什么是对学生需要的分析？
9. 什么是交际教学法？
10. 交际能力由几个部分组成？
11. 请列举你在发音教学中采用的教学活动形式。
12. 课外学习活动设计的主要形式有哪些？教师应起什么作用？
13. 交际课堂环境下教师的角色是怎样的？
14. 教材使用有什么策略？
15. 写作教学的原因是什么？

语言教学知识与能力练习题（十）

一、单项选择题

1. _____ is the first writer in America to win the Nobel Prize in literature.
   A. Sinclair Lewis　　B. Saul Bellow　　C. Ernest Hemingway　　D. Walt Whitman
2. The width of the Niagara Fall is about _____ metres and the drop average _____ metres.
   A. 1240；49　　B. 1650；50　　C. 1540；49　　D. 1350；49
3. _____ has been called the "cradle of American liberty".
   A. New York　　B. Plymouth　　C. Philadelphia　　D. Boston
4. The first inhabitants in Britain were _____.
   A. the Iberians　　B. the Celts　　C. the Normans　　D. the Anglo-Saxons
5. The Columbia River and the Colorado River belong to the system of _____.
   A. the Gulf　　B. the Atlantic　　C. the Indian　　D. the Pacific
6. Which of the following has nothing to do with Easter? _____.
   A. Rabbits　　B. Haggis　　C. Eggs　　D. Chicks

7. Vocabulary building strategies outside classrooms include reviewing regularly,_____, organizing vocabulary effectively, and using a dictionary.

   A. reciting the spelling　　　　　　B. guessing meaning from the context
   C. neglecting the meaning　　　　　D. remembering the translation

8. Among the five Great Lakes, only _____ is wholly within the United States.

   A. Michigan　　　B. Superior　　　C. Erie　　　D. Ontario

9. The state that became the first British settlement is _____.

   A. Queensland　　　　　　　　　B. Western Australia
   C. New south Wales　　　　　　　D. Victoria

10. Which of the following would you NOT agree with? _____.

    A. People have different experiences in learning a foreign language. Some find it easy, some not
    B. People learn languages for different reasons
    C. People have different capacities in language learning
    D. People have the same understanding about language learning

11. According to some scholars, Task-based Language Teaching is, in fact, _____ Communicative Language Teaching.

    A. exactly the same as　　　　　B. a further development of
    C. opposite to　　　　　　　　　D. nothing to do with

12. The ultimate goal of foreign language teaching is to enable students to use the foreign language in work or life when necessary. Thus we should teach _____; and we should teach language in the way it is used in the real world.

    A. that part of the language that will be used
    B. all parts of the language
    C. the language used in works of classical literature
    D. spoken language only

13. In the 19th century, foreign language teachers usually adopted the strategy of combining grammar roles with _____.

    A. reading　　　B. speaking　　　C. writing　　　D. translating

14. One of the objectives by the Natural Approach is to enable the students to make the meaning clear but not necessarily be _____ in all details of grammar.

    A. correct　　　B. accurate　　　C. brief　　　D. concise

15. The Cognitive Approach holds that students' mistakes are _____ in the creative use of language.

    A. useful　　　B. understandable　　　C. unavoidable　　　D. reasonable

二、简答题

1. Who is beating the drum?

   He hit her hard in the face.

2. Last night a thief broke into Mr Brown's house and took away many things.

   A thief broke into and stole a lot of things while we were away for holiday.

3. The sudden cold weather brought on his cold again.

   We also brought in some words from English.

4. The big fire destroyed the whole house.

   I was ruined by that law case; I'm a ruined man.

5. Grasses were moist with dew.

   In the east, the air is humid in summer.

6. We should get rid of the weeds in the fields.

   How did they deal with matters of this sort?

7. We've found oil under the South Sea.

   Can you find out what time the train leaves?

8. He was in disgrace after his ungentlemanly behavior.

   I think it a shame to be so wasteful.

9. He went to Tibet in 1969 and has lived there ever since.

   The flowers grow more beautiful than ever before.

10. He glanced at his watch.

    She stared at him in surprise.

11. He escaped (from) the burning house.

    He fled (from) the burning house.

12. All the girls finished the race except two who gave up half way.

    After a long journey, my strength gave out and couldn't walk any farther.

13. The soldiers had the boy stand.

    The two cheats had their lights burning all night long.

14. I'll have a new suit made of this cloth.

    He had his handbag stolen.

15. Then they knocked a stick into the earth.

    Who is knocking at the door?

三、简要回答下列问题

1. 英语课堂上发生妨碍教学活动的偶发事件时,最好的处理办法是什么?

2. 用英语教学语言例释 introduce。
3. 讲述研究性学习方法的实质。
4. 学习方法指导内容包括哪些方面？
5. 简要说明合作学习的基本理念。
6. 研究性学习的内容包括哪些？
7. 什么是"英语教学内容"？
8. 产生教学策略的途径有哪些？请举例说明。
9. 你认为什么是最好的教学方法？请举例说明。
10. 你选择教学方法和策略的原则有哪些？请加以概要描述。
11. 你选择教学策略的原则有哪些？请加以概要描述。
12. 什么是"学情"？
13. 你怎样理解教师的指导作用？
14. 当学生遇到较复杂的学习任务时，教师应该怎么办？
15. 有效的教学情境要符合哪两点要求？

模块三 英语学科教学设计能力

第一章 大纲描述

考试目标

能够根据英语学科特点,针对高中学生的认知特点、语言水平和学习需要选择并设计合理的教学内容,形成完整合理的教学方案。

考试要求

1. 理解高中学生的认知特点、已有的英语知识、语言能力和学习需求,能够说明教学内容和学生已学知识之间的联系。
2. 理解课程标准的目标要求,能够根据学生的特点选择恰当的教学内容。
3. 能够根据教学内容和学生特点设定合理、明确与具体的教学目标。
4. 能够根据教学目标创设相应的教学情景,设计有效的教学活动,安排合理的教学过程,筛选适当的辅助教学材料。
5. 能够根据教学内容和教学过程,设计有效的学习评估活动。

第二章 考点解读

一、高中英语教学设计的基本概念

高中英语教学设计是在熟悉学情,掌握高中学生的认知特点和通晓教材的基础上,运用现代学习和教学心理学、传播学、教学媒体论、系统论、控制论等相关理论和技术,来分析教学中的问题与需求,确立教学内容,构建教学目标,选择相应的教学策略,教学组织形式和教学媒体,设立教学步骤和组织教学评价,对参与教学的诸要素进行优化整合,使教学效果最优化的一个系统过程。

二、教学设计过程的四个基本要素

(一)制定学习目标

用可观察、可测量的术语明确指出学生通过学习后,在某一认知方面达到何种认知程度,但这必须符合学生的实际认知水平,而不是教师根据自己的意愿凭空炮制,这是教学设计的一项基本要求。

(二)进行任务分析

确定从学生的实际认知水平到学习目标之间所需要获得的能力和子能力及其层次关系。

(三)选择教学方法

包括对教与学的形式、媒体、活动等方面的选择与设计。

(四)开展教学评价

了解学习目标是否达到,教学尺度是否合适,教学效果是否实现,为修正教学系统设计提供实际依据。

三、全方位构建可操作的目标体系

(一)知识与技能目标

1. 准确掌握高中英语语言知识,并以此完成听、说、读、写的训练任务。
2. 迁移所学语言知识,达到真实有效的交际目的。
3. 掌握听说读写的基本技能。
4. 使用地道英语,即时识别和纠正常见语言错误。
5. 熟悉并掌握英语课程标准中六至八级规定的话题。

(二)过程与方法目标

1. 学生能积极、主动、认真地参与教学活动。
2. 师生、生生进行积极互动、交流与合作。
3. 学生对所学内容能进行整理、归纳,使之条理化、系统化、综合化、主题化。
4. 学生在情景中学习英语,并能对所学内容进行举一反三的内化式创造。
5. 学生能运用各种信息工具收集、整理和利用信息。

(三)情感态度和价值观目标

1. 培养学生强烈的自信心和求知欲。
2. 培养学生浓厚的学习兴趣。
3. 培养学生坚强的意志品质。
4. 培养学生的合作和竞争精神。
5. 培养学生的创新精神和实践能力。
6. 帮助学生正确认识社会,提高对跨文化的敏感性,形成正确的人生观与价值观。
7. 培养学生树立热爱祖国,为民族复兴而奋发学习的责任感。

四、教学目标的编写内容

1. 教学对象:教学目标所针对的学生类别及其认知特点。
2. 学生行为:用可观测到的术语说明学生在学习后应该获得的知识与能力状况,以及态度的变化。

3. 行为条件：能影响学生学习结果的限制或范围。

4. 预期程度：即学生达到教学目标的最低衡量依据。

五、教学设计的原则

（一）教学设计要给学生留足自由思维的空间

1. 教学设计在形式上不要过于繁琐。

2. 教学设计的结构上不要过于封闭和程式化。

3. 要体现出内容上的概要性、形式上的模糊性和结构上的不确定性。

这样就能适应新情景，容纳新内容，变换并确立新策略，为教学中师生、生生之间的互动交流、互生新知、互建新情留有余地；这样的预设有利于教师在教学中保持一种开阔的思路与开放的观念，更容易纳入新的内容，适应新的情境，随时改变原有的设计，实现课堂教学的动态化，有效达到课堂教学的生成。

（二）教学设计要注重对课堂教学结构进行实效性的思考

课堂教学结构就是课堂教学步骤。如果对课堂教学结构进行实效性的思考与周密的设计，课堂教学就会收到实质性的效果。教学设计对课堂教学结构的实效性思考主要强调：

1. 依据一定的教育思想、教学理论和学习理论，理清教学思路，设计好一个单元或一节课的整体教学结构。

2. 确定恰当的教学过程、教学方法、教学组织形式和关键的提问、重要的指导语等。

3. 依据学情，整合教学内容，对教材文本作适当的增删并筛选适当的教学资料加以辅助是教学设计的重要一环；教师要创造性地使用教材，把教材内容和相关信息精妙创造为教学内容，以使教学设计个性化，并使自己具有独特的教学风格。

（三）教学设计需要集体智慧、博采众长

在查询学生需求的前提下，同事切磋，同伴互助，讨论交流和合作创新的集体备课模式，有助于提高教学设计的实效。

（四）板书设计是教学设计的重要组成部分

板书是教师创造性劳动的结晶，也是教师风格和教学基本功的具体体现。有效的板书反映出一定的教育理念、教学思想、认知轨迹，以及相关内容的逻辑关系，呈现一堂课的脉络框架，能引导学生理解学习内容，探寻认知规律，进行理性思考，合理归纳总结。板书是英语教学的重要组成部分。

1. 板书要有计划性，布局要合理精当

主题应写在黑板上方的中央。黑板一般分为两个区：左区写主要内容，是当堂教学的逻辑网络；右区用来对左区内容作辅助说明或为学生练习之用，左右区相互呼应，相得益彰，形成有意义的清晰有序的完整组合。

2. 板书要有引导性和启发性，内容要拮精摘要

板书要有梳理贯通的功效，有效地引人入胜，引发思考，便于学生理解和记忆；好的板书能引导学生与教师同步思考，甚至超越教师而思考，起到激活学习兴趣，不断获得印证喜悦的作用。有的板书内容会随着教学进展而成为发散思维的中心，生发新知，延伸新意，具有再生产的功能。

3. 板书要设计精美，有趣味性，在传递教学信息的同时，让学生获得美的享受和熏陶。

第三章　教案示例

教案示例（一）

Unit 1 Friendship（Book 1）
（第六课时　单元小结课）

一、教材内容分析

（一）覆盖内容

第一单元所涉及重要单词、短语、句型结构、直接引语变间接引语的复习和实际运用。本节课进行的前提是学生必须在笔记本上完成一份本单元的"Summing Up"。

（二）教材分析

在单元结束部分，教材设计了一个"Summing Up"版块，旨在让学生养成在单元学习即将结束时，对刚刚掌握到的语言知识进行梳理、总结的学习习惯。而在日常教学中，这个环节往往会被忽视。实际上，只要老师精心设计，早作要求，与学生一起完成一个单元语言知识、语言技能的梳理和巩固操练，就可以帮助学生掌握学习策略，形成良好的学习习惯，对整个高中英语的学习会起到事半功倍的收效。

二、教学目标

By the end of this class, the students will:

1. be more competent in using the core vocabulary (including the awareness of the definition, part of speech, and the proper context of the words).

2. have a good collection of the important phrases that have turned up in this unit, and use them correctly in the various English context.

3. be able to report others' speech appropriately by exchanging direct speech and indirect speech.

4. know how to write an English diary. (It's better if they can imitate some sentence

structures they've learned in this unit.)

> 设计说明
>
> 这节课要达到的主体目标是帮助学生进一步巩固本单元知识内容和语言运用，包括：明确单元核心词汇的词性、英文释义，及在文境中的准确使用；包括收集重点短语及其用法；包括操练直接引语与间接引语的交际功能等。

三、教学过程

Step 1　Vocabulary Part（10 minutes）

1. Sorting Task（分类游戏）

Ask the students to tick out the one that doesn't belong to the category, according to a certain rule.

Show one group as an example:

(On the Screen, all of the six teachers' names are listed out. Among them, the students are required to tick out the only one who doesn't belong to the group according to a certain rule.)

Li Hongying　Li Xia　Liu Danhua　Fu Juan　Yu Jingxiang　Daphne

The answer can be various because of the different rules the students can work out.

Possible Answer 1: Liu Danhua（Because he is the only male teacher among them.）

Possible Answer 2: Daphne（Because only she has an English name.）...

Then, let the students try several groups on the screen. They are required to explain the reasons for their choice.

(examples)

upset　calm　concern　disagree　dislike

entirely　outdoors　secondly　grateful　exactly

gossiper　recovery　loneliness　survey　concern

> 设计说明
>
> 这是一节课的热身。在分类游戏过程中，学生需要一定的词汇积累才能顺利完成任务。借此游戏，进一步清晰所学核心词汇的词性、汉语意思。这就增加了游戏的趣味性，减轻了单纯复习的枯燥感。

2. Guessing Game（猜词游戏）

List out some of the definitions of the core words in this unit. Ask the students to guess it out.（Teacher—Students）

Then list out some words on the screen to ask the students to describe them in English.（Students—Students）

> 设计说明
>
> 英文释义能有效地帮助学生辨析单词的含义和被使用的环境。从高中初始阶段开始慢慢强化学生对英文释义的关注，可有效避免汉语意思对准确运用单词的干扰。游戏的第一环节是师生之间进行。由老师列举出英文释义，学生猜。第二个环节是在学生之间进行的。同桌之间一位学生被允许看屏幕上的单词，并尽其所能用英文解释它的含义，对方如能猜出他所描绘的单词则为成功。

Step 2 Phrase Learning（10 minutes）

1. Brainstorm any verb phrases in this unit

Ask the students to brainstorm any possible phrases that they have already learned and collected in their mind. One student, one phase at a time. No repetition is allowed.

2. Create some sentences showing different situations of Anne's life. Ask the students to fill in the blanks with the right form of the phrases.

> 设计说明
>
> 本环节先让学生尽可能地列举出本单元收集到的重点短语，不允许重复。越到后来难度越大，同时也给了认真学习的学生充分的成就感。第二个环节是一个传统步骤：用短语的适当形式填空，考查学生对短语含义及使用语境的把握，包括形式一致的运用。

Step 3 Reporting Daphne's story（10 minutes）

The teacher tells her story in public. The story is concerned about how she treats a person who is in need of help on the road one day. The story should be told in direct speech by the teacher playing two roles by herself. And then, all the students are asked to retell the story by using indirect speech. In this task, the teacher should remind the students of the changing rules between direct and indirect speech, including the change of pronouns, tenses, time adverbial, and etc.

> 设计说明
>
> 本环节涉及对语法知识的实际语言运用。老师可通过描述自己的故事激起学生的好奇和关注，然后通过本单元学到的直接引语变间接引语的相关知识进行复述。这个设计旨在避开一味重复讲授语法规则所产生的枯燥感，提高学生在实际生活情境中的语言运用能力。

Step 4 Observing the structure（10 minutes）

The teacher is supposed to collect the sentences that the students have used in retelling Daphne's story. Some sentences are right, while some are wrong. Ask the students to observe them and try to identify. They are also required to explain the reasons for their identification.

> 【设计说明】
> 学生对自己在语言产出时出现的问题往往是较为迟钝的,然而,对别人的错误往往是敏感的。本环节借助纠错的过程让学生学会观察、辨析、分析,继而得出正确的结论。通过小组活动、师生对话等形式进一步复习直接引语变间接引语的用法。

Step 5　Model Sentence Imitation（5 minutes）

1. Ask the students to make a collection of all the model sentences that they have learned in this unit.

2. Ask the students to explain the structure of each sentence.

3. Give them two minutes to create two more sentences by using the structure of the model sentences.

> 【设计说明】
> 该环节是一个经典句型的仿写练习。在单元学习的过程中,教师已经有所选择地引导学生注意到了一些经典句型在文章中的运用。在小结课上,侧重将句型结构进一步明确,并鼓励学生仿写。

Step 6　Assessment

1. Evaluate the students' competence in this period of class.

2. Encourage them to improve and perfect their "Summing up".

> 【设计说明】
> 在每节课的教学任务完成时,不论是教师还是学生都应该就自己的收获做一个小结或评论。

Step 7　Homework

1. Ask the students to improve their summing up.

2. Write an English diary, reporting a moving story in daily life.

教案示例（二）

Unit 4　Earthquake（Book 1）

（第二课时　阅读课）

Ⅰ. Three Aims

1. Knowledge Aims:

（1）Get the students to know the basic knowledge of natural disasters.

(2) Get the students to learn the new words and useful expressions in the passage.

2. Ability Aims

(1) Train the students' abilities to collect useful information from the Internet by themselves.

(2) Train the students' abilities to cooperate with others.

3. Emotional Aims

(1) Enable the students to learn the damages earthquake brings about and the ways to reduce losses of it.

(2) Enable the students to know how to protect themselves and help others in the earthquake.

(3) Get students to be aware of a terrible disaster, meanwhile get them to face it, treat it in a proper way and never get discouraged.

II. Teaching difficult and important points

1. Get the students to learn about Tangshan Earthquake.
2. Enable the students to know how to protect themselves and help others in the earthquake.

III. Teaching Method

1. Task-based teaching and learning.
2. Cooperative learning.
3. Discussion and summary.

III. Teaching Aids

The multimedia, postcards and other teaching tools.

V. Teaching Procedures

Step1 Lead-in

Show students the picture of the earth we are living on. Natural disasters happen frequently on the earth, which are caused by nature forces and are beyond the control of human beings.

Step2 Warming-up

Task1: Talking about disasters. (Group-work activity)

1. What natural disasters may cause great damage? (Brainstorm)

2. Have you ever experienced an earthquake? How do you feel?

(*Suggested answer*: **shocked, frightened, nervous**, etc.)

3. What damage did the big earthquake bring about? (showing pictures)

(*Suggested answer*: The city was **in ruins**./ Tall building were **destroyed**./ Roads were **cracked**. / People were **injured**.)

4. Why does an earthquake happen? (listen to the listening practice on Page62)

(*Possible answer*: As a result of the movement of these plates, they meet and then suddenly, they jump and an earthquake is felt.)

Students listen to the listening practice on Page62 and then check the answer.

If possible, they can search for more information on the Internet and share with the class.

Step3 Pre-reading

Task 2: Looking and discussing.

1. What may happen before an earthquake? (looking at the pictures)

(*Suggested answer*: Before an earthquake, animals will become nervous and upset. Mice will run about and fish will jump out of water. Water pipes will have deep cracks and burst. Bright lights can be seen in the sky. The water will rise and fall. Loud noise can be heard.)

2. What shall we do when an earthquake happens? (watching an instructive short video play)

(1) Dos ① Drop, cover your head and hold on the strong furniture.

② Keep away from glass or anything that may fall.

③ Turn off the fire, gas and electricity.

(2) Don'ts ① Don't be nervous.

② Don't try to run out of building without order.

③ Don't use elevators during a quake.

④ Don't jump out of the windows.

3. What should we do after an earthquake? (discussion)

(*Suggested answer*: To rebuild the city. To rescue the injured. To help survivors forget sad experiences and live with strong belief.)

Show students the new look of Tangshan and guide students to bravely face the reality and pick up confidence.

Step4 Activity

Many teenagers of our age suffered a lot in Wenchuan Earthquake. It is vital to help them pick up their confidence and courage in their future life. Therefore, it is advised to write them a postcard to cheer them up. Survivors' names and addresses on the Internet have been listed on the screen. After class, we will mail your postcards to them.

Step5 Homework

Write a summary of what we have learned today and review the new words and expressions in the passage.

教案示例（三）

Unit 2 Cloning （Book 8）

（第二课时 词汇课）

Ⅰ. Teaching Goals

1. To enable students to master key phrases and expressions.

2. To enable students to learn how to use these words and expressions.

3. To enable students to have a right attitude toward cloning.

Ⅱ. Teaching Procedures

Step 1 Language study

Purpose: To train students' listening ability and language capacity.

1. Ask the students to summarize some verbs, nouns, adjectives, and phrases about cloning.

> Verbs: undertake, differ, object, attain, accumulate, forbid
>
> Nouns: breakthrough, procedure, correction, objection, impact,
>
> Adjectives: complicated, straightforward, moral, conservative, exact
>
> Phrases: pay off, cast down, in favor of, in vain, be bound to, bring back ... to life

While the students tell the each word, ask them to make a sentence with it.

2. Complete the sentences using suitable words from the text. The first letter of each word has been given.

(1) In many aspects natural clones, such as identical twins, do not d_____ greatly from man-made ones.

(2) He was c_____ when the procedure he had used to produce a mammal clone ended in failure.

(3) Dust will a_____ in a deserted house.

(4) Her memory is so excellent that she could remember the e_____ names.

(5) She was not a_____ pleased at the corrections he made to her work.

(6) Grey decided to move to the countryside and his wife made no o_____ to it.

(7) According to the constitution, it is compulsory for a citizen to u_____ military service.

(8) The media has a m_____ responsibility to report news truthfully.

Answers: 1. differ   2. cast down   3. accumulate   4. exact
5. altogether   6. objections   7. undertake   8. moral

3. Replace the underlined parts with words that have the same meaning. Rewrite the sentence when necessary.

(1) Compared with her family, and especially her nephew, her niece Daisy is <u>very honest</u> about her opinions.

(2) The decisions of the conservative factory leaders <u>that had been made without any reason</u> caused anger among the workers.

(3) Is the opera house in the <u>business</u> area of Beijing?

(4) The producer of the media program <u>disagreed with</u> Jennifer joining in the chorus.

(5) Before you can make a loaf, you need to <u>get</u> some flour.

(6) You owe the lady an apology. I <u>will not allow</u> you to leave unless you apologize for what you have done.

Answers: 1. straightforward   2. arbitrary   3. commercial
4. made an objection to   5. obtain   6. will forbid

4. Complete the passage using the correct form of the words below.

| complicated   fate   attain   cast   accumulate   reform   carrier |

As Freddy the frog grew older, he only had one ambition left to __1__ — to continue his career forever. To do this he thought that he would have to clone himself. The doctor explained that this was a __2__ procedure that he should consider carefully. Shortly after Freddy did some research, he discovered the __3__ of Dolly the sheep. It seemed as if a clone was a __4__ of more weaknesses than its original. Freddy was __5__ down and looked for some way to __6__ the cloning procedure to avoid this problem. Sadly this seemed impossible. So Freddy made up his mind to enjoy his singing and to __7__ as many happy experiences as he could so that when he retired he would be able to look back on his life with satisfaction.

Answers: 1. attain   2. complicated   3. fate   4. carrier   5. cast   6. reform   7. accumulate

Step 2   Consolidation

Purpose: to consolidate the words and phrases in the text

Ask students to complete the following sentences using suitable words or phrases.

(1) Chinese _____ greatly _____ French in pronunciation.

(2) She _____ the task of monitoring the elections.

(3) Many people _____ experimentation on animals.

(4) You are not legally _____ _____ answer these questions.

(5) It took them three years to _____ _____ the debt.

(6) After a decade of production use, though, no other serious competitor has yet _____.

(7) He was much _____ when he heard of his failure at the examination.

Suggested Answers:

(1) differs... from　(2) undertook　(3) object to　(4) bound to　(5) pay off

(6) arisen　　　(7) cast down

Step 3　Application

Ask the students to express their opinions about cloning. (Divide the students into four groups to discuss the advantages and disadvantages of the cloning.)

Sample:

With the development of science and technology, it is possible for scientists to clone animals or even human beings. People are wondering whether cloning will help or harm us and where it is leading us? People differ with each other on it.

Some people are in favor of cloning animals. They think scientists can find cures for deadly disease by cloning, which can save many patients lives. Besides, cloning can prevent some animals from dying out, which can keep the diversity of species. Though cloning is a long way from being perfect, it is a new science and it is worth doing it.

However, some people object to cloning. Firstly, they think cloning can be made use of by evil leaders to clone themselves to attain their ambitions, which will be terrible for the whole world. Secondly, cloned animals can suffer from illnesses more easily and survive shorter than normal animals. In addition, cloning can also raise some moral and religious questions. In a sense, it is a waste of time and money to clone animals. We can spend the money spent in cloning animals in protecting animals.

Step 4　Homework

1. Ask students to review the language points in this period.

2. Ask students to finish the following exercises.

(1) Ask students to use "happen, occur, take place, come about" to fill the following blanks.

① When did the accident _____?

② Our school sports meeting will _____ next week.

③ How did it _____ that he was dismissed?

④ It _____ to me that Mary knew him very well.

⑤ He _____ to be out when I called.

Suggested Answers:

① happen ② take place ③ come about ④ occurred ⑤ happened

(2) Ask students to use "raise" or "rise" to fill the following blanks.

① The guests _____ to their feet, applauding the golden couple.

② The heavy rains _____ the river stage, which was worrying.

③ The government is trying to _____ the living standard of the working people.

④ His voice _____ as he got excited.

⑤ We are about to leave when the wind is _____.

⑥ Her parents died when she was a baby and she was _____ by her grandparents.

Suggested Answers:

① rose ② raised ③ raise ④ rose ⑤ rising ⑥ raised

第四章　题型训练

一、教学设计题（一）

请根据以下提供的信息和语言素材进行教学设计。（本题用英文作答）

设计任务：阅读以下信息和语言素材。假设你将利用此语言素材提高学生的阅读能力，请根据学生情况设计针对此素材的教学目标，以及实现该目标的课堂活动。

学生概况：本班为中等城市普通学校高中一年级的学生，班级人数为50人。学生刚入高一，具备初步的英语语言能力。学生能够积极参与课堂活动，合作意识较强。

教学时间：25分钟。

教学设计需包括：
- 教学目标；
- 教学步骤及设计意图；
- 教学活动方式、具体内容及设计意图；
- 教学时间规划；
- 学习评价。

语言素材：（加粗单词为学生首次接触的词汇）

SEFC B1　Unit 2　The Road to Modern English

At the end of the 16th century, above five to seven million people spoke English. Nearly all of them lived in England. Later in the next century, people from England made **voyages** to conquer other parts of the world and **because of** that, English began to be spoken in many other countries. Today, more people speak English as their first, second or a foreign language than ever before.

Native English speakers can understand each other even if they don't speak the same kind of English. Look at this example:

British Betty: Would you like to see my flat?

American Amy: Yes, I'd like to **come up** to your **apartment**.

So why has English changed over time? **Actually** all languages change and develop when cultures meet and communicate with each other. At first, the English language spoken in England between about **A.D.** 450 and 1150 was very different from the English spoken today. It was **based** more on German than the English we speak **at present**. Then **gradually** between about A.D. 800 and 1150, English became less like German because those who ruled England spoke first **Danish** and later French. These new settlers enriched the English language and especially its **vocabulary**. So by the 1600s Shakespeare was able to **make use of** a wider vocabulary than ever before. In 1620 some British settlers moved to America. Later in the 18th century some British people were taken to Australia too. English began to speak in both countries.

Finally by the 19th century the language was settled. At that time two big changes in English **spelling** happened: first Samuel Johnson wrote his dictionary and later Noah Webster wrote The American Dictionary of English Language. The latter gave a separate **identity** to American English Spelling.

English now is also spoken as a foreign or second language in South Asia. For example, India has a very large number of **fluent** English speakers because Britain ruled India from 1765 to 1947. During that time English became the language for government and education. English is also spoken in **Singapore** and **Malaysia** and countries in Africa **such as** South Africa. Today the number of people learning English in China is increasing rapidly. In fact, China may have the largest number of English learners. Will Chinese English develop its own identity? Only time will tell.

二、教学设计题(二)

请根据以下提供的信息和语言素材进行教学设计。(本题用英文作答)

设计任务：阅读以下信息和语言素材。假设你将利用此语言素材提高学生的阅读能力，请根据学生情况设计针对此素材的教学目标，以及实现该目标的课堂活动。

学生概况：本班为大城市普通学校高中一年级的学生，班级人数为50人。学生具备初步的英语语言能力。学生能够积极参与课堂活动，合作意识较强。

教学时间：25分钟。

教学设计需包括：
- 教学目标；
- 教学步骤及设计意图；
- 教学活动方式、具体内容及设计意图；
- 教学时间规划；
- 学习评价。

语言素材：（加粗单词为学生首次接触的词汇）

SEFC B2　Unit 5　Music

　　Have you ever wanted to be part of a band as a famous singer or **musician**? Have you ever **dreamed of** playing in front of thousands of people at a concert, at which everyone is clapping and appreciating your music? Do you sing karaoke and **pretend** you are a famous singer like Song Zuying or Liu Huan? **To be honest**, a lot of people **attach** great importance to becoming rich and famous. But just how do people **form** a band?

　　Many musicians meet and form a band because they like to write and play their own music. They may start as a group of high-school students, for whom practising their music in someone's house is the first step to fame. Sometimes they may play to **passers-by** in the street or subway so that they can **earn** some **extra** money for themselves or to pay for their **instruments**. Later they may give **performances** in **pubs** or clubs, for which they are paid **in cash**. Of course they hope to make records in a **studio** and sell millions of copies to become **millionaires**!

　　However, there was one band that started in a different way. It was called the Monkees and began as a TV show. The musicians were to **play jokes on** each other as well as play music, most of which was based loosely on the Beatles. The TV organizers had planned to find four musicians who could act as well as sing. They put an advertisement in a newspaper looking for rock musicians, but they could only find one who was good enough. They had to use **actors** for the other three members of the band.

　　As some of these actors could not sing well enough, they had to **rely on** other musicians to help them. So during the **broadcasts** they just pretended to sing. Anyhow their performances were **humorous** enough to be copied by other groups. They were so popular that their fans formed clubs in order to **get** more **familiar with** them. Each week on TV, the Monkees would play and sing songs written by other musicians. However, after a year or so in which they became more serious about their work, the Monkees started to play and sing their own songs like a real band. Then they produced their own records and started touring and playing their own music. In the USA they became even more popular than the Beatles and sold even more records. The band **broke up** about 1970, but happily they reunited in the mid-1980s. They produced a new record in 1996, with which they celebrated their former time as a real band.

三、教学设计题(三)

请根据以下提供的信息和语言素材进行教学设计。(本题用英文作答)

设计任务：阅读以下信息和语言素材。假设你将利用此语言素材提高学生的阅读能力，请根据学生情况设计针对此素材的教学目标，以及实现该目标的课堂活动。

学生概况：本班为中等城市普通学校高中二年级的学生，班级人数为50人。学生具备较好的英语语言能力。学生能够积极参与课堂活动，合作意识较强。

教学时间：25分钟。

教学设计需包括：
- 教学目标；
- 教学步骤及设计意图；
- 教学活动方式、具体内容及设计意图；
- 教学时间规划；
- 学习评价。

语言素材：(加粗单词为学生首次接触的词汇)

SEFC B6　Unit 5　AN EXCITING JOB

I have the greatest job in the world. I travel to unusual places and work **alongside** people from all over the world. Sometimes working outdoors sometimes in an office sometimes using scientific **equipment** and sometimes meeting local people and tourists I am never bored. Although my job is occasionally dangerous I don't mind because danger excites me and makes me feel alive. However the most important thing about my job is that I help protect ordinary people from one of the most powerful forces on earth — the volcano.

I was **appointed** as volcanologist information for a database about Mount Kilauea which is one of the most active volcanoes in Hawaii. Having collected and evaluated the information I help other scientists to predict where lava from the volcano will flow next and how fast. Our work has saved man lives because people in the path of the lava can be warned to leave their houses. Unfortunately we cannot move their homes out of the way and many houses have been covered with lava or burned to the ground.

When boiling rock erupts from a volcano and crashes back to earth it causes less damage than you might imagine. This is because no one lives near the top of Mount Kilauea where the rocks fall. The lava that flows slowly like a wave down the mountain causes far more damage because it buries everything in its path under the molten rock. However the **eruption** itself is really exciting to watch and I shall never forget my first sight of one.

It was in the second week after I arrived in Hawaii. Having worked hard all day I went to bed early. I was fast asleep when suddenly my bed began shaking and I heard a strange sound like a railway train passing my window. Having experienced quite a few earthquakes in Hawaii already I didn't take much notice. I was about to go back to sleep when suddenly my bedroom became as bright as day. I ran out of the house into the back garden where I could see Mount Kilauea in the distance. There had been an eruption from the side of the mountain and red hot lava was fountaining hundreds of metres into the air. It was an **absolutely** fantastic sight.

　　The day after this eruption I was lucky enough to have a much closer look at it. Two other scientists and I were driven up the mountain and dropped as close as possible to the crater that had been formed during the eruption. Having earlier collected special clothes from the observatory we put them on before we went any closer. All three of us looked like spacemen. We had white protective **suits** that covered our whole body, **helmets**, big **boots** and special gloves. It was not easy to walk in these suits but we slowly **made our way** to the edge of the crater and looked down into the red boiling centre. The other two climbed down into the crater to collect some lava for later study but this being my first experience I stayed at the top and watched them.

　　Today I am just as enthusiastic about my job as the day I first started. Having studied volcanoes now for many years I am still amazed their beauty as well as their **potential** to cause great damage.

四、教学设计题（四）

　　请根据以下提供的信息和语言素材进行教学设计。（本题用英文作答）

　　设计任务：阅读以下信息和语言素材。假设你将利用此语言素材提高学生的阅读能力，请根据学生情况设计针对此素材的教学目标，以及实现该目标的课堂活动。

　　学生概况：本班为县级城市普通学校高中一年级的学生，班级人数为50人。学生具备初步的英语语言能力。学生能够积极参与课堂活动，合作意识较强。

　　教学时间：25分钟。

　　教学设计需包括：

　　● 教学目标；

　　● 教学步骤及设计意图；

　　● 教学活动方式、具体内容及设计意图；

　　● 教学时间规划；

　　● 学习评价。

　　语言素材：（加粗单词为学生首次接触的词汇）

SEFC B3　Unit 1　FESTIVALS AND CELEBRATIONS

Festivals and celebrations of all kinds are held everywhere. The most ancient festivals would celebrate the end of the cold weather planting in spring and harvest in autumn. Other celebrations were held after **hunters** had caught animals. They would **starve** if food was difficult to find.

Festivals of the Dead

Some festivals are held to honour the dead or satisfy and please the ancestors who could return either to help or to do harm. In Japan the festival is called Obon when people should go to clean the graves and light incense in memory of their ancestors. They light lamps and play music because they think that this will lead the ancestors back to earth. In Mexico they have the Day of the Dead in early November. On this important feast day people might eat food in shape of skull sand cakes with "bones" on them. They offer food flowers and gifts to the dead. The festival of Halloween had its origin as an event in memory of the dead. It is now a children's festival when they can go to their neighbours' homes and ask for sweets. They dress up and try to frighten people. If they are not given anything the children might play a trick.

Festivals to Honour People

Festivals can be held as an honour to famous people or to the gods. One of these is the Dragon Boat Festival in China which honours the famous ancient **poet** Qu Yuan. Another is Columbus Day in the USA in memory of the **arrival** of Christopher Columbus in America. In India there is a national festival on October 2 to honour Mahatma Gandhi the leader who helped gain India's **independence** from Britain.

Harvest Festivals

Harvest and Thanksgiving festivals can be very happy events. People are grateful because their food is **gathered** for the winter and because a season of **agricultural** work is over. In European countries it is the custom to decorate churches and town halls with flowers and fruit and people get together to have meals. Some people might win **awards** for their animals flowers fruits and vegetables like the biggest watermelon or the most handsome rooster. In China and Japan there are mid-autumn festivals when people admire the moon and give gift of mooncakes.

Spring Festivals

The most energetic and important festivals are the ones that **look forward to** the end of winter and to the coming of spring. At the Spring Festival in China people eat dumplings fish and meat and may give children lucky money in the red paper. There are dragon dances and carnivals and families celebrate the lunar New Year together. In some Western countries there are very exciting carnivals which take place forty days before **Easter** usually in February. They might include parades dancing in the streets **day and night** loud music and colourful **clothing** of all kinds. Easter is an important religious and social festival in Christian countries. It celebrates the return of Jesus for **Christians** and it also celebrates the coming of spring. In Japan the Cherry Blossom Festival happens a little later. The country is covered with cherry tree flowers so that it looks as though it might be covered with pink snow.

People love to get together to eat and drink and have fun with each others. Festivals let us enjoy life and be proud of our customs and forget our daily life for a little while.

五、教学设计题(五)

请根据以下提供的信息和语言素材进行教学设计。(本题用英文作答)

设计任务：阅读以下信息和语言素材。假设你将利用此语言素材提高学生的阅读能力，请根据学生情况设计针对此素材的教学目标，以及实现该目标的课堂活动。

学生概况：本班为地级城市普通学校高中二年级的学生，班级人数为50人。学生具有一般的英语语言能力。但学生能够积极参与课堂活动，合作意识较强。

教学时间：25分钟。

教学设计需包括：
- 教学目标；
- 教学步骤及设计意图；
- 教学活动方式、具体内容及设计意图；
- 教学时间规划；
- 学习评价。

语言素材：(加粗单词为学生首次接触的词汇)

SEFC B6 Unit 4 THE EARTH IS BECOMIG WARMER-BUT DOES IT MATTER

During the 20th century the temperature of the earth rose about one degree Fahrenheit. That probably does not seem much to you or me but it is a rapid increase when compared to other natural changes. So how has this **come about** and does it matter Earth cares Sophie Armstrong explores these questions.

There is no doubt that the earth is becoming warmer and that it is human activity that has caused this global warming rather than a **random** but natural **phenomenon**.

All scientists **subscribe to** the view that the increase in the earths temperature is due to the burning of fossil **fuels** like coal natural gas and oil to produce energy. Some byproducts of this process are called "greenhouse" gases the most important one of which is carbon dioxide. Dr. Janice Foster explains: "There is a natural phenomenon that scientists call the "greenhouse effect". This is when small amounts of gases in the atmosphere like carbon dioxide methane and water vapour trap heat from the sun and therefore warm the earth. Without the greenhouse effect the earth would be about thirty-three degrees Celsius cooler than it is. So we need those gases. The problem begins when we add huge **quantities of** extra carbon dioxide into the atmosphere. It means that more heat energy **tends to** be trapped in the atmosphere causing the global temperature to **go up**.

We know that the levels of carbon dioxide have increased greatly over the last 100 to 150 years. It was a scientist called Charles Keeling who made accurate measurements of the amount of carbon dioxide in the atmosphere from 1957 to 1997. He found that between these years the carbon dioxide in the atmosphere went up from around 315 parts to around 370 parts per million.

All scientists accept this **data**. They also agree that it is the burning of more and more fossil fuels that has **resulted in** this increase in carbon dioxide. So how high will the temperature increase go Dr. Janice Foster says that over the next 100 years the amount of warming could be as low as 1 to 1.5 degrees Celsius but it could be as high as 5 degrees.

However the attitude of scientists towards this rise in completely different. On the one hand Dr. Foster thinks that the **trend** which increases the temperature by 5 degrees would be a catastrophe. She says "We can't predict the climate well enough to know what to expect but it could be very serious." Others who agree with her think there may be a rise of several metres in the sea level or predict severe storms **floods** droughts famines the spread of diseases and the disappearance of species. On the other hand there are those like George Hambley who **are opposed to** this view believe that we should not worry about high levels of carbon dioxide in the air. They predict that any warming will be **mild** with few bad environmental **consequences**. In fact Hambley **states** "More carbon dioxide is actually a positive thing. It will make plants grow quicker crops will produce more it will encourage a greater **range** of animals-all of which will make life for human beings better."

Greenhouse gases continue to build up in the atmosphere. **Even if** we start reducing the amount of carbon dioxide and other greenhouse gases the climate is going to **keep on** warming for decades or centuries. No one knows the effects of global warming. Does that mean we should do nothing?

六、教学设计题（六）

请根据以下提供的信息和语言素材进行教学设计。（本题用英文作答）

设计任务：阅读以下信息和语言素材。假设你将利用此语言素材提高学生的阅读能力，请根据学生情况设计针对此素材的教学目标，以及实现该目标的课堂活动。

学生概况：本班为大型林区普通学校高中一年级的学生，班级人数为 50 人。学生具备中等的英语语言能力。但学生能够积极参与课堂活动，合作意识较强。

教学时间：25 分钟。

教学设计需包括：
- 教学目标；
- 教学步骤及设计意图；
- 教学活动方式、具体内容及设计意图；
- 教学时间规划；
- 学习评价。

语言素材：（加粗单词为学生首次接触的词汇）

SEFC B4　Unit 5　THEME PARKS — FUN AND MORE THAN FUN

Which theme park would you like to visit? There are **various** kinds of theme parks, with a different park for almost everything: food, culture, science, **cartoons**, movies or history. Some parks **are famous for** having the biggest or longest roller coasters, others for showing the famous sights and sounds of a culture. **Whichever** and whatever you like, there is a theme park for you!

The theme park you are probably most familiar with is Disneyland. It can be found in several parts of the world. It will bring you into a magical world and make your dreams come true, whether traveling through space, visiting a pirate ship or meeting your favourite fairy tale or Disney cartoon character. As you wander around the **fantasy** amusement park, you may see Snow White or Mickey Mouse in a parade or on the street. Of course Disneyland also has many exciting rides, from giant **swinging** ships to terrifying free-fall drops. With all these **attractions, no wonder tourism** is increasing **wherever** there is a Disneyland. If you want to have fun and more than fun, come to Disneyland!

Dollywood, in the beautiful Smoky Mountains in the southeastern USA, is one of the most **unique** theme parks in the world. Dollywood shows and celebrates America's traditional southeastern culture. Although Dollywood has rides, the park's main attraction is its culture. Famous country music groups perform there all year in indoor and outdoor theatres. People come from all over America to see **carpenters** and other craftsmen make wood, glass and iron objects in the old-fashioned way. Visit the candy shop to try the same kind of candy that American southerners made 150 years ago, or take a ride on the only steam-**engine** train still working in the southeast USA. You can even see beautiful bald eagles in the world's largest bald eagle **preserve**. And for those who like rides, Dollywood has one of the best old wooden roller coasters, Thunderhead. It is world-famous for having the most length in the smallest space.

Come to Dollywood to have fun learning all about America's historical southeastern culture!

If you want to experience the ancient days and great **deeds** of English knights and ladies, princes and queens, then England's Camelot Park is the place for you. Every area of the park **is modelled after** life in the days of King Arthur and the Knights of the Round Table. In one place, you can watch magic shows with Merlin the Wizard. If you want to see fighting with **swords** or on horseback, then the jousting area is a good place to visit. If you do well there, King Arthur may choose you to fight in the big jousting **tournament**. Do you like animals? Then visit the farm area, and learn how people in ancient England ran their farms and took care of their animals. To enter a world of fantasy about ancient England, come to Camelot Park!

七、教学设计题(七)

请根据以下提供的信息和语言素材进行教学设计。(本题用英文作答)

设计任务：阅读以下信息和语言素材。假设你将利用此语言素材提高学生的阅读能力，请根据学生情况设计针对此素材的教学目标，以及实现该目标的课堂活动。

学生概况：本班为乡镇普通学校高中一年级的学生，班级人数为50人。学生具备初步的英语语言能力。学生能够积极参与课堂活动，合作意识较强。

教学时间：25分钟。

教学设计需包括：
- 教学目标；
- 教学步骤及设计意图；
- 教学活动方式、具体内容及设计意图；
- 教学时间规划；
- 学习评价。

语言素材：(加粗单词为学生首次接触的词汇)

SEFC B4　Unit 2　A PIONEER FOR ALL PEOPLE

Although he is one of China's most famous scientists, Yuan Longping considers himself a farmer, for he works the land to do his research. Indeed, his sunburnt face and arms and his slim, strong body are just like those of millions of Chinese farmers, for whom he has **struggled** for the past five **decades**. Dr. Yuan Longping grows what is called **super** hybrid rice. In 1974, he became the first agricultural pioneer in the world to grow rice that has a high **output**. This special strain of rice makes it possible to produce one-third more of the **crop** in the same fields. Now more than 60% of the rice produced in China each year is from this hybrid strain.

Born into a poor farmer's family in 1930, Dr. Yuan graduated from Southwest Agricultural College in 1953. Since then, finding ways to grow more rice has been his life goal. As a young man, he saw the great need for increasing the rice output. At that time, **hunger** was a **disturbing** problem in many parts of the countryside. Dr. Yuan searched for a way to increase rice harvests without **expanding** the area of the fields. In 1950, Chinese farmers could produce only fifty million tons of rice. In a recent harvest, however, nearly two hundred million tons of rice was produced. These increased harvests mean that 22% of the world's people are fed from just 7% of the farmland in China. Dr. Yuan is now **circulating** his knowledge in India, **Vietnam** and many other less developed countries to increase their rice harvests. **Thanks to** his research, the UN has more tools in the **battle** to **rid** the world of hunger. Using his hybrid rice, farmers are producing harvests twice as large as before.

Dr. Yuan is quite **satisfied with** his life. However, he doesn't care about being famous. He feels it gives him less **freedom** to do his research. He **would** much **rather** keep time for his hobbies. He enjoys listening to violin music, playing mah-jong, swimming and reading. Spending money on himself or leading a comfortable life also means very little to him. Indeed, he believes that a person with too much money has more rather than fewer troubles. He therefore gives millions of yuan to **equip** others for their research in agriculture. Just dreaming for things, however, costs nothing. Long ago Dr. yuan had a dream about rice plants as tall as sorghum. Each ear of rice was as big as an ear of corn and each grain of rice was as huge as a peanut. Dr Yuan awoke from his dream with the hope of producing a kind of rice that could feed more people. Now, many years later, Dr. Yuan has another dream: to **export** his rice so that it can be grown around the globe. One dream is not always enough, especially for a person who loves and cares for his people.

八、教学设计题（八）

请根据以下提供的信息和语言素材进行教学设计。（本题用英文作答）

设计任务：阅读以下信息和语言素材。假设你将利用此语言素材提高学生的阅读能力，请根据学生情况设计针对此素材的教学目标，以及实现该目标的课堂活动。

学生概况：本班为中等城市普通学校高中一年级的学生，班级人数为50人。学生具备初步的英语语言能力。学生能够积极参与课堂活动，合作意识较强。

教学时间：25分钟。

教学设计需包括：
- 教学目标；
- 教学步骤及设计意图；
- 教学活动方式、具体内容及设计意图；
- 教学时间规划；
- 学习评价。

语言素材：（加粗单词为学生首次接触的词汇）

SEFC B4 Unit 1 A STUDENT OF AFRICAN WILDLIFE

It is 5:45 a.m. and the sun is just rising over Gombe National Park in East Africa. Following Jane's way of studying chimps, our group are all going to visit them in the forest. Jane has studied these families of chimps for many years and helped people understand how much they **behave** like humans. Watching a family of chimps wake up is our first activity of the day. This means going back to the place where we left the family sleeping in a tree the night before. Everybody sits and waits in the **shade** of the trees while the family begins to wake up and **move off**. Then we follow as they wander into the forest. Most of the time, chimps either feed or clean each other as a way of showing love in their family. Jane warns us that our group is going to be very tired and dirty by the afternoon and she is right. However, the evening makes it all **worthwhile**. We watch the mother chimp and her babies play in the tree. Then we see them go to sleep together in their **nest** for the night. We realize that the **bond** between members of a chimp family is as strong as in a human family.

Nobody before Jane fully understood chimp **behaviour**. She spent years **observing** and recording their daily activities. Since her **childhood** she had wanted to work with animals in their own environment. However, this was not easy. When she first arrived in Gombe in 1960, it was unusual for a woman to live in the forest. Only after her mother came to help her for the first few months was she allowed to begin her project. Her work changed the way people think about chimps. For example, one important thing she discovered was that chimps hunt and eat meat. Until then everyone had thought chimps ate only fruit and nuts. She actually observed chimps as a group hunting a monkey and then eating it. She also discovered how chimps communicate with each other, and her study of their body language helped her work out their social system.

For forty years Jane Goodall has been **outspoken** about making the rest of the world understand and **respect** the life of these animals. She has **argued** that wild animals should be left in the wild and not used for **entertainment** or advertisements. She has helped to set up special places where they can live safely. She is **leading** a busy **life** but she says: "Once I stop, it all comes **crowding in** and I remember the chimps in laboratories. It's terrible. It affects me when I watch the wild chimps. I say to myself," Aren't they lucky? "And then I think about small chimps in cages though they have done nothing wrong. Once you have seen that you can never forget …"

She has achieved everything she wanted to do: working with animals in their own environment, gaining a doctor's degree and showing that women can live in the forest as men can. She **inspires** those who want to cheer the achievements of women.

九、教学设计题(九)

请根据以下提供的信息和语言素材进行教学设计。(本题用英文作答)

设计任务：阅读以下信息和语言素材。假设你将利用此语言素材提高学生的阅读能力，请根据学生情况设计针对此素材的教学目标，以及实现该目标的课堂活动。

学生概况：本班为大城市普通学校高中一年级的学生，班级人数为 50 人。学生具备较好的英语语言能力。学生能够积极参与课堂活动，合作意识较强。

教学时间：25 分钟。

教学设计需包括：
- 教学目标；
- 教学步骤及设计意图；
- 教学活动方式、具体内容及设计意图；
- 教学时间规划；
- 学习评价。

语言素材：(加粗单词为学生首次接触的词汇)

SEFC B3　Unit 2　COME AND EAT HERE(1)

Wang Peiwei sat in his empty restaurant feeling very frustrated. It had been a very strange morning. Usually he got up early and prepared his menu. Then by lunchtime they would all be sold. His restaurant **ought to** be full of people. But not today Why was it so What could have happened He thought of his mutton kebabs and fatty pork cooked in the hottest finest oil. His fried rice was hot but did not taste of fat. His cola was sugary and cold and his ice cream was made of eggs milk cream and fruit. "Nothing could have been better", he thought. Suddenly he saw his friend Li Maochang hurrying by. "Hello Maochang",he called. "Your usual." But Maochang seemed not to hear. What was the matter? Something terrible must have happened if Maochang was not coming to eat with him as he always did.

Wang followed Li Chang into a newly-opened small restaurant at the end of the street. There was a sign in the window.

Tired of all that fat？

Want to **lose weight**？

Come inside to Yong Hui's **slimming** restaurant.

Only slimming foods served here.

Make yourself thin again.

Curiosity drove Wang Pengwei inside. It was full of people. A very thin lady came forward. "Welcome." she said, "My name is Yong Hui. I will take all that fat off you in two weeks if you eat here every day." Then she gave a menu to Wang Peiwei. There were only two kinds of food and one drink on it: **raw** vegetables fruit and water. Wang Peiwei was amazed at this and especially at the prices. It cost more than a good meal in his own restaurant. He could not believe his eyes. He threw away the menu and hurried outside. On his way home he thought about his own menu. Did it make people fat? He wondered if he should go to the library to find out. He couldn't have Yong Hui **getting away with telling** people **lies**. He had better do some research.

After reading he realised what was wrong with Yong Hui's restaurant. It was not giving its customers energy-giving food. After eating in her restaurant, people would become tired very quickly. Perhaps this was a way to **win** his **customers back.** Peng Wei wrote his own sign. It said, want to feel fit? Come and eat here. Our food gives you energy all day. The competition between the two restaurants was on!

十、教学设计题(十)

请根据以下提供的信息和语言素材进行教学设计。(本题用英文作答)

设计任务：阅读以下信息和语言素材。假设你将利用此语言素材提高学生的阅读能力，请根据学生情况设计针对此素材的教学目标，以及实现该目标的课堂活动。

学生概况：本班为地级城市普通学校高中一年级的学生，班级人数为 50 人。学生具备较好的英语语言能力。学生能够积极参与课堂活动，合作意识较强。

教学时间：25 分钟。

教学设计需包括：
● 教学目标；
● 教学步骤及设计意图；
● 教学活动方式、具体内容及设计意图；
● 教学时间规划；
● 学习评价。

语言素材：(加粗单词为学生首次接触的词汇)

SEFC B4   Unit 3 A TASTE OF ENGLISH HUMOR

As Victor Hugo once said, "Laughter is the sun that drives winter from the human face", and **up to now** nobody has been able to do this better than Charlie Chaplin. He brightened the lives of Americans and British through two world wars and the hard years in between. He made people laugh at a time when they felt depressed, so they could feel **more content with** their lives.

Not that Charlie's own life was easy! He was born in a poor family in 1889. His parents were both poor music hall **performers**. You may find it **astonishing** that Charlie was taught to sing as soon as he could speak and dance as soon as he could walk. Such training was common in acting families at this time, especially when the family income was often uncertain. **Unfortunately** his father died, leaving the family even **worse off**, so Charlie spent his childhood looking after his sick mother and his brother. By his teens, Charlie had, through his humour, become one of the most popular child actors in England. He could mime and act the fool doing ordinary everyday tasks. No one was ever **bored** watching him — his subtle acting made everything entertaining. As time went by, he began making films. He grew more and more popular as his charming character, the little tramp, became known **throughout** the world. The tramp, a poor, **homeless** man with a **moustache**, wore large trousers, **worn-out** shoes and a small round black hat. He walked around stilly carrying a walking stick. This character was a social **failure** but was loved for his optimism and determination to **overcome** all difficulties. He was the underdog who was kind even when others were unkind to him.

How did the little tramp make a sad situation entertaining? Here is an example from one of his most famous films, The Gold Rush. It is the mid-nineteenth century and gold has just been discovered in California. Like so many others, the little tramp and his friend have rushed there in search of gold, but without success. Instead they are hiding in a small hut on the edge of a mountain during a snowstorm with nothing to eat. They are so hungry that they try boiling a pair of leather shoes for their dinner. Charlie first **picks out** the laces and eats them as if they were spaghetti. Then he **cuts off** the leather top of the shoe as if it were the finest steak. Finally he tries cutting and chewing the bottom of the shoe. He eats each mouthful with great enjoyment. The acting is so convincing that it makes you believe that it is one of the best meals he has ever taste!

Charlie Chaplin wrote, **directed** and produced the films he **starred in**. In 1972 he was given a special Oscar for his **outstanding** work in films. He lived in England and the USA but spent his last years in **Switzerland**, where he was buried in 1977. He is loved and remembered as a great actor who could inspire people with great confidence.

模块四　英语学科教学实施能力

第一章　大纲描述

考试目标

理解高中英语课堂教学实施的基本原则和方法，具备实施语言课堂教学的基本能力；能够根据教学设计，结合教学实际情况，采用恰当的教学手段，引导学生进行有效学习。

考试要求

1. 掌握英语课堂教学的基本步骤与方法，能够创设教学情景，激发学习动机，引导学生参与语言学习活动。
2. 掌握指导学生学习的方法与策略，能依据英语学科和学生的特点，根据教学实际情况，恰当地运用语言讲解、练习、提问、反馈等方法，帮助学生有效学习。
3. 掌握课堂管理的基本方法，熟悉课堂活动常用的组织形式，能在教学活动中以学生为中心组织教学，能在课堂教学的不同阶段发挥教师的作用。
4. 掌握课堂总结的方法，能适时地对教学内容进行归纳、总结和评价，科学合理地布置作业。
5. 掌握基本的现代教育技术，能够针对不同的教学内容与教学目标，整合多种资源，选择恰当的辅助教学手段进行有效教学。

第二章　考点解读

一、高中英语教学实施的基本原则

（一）关注学生发展方面

1. 导向性原则：确立并构建符合课程标准要求、教材特点和学情的教学目标，为教学内容、方法与评价提出明确的导向依据。
2. 主体性原则：课堂教学要以学生为主体，教师要充分调动和发挥学生的积极性和主动性，师生互动，通过交流和研讨，达成共识，达到共享，实现共进。

3.全面性原则:课堂教学既要面向全体学生,分类推进,满足各个层面学生的学习要求,又要照顾到学生个体的全方位提高,使他们在知识、能力、情感态度价值观等方面全面发展。

4.知情并重原则:在课堂教学中,教师要高度关注学生的智力因素和非智力因素的协调发展,促进学生的学习动机、学习兴趣、情感态度和学习过程协调一致,以保证课堂教学目标的实现。

5.开放性原则:课堂教学要以教材为媒介,紧密结合英语国家人文、科技的渊源和沿革进行可理解的联想与拓展,注意跨文化交流和跨学科的知识综合积累。

(二)关注英语习得方面

1.情景性原则:英语课堂教学中,师生要不断地创设情景,构建真实的课堂语境和浓厚的英语氛围,以便真切感知体验英语,形成有效习得。

2.交际性原则:在语言课堂教学中,通过精心设计的听、说、读、写等交际活动,使学生学会运用英语思考问题、解决问题、发展综合素质。

3.阶段侧重原则:英语教学,初中阶段侧重于听说,高中阶段侧重于读写,要合理利用学生已有的知识与能力,培养学生良好的读写习惯,适当加大阅读量,指导学生的阅读技巧和写作技巧,努力提高学生的阅读理解和书面表达能力。

4.艺术性原则:英语教学是一门科学,也是一门艺术,教师要精心安排教学步骤,巧妙设计教学内容,恰当使用教学手段,灵活运用教学方法,合理分配教学时间,精明点评智慧碰撞,使课堂教学成为师生互动、心灵对话的舞台,构成课堂动态生成美。

二、英语课堂教学的基本步骤与方法

(一)英语课堂教学的基本步骤

一般来说,课堂教学是师生之间从"教学启动、导入、展示、讲授、训练到评价和反馈"等连续不断的结构或形态序列。从本质上讲,教学过程是学生在教师以及教师所提供的学习环境引导下,通过与教师的经验互动,学生自己的主体性和认知得到确认、生成和发展的过程,同时是学生通过与教师主体间互动(感悟、理解和体验等)展示自我,发现自我,发展自我的过程。

英语课堂教学的基本步骤是:教学导入、新知呈现、学习开展、巩固复习、运用提高、检测评价等。

(二)英语课堂教学的基本方法

1.目前对我国英语课堂教学有一定影响的外语教学法

(1)语法翻译法(Grammar Translation Method),现行的教学模式是:教师带读生词——教师解读课文——切合原意的课文翻译——课文句子结构分析——语法项目练习——翻译练习——背诵课文。

(2)认知法(Cognitive Approach),它提倡"先理解、后操练"。其教学模式是:理解(句子结构和所学的内容）——形成（语言能力）——运用（语言行为）。

（3）听说法（Audio-lingual Method），其教学模式是：教师讲授教学内容（学生听）——教师示范（学生模仿）——学生复述——句型替换、转换和拓展练习——口语交流活动。

（4）交际法（Communicative Approach），又称功能法（Functional Approach）或功能—意念法（Functional-notional Approach），其教学模式是 PPC 模式：呈现（Presentation）——操练（Practice）——交际活动（Communicative Activities）。

（5）结构—功能法（Structure-function Approach），倡导的是 RPDPC 模式：复习（Revision）——呈现（Presentation）——操练（Drill）——实践（Practice）——巩固（Consolidation）。

2. 英语课程标准提倡任务型教学（Task-based Language Teaching）

任务型教学就是以具体任务为载体，以完成任务为动力，用所学的语言去做事，在做事的过程中发展运用自己所学的语言。任务型教学也就是把综合语言运用能力的培养落实到教学过程中，它丰富了课堂语言输入，使得语言输入更有效。

（1）任务型教学的五种类型活动：

① Story Chain（故事链任务）；

② Information Gap（信息差任务）；

③ Problem Solving（解决问题任务）；

④ Decision Making（做决定任务）；

⑤ Exchanging Ideas（观点交换任务）。

（2）任务型教学的五个鲜明特点：

① 目的性：有目的地搜集整理信息，分析解决问题；

② 与人们日常交际活动过程相似，使交际语境有较强的真实性；

③ 主要关注语言的意义，也注意语言形式的正确性；

④ 着重于听、说、读、写等语言技能的综合运用；

⑤ 任务是一个完整的交际过程。

（3）任务型教学包括四个阶段：

① Pre-task 任务呈现阶段：主要引出话题，交代任务要求，提出相关的词语和语法；

② While-task 实施任务阶段：主要通过 pair-work, group-work 实施分工明确的操作；

③ Post-task 阶段：主要是评估任务完成情况；

④ Language Learning 语言学习阶段：分析文章，学习词语的用法和语法结构，纠正并学习在前面运用过程中出现的语言问题等。

3. 高中英语课堂教学常用的教学方法大致分为四类

（1）语言的方法：包括讲授法（讲述法、讲解法、讲读法、讲演法），谈话法（启发式谈话、问答式谈话、指导性谈话）；

(2)直观的方法:包括演示法、参观法;
(3)实践的方法:包括口头练习、笔头练习、操作练习;
(4)自学的方法:包括读书指导法(半独立性阅读、独立性阅读、合作性阅读)、讨论法。

4.高中英语课堂比较具体的教学方法

视听法、情景法、归纳法、导读法、发现法、暗示法、协作探究法等。

5.高中英语课堂还常针对各种课型采用不同的微型教学法

如:复习课主要以知识为目标,梳理知识以期系统化,或帮助学生查漏补缺,达到举一反三的目的,其教学步骤通常是:呈现问题(或学生的错误)——让学生呈现当时的思维过程——分析错误的原因——针对问题或错误进行练习或运用——反馈。

6.启发式教学仍然是诸多教学法中的精髓。

三、指导学生学习的方法和策略

(一)指导的内容

1.认知策略方面的指导,教师应指导学生做到:
(1)善于总结所学的语篇中的语言精华和语言规律并加以运用;
(2)善于抓住重点,做好学习笔记,并对所学内容进行归纳整理;
(3)善于在听或读的过程中,利用语境猜测词义或段落大意;
(4)善于发挥联想建立相关知识之间的联系;
(5)善于利用图表等非语言信息进行理解和表达;
(6)善于利用逻辑推理分析解决问题。

2.调控策略方面的指导,教师应指导学生做到:
(1)善于根据自己的学习情况制定英语学习计划;
(2)善于把握并创造学习英语的机会;
(3)善于拓宽英语学习的渠道;
(4)善于寻求帮助以解决英语学习的困难;
(5)善于与教师或同学交流分享学习英语的体会和经验;
(6)善于评价自己的学习过程与效果,总结有效的学习方法,遵循记忆规律,提高记忆效果。

3.交际策略方面的指导,教师应指导学生做到:
(1)善于争取更多的交际机会,在课内外用英语与同学交流沟通;
(2)善于克服语言障碍,维持交际;
(3)善于用手势、表情等非语言手段提高交际效果;
(4)善于把握分寸,在交际中注意并遵守英语交际的基本礼仪。

4.资源策略方面的指导,教师应指导学生做到:
合理、有效地利用各种媒体(如图书馆、网络、电视、广播)来获取更广泛的英语信息,提高英语水平。

(二)指导的方法

1. 教师要转变在教学中的角色:既当知识的传播者,又当学生学习的促进者、指导者、组织者、帮助者、参与者和合作者。

2. 本书前三章所阐述的英语语言知识、技能的教学方法,以及英语课堂教学方法都是指导学生学习英语的方法和策略。

3. "爱生"是指导学生学习的方法和策略的核心。

四、英语课堂管理

(一)英语课堂管理的实质

英语课堂管理,实质上是用系统论、信息论、控制论、心理学、管理学、教育学等原理协调教学活动中的师生关系,促进课堂中的消极因素向积极因素转化,从而保证教与学有机统一,获取预期效果的行为方式与过程。

(二)英语课堂管理的特点

1. 协调性:英语课堂管理要以学生为中心,并达到学生的主体性和教师的主导性高度协调。

2. 民主性:英语课堂是师生共同参与的,具有强烈的民主性。教学计划的制定,教学内容的选择,习题的布置,都应广泛听取学生的意见;教师还要依据学生学习心理因素的变化适时调整教学节奏或进度。

3. 严肃性和强制性:为了保证课堂教学步调一致的常规进程不受意外干扰,课堂管理必须具有严肃性和一定的强制性。

4. 目的性:管理只是手段,而教师为学生服务,创造宽松和谐的课堂氛围,让学生自我开发潜能,乐于学习英语才是课堂管理的真正目的。

(三)英语课堂管理的原则

1. 热爱学生:热爱每一个学生,不让一个学生掉队,形成尊师爱生的良好师生关系。

2. 严格要求:在组织课堂教学活动时,要预示明确的要求,而且随时调控,使课堂规范化。

3. 管理育人:培养学生高度的纪律性和互相尊重、互相帮助、互相协作的集体主义精神。

4. 内外结合:课内管理与课外的学校管理、社会管理、家庭管理相结合,形成全方位的管理网络。

5. 区别对待:课堂管理中要因人而异,"因材施教",因势利导。

6. 以身作则:教师要身正为范,身教重于言教,而且要以情感人,以理服人。

7. 创造环境:优化课堂内外的文化环境,达到隐性管理育人的效果。

（四）英语课堂管理的基本方法

1. 冷处理：对课堂突发事件，要冷静对待，不能激化矛盾，更不能弃其他学生和教学进程而不顾去耗时处理，要巧妙泰然地平息，留待课后解决，以保证教学正常进行。

2. 奖优罚劣：树立正气，鼓励积极行为，转化消极因素，奖优以精神鼓励为主，罚劣以"动之以情、晓之以理"的劝诫为主，点到为止；力戒嘲讽挖苦。

3. 自我管理：结合校风、班风建设，促进学生良好的学风养成，引导学生提高自控力、自制力、专注力和创优争先的意识，使课堂管理达到"管"是为了"不管"、"活而不乱，静而不呆"的境界。

五、英语课堂活动常见的组织形式

1. 个体练习（Individual Work）。
2. 结对练习（Pair Work）。
3. 小组练习（Group Work）。
4. 全班练习（Class Work）。

六、英语课堂总结的方法

1. 归纳总结

（1）从课的内容，所采用的教学方法、教学效果方面进行总结。

（2）突出重难点的归纳，用简明扼要的语言或口诀加深学生记忆。

（3）尽量让学生总结归纳，教师进行点拨引导。

2. 拓展延伸，用名言谚语画龙点睛，进而设置悬念，一让学生带着问题离开课堂，二让学生对下一堂课充满期待。

七、合理利用现代教育技术，辅助英语教学

以信息技术为主体的现代教育技术在辅助英语教学中发挥着越来越重要的作用，多媒体信息技术集文字、图形、动画、声音于一体，创造了生动形象的教学环境，使学生置身于真实的语言环境之中，促进他们积极应对课堂生态的变化，提高了教学效率。

1. 合理利用现代教育技术辅助英语教学要立足于结合具体教学内容创设语言情境，激发学生学习兴趣，吸引其主动参与语言实践，促进学习的正迁移，提高学生的英语交际能力。

2. 合理利用现代教育技术辅助英语教学要立足于教学目标的需要，突出教学的重难点，适度增加语言练习的呈现，节省板书时间，用来提高语言信息的活动强度，提高语言输入的有效性，更好地达到预期教学效果。

3. 利用现代教育技术搜集整理相关的文化背景资料，用于语篇教学，丰富语言学习的意境，提高学生的文化修养。

第三章　课堂教学实录示例

授课内容：高一英语必修 2

第四单元 Wildlife Protection

第一课时 Warming up, pre-reading and reading

授课人：孟红生（武汉市第二中学英语高级教师，2011 年湖北省高中英语好课竞赛一等奖第一名）

参与学生：湖北省宜昌市夷陵中学 1108 班 30 名学生

教学目标：通过阅读文本，让学生树立保护野生生物的意识

教学重点：Daisy 在神奇之旅中发现不同的野生动物的不同生存状况

教学难点：Daisy 在神奇之旅中的情感变化

教学环节	活动设计	教师指令	学生反馈
Warming up	Guess what impressed me most in Yichang.	I'm Mr. Meng from Wuhan NO.2 High school. I came here 3 days ago, when I was shown around the beautiful city of Yichang. Can you guess what impressed me most in Yichang?	Student A: the delicious food here Student B: the beautiful scenery Student C: the Three Gorges
	Show the student 3 pictures (famous school, talented students and colorful English).	What impressed me most is your famous school, talented students and colorful English. You like colorful English activities, so do I, especially brainteasers. Do you like them?	Yes.
	Show the students a brainteaser. Why don't polar bears eat penguins?	Now, Let's try one.	Student D: Because polar bears live in the north pole while penguins live in the south pole.
	—	Correct. I think you will make a brainteaser expert. Yes, penguins live in the south pole. How many students think they never existed in the north pole? To tell you the truth, penguins did exist in the north pole thousands of years ago. But the astonishing fact is that they died out 400 years ago due to over-hunting.	All the students raised their hands.
	—	Another shocking fact is that the last Yangtze River dolphin, Qiqi, died in 2007. They used to exist in large numbers in the Yangtze River, both in Yichang and Wuhan. But they have died out, so we will never have a chance to appreciate their beauty and elegance.	The students look sad.

续表

教学环节	活动设计	教师指令	学生反馈
Pre-reading	Question: what other endangered species can you name?	It's true that many animal species have died out, what's worse, more are endangered, including red-crowned crane.	——
	Show the students pictures of endangered species (panda, South China tiger, Tibetan antelope, golden monkey).	——	——
	Show a picture of polar bears.	Even polar bears, the Arctic rulers became endangered due to global warming, lack of food source and shrink of habitat.	——
	Show the students a picture of a mother polar bear with her baby.	Can you read any message in the mother bear's eyes?	Deep in thought. Student E: she is uncertain about her baby's future. She is hopeless.
	——	I think she is both hopeless and hopeful. She hopes that we can help them.	——
	——	Will you help them?	Yes!
	——	Fortunately, many people do care about wildlife protection, including a girl named Daisy. Let's read the text: How Daisy learned to help wildlife.	——
Reading	The first reading	Let's read the whole passage quickly to get some information from the text.	
	Now the four questions: 1. Who took the journey? 2. How did she travel? 3. Where did she go? 4. What animals did she see?	Answers to the 4 questions	
	——	——	Student F: Daisy By flying carpet. Tibet, Zimbabwe and a rainforest. Tibetan antelopes, elephants, a monkey and a millipede
	——	You are king of speed and efficiency in reading comprehension. Can we be friends?	——

续表

教学环节	活动设计	教师指令	学生反馈
Reading	—	—	Yes. Shake hands with the teacher.
	—	Now, let's read it again one paragraph after another to see what Daisy found about the wildlife.	—
	Read the paragraphs in different ways.	Read the first paragraph silently.	Students read the first paragraph silently.
Paragraph 1	Read silently.	What is happening to Tibetan antelopes?	Student G: They are being killed.
	—	By the way, why are they being killed.	Student H: For wool to make sweaters. A boy raised his hand and said "Mr. Meng, why are you wearing a sweater?"
	—	Surprised, I answered, "Yes, I'm wearing a sweater. But it is not made of real wool. It's artificial wool, man-made. Come and touch it."	The boy touched my sweater, "Yes, it's not real wool." The others (including other teachers present) burst into laughter.
Paragraph 2	Read silently while listening to the tape.	Now, Let's read the second paragraph silently while listening to the tape and see what is happening to the elephants in Zimbabwe.	Read silently while listening to the tape.
		—	Student I: They used to be hunted without mercy. Now their numbers are increasing thanks to the government's help.
Paragraph 3	Read aloud along with the tape.	Now, Let's read the third paragraph aloud along with the tape and see what the monkey is doing with the millipede.	Student read aloud along with the tape.
	—	—	Student J: The monkeys used the drug in the millipede to protect themselves from mosquitoes.
	—	What's the relationship between them?	—
	—	If we help each other to improve our English studies, we cooperate.(write cooperate on the blackboard.) If we help each other to found a company, we are co-founders. (write co-founder on the blackboard.)	puzzled

续表

教学环节	活动设计	教师指令	学生反馈
Paragraph 3	——	They depend on each other to exist.	Student K: They co-exist.
	——	Wonderful answer. If all species co-exist, they form a wildlife...	Wildlife chain
	——	What's the relationship between them?	——
	——	Do remember we human beings are a member of the chain. So protecting wildlife is ...	Protecting ourselves!
Paragraph 4	Read aloud together	Now read the fourth paragraph aloud to see if Daisy continued her journey.	Students read aloud together.
	——		Student L: No. She was back in reality.
	The third reading	Now, let's read it a third time to see how Daisy felt during her magical journey. But you don't need to read every sentence. Read bits here and bits there.	——
	——	Human feelings or emotions are hidden behind actions. So pay attention to the verbs that may communicate human feeling or emotions. Let me show you an example.	——
	——	Before she started her journey, she longed to help wildlife. If you long to do something, you can't wait to do it, you are eager to do it. (Show eager on the screen.)	——
	——	It's your turn now.	Students read silently to pick out the verbs which communicate human feelings or emotions. Cried → sad Burst into laughter → relieved Smiled → cheerful
	——	eager→sad→relieved→cheerful→amazed. That's the emotional development of Daisy in her journey. No wonder the writer says "What an experience!"	amazed
	——	Now, let's come to the ending of the text. What an ending! And there was always WWF ... How do you understand it?	Discussion
	——		student M: Whatever difficulty we may meet with in wildlife protection, we can always turn to WWF.

续表

教学环节	活动设计	教师指令	学生反馈
Post-reading	Show the students information about WWF.	Yes. WWF stands for world wildlife fund. Let's get familiar with this organization.	——
	——	There is a WWF whose base is in Switzerland. Can't we have WWF branches elsewhere?	——
	——	——	Student N: We can have WWF branches in our family, our class and our school.
	——	Do you want to set up the first WWF branch in your school?	Yes! (All the students)
	——	They have a slogan "for a living planet". Can you think of a similar sentence like the one in our text "No rainforest, no animals, no drugs." to raise awareness of wildlife protection?	Students began to write "no ... no..., no..." on heart-shaped sheets of paper.
	——	Now let's stick our paper to the blackboard.	Students came to the blackboard one after another to stick the paper to it, forming a big WWF on it.
	Let the student vote for their favourite sentence. "No mercy, no wildlife protection."	I solemnly announce the first WWF branch in Yiling Senior Middle School is founded today!	All the students stood up to applaud warmly.
	——	Do you want to know my sentence?	Yes!
	——	It's "No wildlife protection, no human beings!"	——
Summary	Show a picture with "Protecting wildlife is protecting ourselves. Act now before it is too late" on the screen.	Because protecting wildlife is protecting ourselves, so let's act now before it is too late!	——

板书设计

How Daisy learned to help wildlife?

situation   longed to —— eager

solution   cried —— sad / upset

importance   burst into laughter —— relieved

action   smiled —— cheerful

课后反思

课前设计时对阅读文本的深入研究，尤其是对 Daisy 在神奇之旅中情感变化这条暗线的挖掘，是这堂阅读课最大的亮点，也是它成功的重要保证。"野生动物保护"这一话题本身就涉及人类美好情感的投入，也符合新课标所倡导的：通过语言学习，培养、塑造学生"情感、态度、价值观"这一理念。所以上阅读课，一定要忠于文本，挖掘文本，将文本的价值最大限度地发挥出来，阅读课才能算是成功的。

在对文本进行三遍阅读时，指导学生用不同的方法来读，如默读、跟着磁带默读、跟着磁带朗读、朗读等，也是这堂阅读课的亮点之一。专家在点评时，也对"阅读课上听到了琅琅的读书声"给予了高度肯定。

课堂上对学生恰当和适时的肯定，是整堂课 40 分钟所有学生都乐于配合的一个至关重要的因素。如第一次快速阅读后，一名男生最先找出了 4 个问题的答案。教师对他说："You are king of speed and efficiency in reading in this class." 一名女生恰当运用 relieved 来说明 Daisy 的情感时，教师对她说："May I know your name?" "Can we be friends?" 所以这次课体现出：英语教学应该是一个优雅的过程，而教师对学生的欣赏与肯定是保证这一过程优雅的必要条件。

第四章　题型训练

教学情景分析题

1. 分析以下教学片段：

T: What did your mummy do yesterday, Wang Lin?

S: My mummy **drived** me to the school.

T: Oh, that is nice, your Mummy **drove** you to the school, did she?

S: Yes.

T: How fast did she drive?

S: She **drived** at the speed of 40km an hour.

T: Oh, she **drove** at the speed of 40km an hour. Well, it is very nice.

2. 分析以下教学片段：

T: What did you do yesterday?

S: I **swimed** with Tom.

T: Oh, that is nice, you **swam** with Tom, did you?

S: Yes.

T: Where did you swim?

S: I **swimed** in the Changjian River.

T: Oh, you swam in the Changjian River. Well, it is very nice.

3. 分析以下教学片段：

T: What did you do yesterday?

S: I **selled** newspaper with Tom.

T: Oh, that is nice, you **sold** newspaper with Tom, did you?

S: Yes.

T: Where did you sell it?

S: I **selled** it along the Jiefang Road.

T: Oh, you **sold** it along the Jiefang Road. Well, it is very nice.

4. 分析以下教学片段：

T: What did you do yesterday?

S: I played with Tom and **breaked** my leg.

T: Oh, sorry to hear that, you **broke** your leg, did you?

S: Yes.

T: Where did you break it?

S: I **breaked** it in the yard.

T: Oh, you **broke** it in the yard. Well, be careful next time.

5. 分析以下教学片段：

T: What did you do yesterday?

S: I **spended** a whole day preparing my coming exam.

T: Oh, nice to hear that, you **spent** a whole day preparing your coming exam, did you?

S: Yes.

T: Where did you spend it?

S: I **spended** it in my study.

T: Oh, you **spent** in my study. Well, have a good luck.

6. 分析以下教学片段：

T: What did you do yesterday?

S: I **teached** Tom to learn Chinese a whole day.

T: Oh, nice to hear that, you **taught** Tom to learn Chinese, did you?

S: Yes.

T: Where did you teach him?

S: I **teached** him in my study.

T: Oh, you **taught** him in your study. Well, nice to hear that.

7. 分析以下教学片段：

T: What did you do yesterday?

S: I **writed** Tom a letter.

T: Oh, nice to hear that, you **wrote** Tom a letter, did you?

S: Yes.

T: Where did you write him?

S: I **writed** him in my study.

T: Oh, you **wrote** him in your study. Well, nice to hear that.

8. 分析以下教学片段：

T: What did you do yesterday?

S: I **sitted** by the seashore.

T: Oh, nice to hear that, you **sat** by the seashore, did you?

S: Yes.

T: Whom did you sit with?

S: I **sitted** with Tom.

T: Oh, you **sat** with Tom. Well, nice to hear that.

9. 分析以下教学片段：

T: What did you do yesterday?

S: I **bringed** my little sister to the market.

T: Oh, nice to hear that, you **brought** your little sister to the market, did you?

S: Yes.

T: Why did you bring her?

S: I **bringed** her because my mum is busy.

T: Oh, you **brought** her because your mum is busy. Well, nice to hear that.

10. 分析以下教学片段：

T: What did you do yesterday?

S: I **drawed** pictures at home.

T: Oh, nice to hear that, you drew picture, did you?

S: Yes.

T: Why did you draw pictures?

S: I **drawed** them because I'm interested.

T: Oh, you **drew** them because you're interested. Well, nice to hear that.

模块五　英语学科教学评价知识与能力

第一章　大纲描述

考试目标

了解高中英语课堂教学评价的基本知识和方法,能够对学生的语言学习进行恰当的评价;了解教学反思的基本方法和策略,能够对自己的课堂教学实践进行反思,提出改进的思路。

考试要求

1. 了解形成性评价和终结性评价的知识与方法,并在高中英语教学中合理运用。
2. 了解教学案例评析的基本方法,能够对教学案例进行评价。
3. 了解教学反思的基本方法和策略,能够对自己的教学进行反思并提出改进思路。

第二章　考点解读

一、形成性评价和终结性评价的知识与方法

(一)形成性评价

1. 形成性评价的含义

课程标准指出:形成性评价是教学的重要组成部分和推动因素。形成性评价的任务是对学生日常学习过程中的表现、所取得的成绩以及反映出的情感、态度、策略等方面的发展做出评价。其目的是激励学生学习,帮助学生有效调控自己的学习过程,使学生获得成就感,增强自信心,培养合作精神。

2. 形成性评价的内容

(1)学习条件

包括以前英语学习的经验、教育设施、班级规模、教师能力、学生关系、师生关系、课堂环境、家庭背景、社区环境等。

(2)学习过程

包括接受语言材料的方式、课堂活动方式、学生行动的质与量、教师行为的方式、教学进度、教材内容和使用方式、学生合作形式、学习任务的智力水平、情感过程等。

(3)学习成效

包括语言知识的记忆量、语言知识的组织形式、话题范围和内容、功能范围和内容、语篇知识和运用、口头交际技能、书面表达技能、语用因素的参与(如策略、情感、文化等)、学习策略(如学习技能、学习意识和习惯、反思能力)等。

3.形成性评价的方法

课程标准指出:为了使评价有机地融入教学过程,应建立开放、宽松的评价氛围,以测试和非测试的方式以及个人与小组结合的方式进行评价,鼓励学生、同伴、教师和家长共同参与评价,实现评价主体的多元化。形成性评价的形式可有多种,如课堂学习活动评比、学习效果自评、学习档案、问卷调查、访谈、家长对学生学习情况的反馈与评价、平时测验等。形成性评价可采用描述性评价、等级评定或评分等评价记录方式。无论何种方式,都应注意评价的正面鼓励和激励作用。教师要根据评价结果与学生进行不同形式的交流,充分肯定学生的进步,鼓励学生自我反思,自我提高。

(二)终结性评价的知识与方法

课程标准指出:终结性评价(如期末考试、结业考试等)是检测学生语言综合运用能力发展程度的重要途径,也是反映教学效果、学校办学质量的重要指标之一。终结性评价必须以考查学生语言综合运用能力为目标,力争科学地、全面地考查学生在经过一段学习后所具有的语言水平。测试应包括口试、听力考试和笔试等形式,全面考查学生综合语言运用能力。听力测试在学期、学年考试和结业考试中所占比例应不少于20%。听力测试应着重测试学生理解和获取信息的能力,不应把脱离语境的单纯辨音题作为考试内容。笔试应避免单纯语音知识题和单纯语法知识题;增加具有语境的应用型试题;适当减少客观题、增加主观题。不得公布学生考试成绩并按考试成绩排列名次。

二、教学案例评析的基本方法

(一)教学案例的含义

教学案例是教师在教学中,对教学的重难点、偶发事件、有意义而又典型的教学事例处理的过程、方法和具体的教学行为与艺术的记叙,以及对该个案记录的剖析、反思、总结。教学案例不仅记叙教学行为,还记录伴随行为而产生的思想、情感及灵感,反映教师在教学活动中遇到的问题、矛盾、困惑,以及由此产生的想法、思路、对策等。教学案例既有具体的情节、过程、真实感人的故事,又从教育理论、教学方法、教学艺术的高度进行归纳、总结,悟出育人真谛,给人以启发。

简言之,教学案例是真实而又典型且含有问题的事件。一个教学案例就是一个含有疑难问题的实际情境的描述,是一个教学实践过程中的故事。

(二)教学案例的五要素

1. 背景:"故事"发生的时间、地点、人物、起因等,并着重说明"故事"发生的特别原因和条件。

2. 主题:主要关注对某个教学理念的认识、理解和实践;教师角色如何转变,教法和学法指导如何变化,或对教材的重难点的把握与处理。

3. 细节:有针对性地筛选最能反映主题的特定的内容,把关键性的细节写清楚,尤其要真实描述人物的心理和教师当时的所思所为,以及教学行为的内在逻辑联系,让读者知其然并知其所以然。

4. 结果:在说明教学思路和教学流程的同时,还要记叙教学结果,即某种教学措施的即时效果,包括学生的反应和教师的态度、应变等。

5. 评析:评析是在记述的基础上的议论,表明对教学案例所反映的主题和内容的看法与分析,以揭示"故事"的意义和价值。

(三)教学案例的基本结构形式

1. 案例过程——案例反思

2. 案例背景——案例描述——案例分析

3. 主题背景——情景描述——问题探讨——诠释与研究

(四)教学案例的特点

1. 以记述为主,兼有议论:是通过讲故事说明道理。

2. 教学案例的写作是一种归纳思维,思维的方式是从具体到抽象。

3. 客观性:教学案例是已经发生的教学过程的反映,是教学的结果,必然写在教学之后。

4. 选择性:教学案例不是教学全过程的实录,而是有选择性地描述、议论。

(五)教学案例评析方法

1. 自己评析和研究是最好的方法,评析不一定要理论阐述,就事论事,有感而发。

2. 教学案例主要评析学生的学习效果,反思自己或他人的教学理念,提炼教学经验与教训,把自己或他人的教学行为提升到教学理念的高度进行审视,可以从教育学、心理学等不同的理论角度切入,揭示成功的原因和科学的规律。也可对课堂教学行为作技术分析。

3. 教学案例评析也可在教研组进行讨论,协作研究。

4. 还可对照文献研究评析教学案例,发现课堂教学现象的理论依据,从而挖掘案例中的教育思想。

三、教学反思的基本方法和策略

(一)教学反思的含义

教学反思是教师以自己的教学活动为思考对象,对自己在教学活动过程中的行为及其产生的结果进行审视和分析的过程,其实质就是自己与自己的教学实践对话,以求对教学产生更深的理解。教学反思不是简单的教学回顾,而是教师通过提高自我觉察水平来促进能力发展的重要途径。

(二)教学反思的内容

1. 教育理论的反思

是否正确理解与有效实施英语课程标准提出的六个基本理念:

(1)面向全体学生,注重素质教育;

(2)整体设计目标,体现灵活开放;

(3)突出学生主体,尊重个体差异;

(4)采用活动途径,倡导体验参与;

(5)注重过程评价,促进学生发展;

(6)开发课程资源,拓展学用渠道。

2. 教育目标的反思

(1)是否帮助学生明确学习目的,增强英语学习动力;

(2)是否有效培养学生的英语综合运用能力;

(3)是否有效促进学生自主学习和通过合作学习获得英语知识与能力;

(4)是否引导学生优化学习方法和策略。

3. 教学内容的反思

是否按学生的需要,恰当整合英语教学内容,保证了教学内容的质与量;英语练习是否经过精选而具有典型性和操练价值。

4. 教学策略的反思

是否在英语教学中保证以学生为主体,倡导"发现式学习,启发式引导"的教学模式,从而促进学生自主学习并形成有效的学习策略。

(三)教学反思的方法

1. 内省式反思。

2. 交流式反思。

3. 学习式反思。

4. 研究式反思。

仿真试题一

一、语言知识与能力

（一）单项选择题

1. We tried our best to head Henry off the topic, because we knew he'd reveal _____ information.
   A. spectacular   B. confidential   C. spatial   D. profound

2. Mildred and I are very _____. She's interested in the things that interest me, including thrilling bungee jumping.
   A. composite   B. civilian   C. comparable   D. compatible

3. This motto "Embrace Diversity. End Discrimination" is particularly _____ in the contemporary world that has become more diverse than ever before.
   A. acute   B. consistent   C. pertinent   D. persistent

4. Infection causes a wide _____ of diseases, from mild symptoms to severe illnesses and death.
   A. auditorium   B. spectrum   C. census   D. optimum

5. We stand in _____ with peace-loving people all over the world in our condemnation of these terrorist acts.
   A. solidarity   B. priority   C. superiority   D. hospitality

6. In other words, our continued dependence on imported fossil fuels will _____ our national security.
   A. visualize   B. jeopardize   C. stabilize   D. minimize

7. In the museum one room contained a gallery of paintings _____ great moments in baseball history.
   A. commencing   B. commemorating   C. commuting   D. compensating

8. Using murder to _____ a society of one of its voices is contrary to democracy and to human rights.
   A. deprive   B. corrode   C. suspect   D. despise

9. Meanwhile, most children are vulnerable to the enormous influence _____ by grandchildless

parents aiming to persuade their kids to produce children.

  A. exerted   B. alleged   C. boosted   D. conferred

10. Anger can be used to make others back down, grief attracts help and fear may stop us _____ attempting difficult or dangerous tasks.

  A. hastily   B. readily   C. rashly   D. respectively

11. Cordelia's devotion to Your Majesty is beyond question. What actually happens according to the statement?

  A. Cordelia truly loves you.   B. Cordelia doesn't truly love you.

  C. Cordelia betrays you.   D. Cordelia cheats you.

12. Kent, if you value your life, say no more. What does the statement imply?

  A. Saying more means valuing your life.   B. I will kill you if you say more.

  C. I admire those speaking out.   D. Those speaking out live a short life.

13. Pack up your things and be gone from my kingdom. What does the statement imply?

  A. Get out of my sight.   B. Go abroad.

  C. Traveling is worthwhile.   D. Time and tide wait for no man.

14. I have had enough of your soldiers. What does the statement imply?

  A. I owe thanks to your soldiers.

  B. I have helped your soldiers.

  C. I have wiped out your soldiers.

  D. I can't tolerate your soldiers any more.

15. For whichever of you has for me the most devotion I will give to her the best part of everything I own. What will actually happen according to the statement?

  A. I will give my best thing to whoever loves me most.

  B. I will give my best thing to whoever helps me most.

  C. Whoever supports me most will get the best thing from me.

  D. Whoever accompanies me most will get the best thing from me.

16. The university is trying to make more accommodation available for students. What actually happens according to the statement?

  A. The university is trying to help students have more tutors.

  B. The university is trying to help students have more courses.

  C. The university is trying to help students have more rooms.

  D. The university is trying to help students have more food.

17. Nothing can wipe out the bitter memories of the past. What actually happens according to

the statement?

   A. The bad memories of the past will last forever.

   B. The bad memories of the past won't last long.

   C. The sweet memories of the past will last forever.

   D. The sweet memories of the past won't last forever.

18. The government is considering a proposal for a green energy policy. What actually happens according to the statement?

   A. The government wants to plant more trees.

   B. The government wants to save energy.

   C. The government wants to develop eco-friendly energy.

   D. The government wants to produce more energy.

19. As you have a tight schedule, I will not take up more of your time. What will actually happen according to the statement?

   A. I will change your schedule.   B. You are very busy now.

   C. You are very nervous now.   D. I will not disturb you.

20. All that walking has given me an appetite for dinner. What actually happened according to the statement?

   A. I had a huge meal.   B. I was too tired to have a meal.

   C. I went to bed hungry.   D. I began cooking a meal.

21. They are always so rude that I've almost become immune to it. What actually happens according to the statement?

   A. I've been used to their rudeness.   B. I can hardly put up with their rudeness.

   C. I am so angry with their rudeness.   D. I have become rude like them.

22. The smell is, as usual, almost unbearable, being a mixture of sweat, seal oil fat, and dirty underwear. What actually happens according to the statement?

   A. The smell is pleasant.   B. The smell is terrible.

   C. The smell is strong.   D. The smell is light.

23. The first theory suggested that cholera multiplied in the air. What can be learned from the statement?

   A. The first theory stated that cholera polluted air.

   B. The first theory stated that cholera didn't pollute air.

   C. The first theory stated that cholera circulated in the air.

   D. The first theory stated that cholera didn't circulate in the air.

24. He was so busy dreaming about all the fish he would catch that he was unaware of the swarm of

bees around him. Why did he fail to notice the swarm of bees earlier?

A. He was riding to school.

B. He was listening to a strange sound.

C. He was going fishing alone.

D. He was lost in the thought of the fishing trip.

(二)阅读理解

For a time, Americans were turning in their new cars at a breakneck pace. Cheap financing, good deals, a strong used car market, and a robust economy meant that we could justify keeping a car for less time than a traditional lease, and only see a modest increase in our monthly payment, if any increase at all.

Those days are apparently over, at least for the short term.

R.L. Polk, which collects and measures data in the automotive industry like Nielsen records our television habits, says that we're now keeping our cars longer than we ever have. According to Polk's study of registration data, Americans are keeping new cars for an average 63.9 months — five-and-a-quarter years — up 4.5 months from the same period in 2009. We are keeping used cars longer, too. The average length of ownership for a used car is 46.1 months, up 3.7 months from the same period in 2009. Data for new and used cars combined sees an average length of ownership to 52.2 months.

In truth, there's not much need to turn a car in on any kind of schedule. By following proper maintenance, it's relatively simple to squeeze a decade or 150,000 miles out of a new car with no major issues. The routine "tune-up" items that used to require replacement every 15,000 miles — spark plugs, plug wires, distributor caps, rotors — are now good for 100,000 miles, if they're even in the car anymore. Platinum spark plugs, combined with an incredibly efficient internal combustion engine, can last just as long. Newer ignitions, with an ignition coil pack for every cylinder, means that the caps and rotors are history.

In 2006, the sticker price on a Silverado was $32,000, but thanks to a model change over for 2007 and a timely purchase in October when dealers were trying to move any remaining inventory, Whelan purchased the truck for $22,700. At five years of age, with 75,000 miles showing on the odometer, he has no intention of turning it in at any point in the near future. "My goal is to run it to 160,000 miles and evaluate my options from there," he says.

Like a long weekend on the Cape, a spa treatment or a change in hairstyle, there's a limitless number of tweaks and modifications we can perform to reignite the romance. The Specialty Equipment Market Association (SEMA) — the trade association that represents the aftermarket industry — noted that in the first quarter of 2010, consumer demand for aftermarket products reached a frenzied pace.

SEMA produces a Consumer Demand Index Report that retailers use as a forecasting tool, and late in 2010 it showed that consumer demand for aftermarket products had recovered since the economic downturn, and reached its highest level since July 2009. The index predicted that 15 percent of American households would purchase some kind of accessory for their car by the end of the year, and that car dealerships were the most popular purchase destinations.

In an effort to stave off the impulse to purchase another truck, Whelan has been regularly upgrading the truck he has. Soon after he purchased it, he bought chrome steps for $300. In 2007, he added a custom dual exhaust with Flowmaster mufflers for another $300. In 2008, it was a set of new 17-inch alloy wheels and tires — takeoffs from a new Cadillac Escalade that was fitted with aftermarket wheels — that he found on Craigslist for $600. "I needed new tires anyway, and the whole package cost me less than a set of new tires," says Whelan.

Whelan figures he's put the average of about two payments a year into regular improvements meant to keep the truck fresh. "I've found that making a modification here and there keeps me happy. That, and the thought of having a payment again, with big excise tax bills and another sales tax payment has been enough to suppress my urges," he says. "The truck's five years old now, and I have a couple of scuffs and scratches, but I think I prefer that now, rather than having to worry about getting scratches in a new truck."

1. There was a time when Americans tended to _____.
   A. sell their cars at a frightening speed
   B. make a high monthly payment on cars
   C. receive a larger income than nowadays
   D. shorten the period of use of their cars
2. Whelan won't consider buying a new truck until _____.
   A. his wife divorces him or passes away
   B. he gets bored of driving it every day
   C. a fantastic model is placed on a car
   D. the expected miles of driving is reached
3. The author employs the example of Whelan to show _____.
   A. weak economy results in decreasing expense
   B. resisting new car purchases can pay off is reach
   C. saving money is better than saving face
   D. some people prefer old things than new ones

二、语言教学知识与能力

(一)单项选择题

1. The famous Yellowstone National Park is situated in northwestern part of _____.
   A. California   B. Arizona   C. Wyoming   D. Utah
2. McCarthy was notorious for his harsh _____ persecution of the progressive people.

A. religious　　　B. spiritual　　　C. political　　　D. historical

3. The Great Depression of _____ shook the US and the whole capitalist world to its foundations.

　　A. 1929—1933　　B. 1933—1937　　C. 1924—1929　　D. 1929—1934

4. Which of the following activities is most suitable for whole-class work?

　　A. Presenting new language.　　B. Role-play.

　　C. Information gap.　　D. Writing summaries.

5. Which of the following belongs to physical factors that affect the designing of a lesson plan?

　　A. Students' needs.　　B. Students' background.

　　C. Students' language proficiency.　　D. Syllabus' requirements.

6. _____ was the only American president who was re-elected three times in succession.

　　A. Theodore Roosevelt　　B. George Washington

　　C. Franklin D. Roosevelt　　D. Thomas Jefferson

7. For a teacher, who teaches young learners English pronunciation, which principle is he suggested following?

　　A. Maximum quantity of spoken input.　　B. Conscious effort.

　　C. Tolerance of errors in continuous speech.　　D. Correct the errors as soon as possible.

8. Which one of the four aspects included in communicative competence is roughly equivalent to Chomsky's linguistic competence?

　　A. Possibility.　　B. Feasibility.　　C. Appropriateness.　　D. Performance.

9. Considering our English learning context, our realistic goals of teaching pronunciation should include the following except _____.

　　A. consistency　　B. intelligibility

　　C. communicative efficiency　　D. native-like pronunciation

10. _____ is generally regarded as Shakespeare's most popular play on the stage, for it has the qualities of a "blood and thunder" thriller and a philosophical exploration of life and death.

　　A. Hamlet　　B. King Lear　　C. Romeo and Juliet　　D. Othello

(二)简答题

1. How long have you been waiting for me?

　　We are anxiously awaiting your reply.

2. The flowers have withered away.

　　The blue rug has faded over the year.

3. The fierce robbers come down from the mountains.

　　I have never met such savage manners.

4. Industrial waste must be prevented from polluting our rivers.

   The rubbish must be thrown away.

5. The soldiers are striding with a dignified gait.

   A huge crowd strolled down Fifth Avenue in the Easter Parade.

（三）简要回答下列问题

1. 课堂教学中全班学生突然十分安静，学习活动（听、说、读、写）也不活跃。这时你认为这是哪些情况的反映？
2. 语音教学的主要内容是什么？
3. 评价学生可以采用以下哪些途径？
4. 教会学生学习是新世纪各科教学的共同要求，英语教师必须向学生介绍学习方法。你认为应当怎样介绍？
5. 课程资源有校内资源、校外资源和网络化资源。它们分别有什么资源？

三、教学设计

教学设计题：根据所提供的信息和语言素材进行教学设计，本题用英文作答。

根据所提供的语言素材设计教学活动，要求教学设计目标具体、教学内容分析恰当、教学重点和难点突出、教学过程完整、师生任务明确。

学生概况：本班为中等城市普通学校高中二年级的学生，班级人数为40人。多数学生已具备一定的英语语言能力。学生能够积极参与课堂活动，合作意识较强。

教学时间：25分钟

语言素材：（加粗单词为学生首次接触的词汇）

英语必修5 Unit4 Making the News-reading

MY FIRST WORK ASSIGNMENT

"Unforgettable", says new journalist.

Never will Zhou Yang (ZY) forget his first assignment at the office of a popular English newspaper. His discussion with his new boss, Hu Xin (HX), was to strongly **influence** his life as a journalist.

HX: Welcome. We're **delighted** you're coming to work with us. Your first job here will be an **assistant** journalist. Do you have any questions?

ZY: Can I go out on a story immediately?

HX: (Laughing) That's admirable, but I'm afraid it would be unusual! Wait till you are more experienced. First we'll put you as an assistant to an experienced journalist. Later you can **cover** a story and **submit** the article yourself.

ZY: Wonderful. What do I need to take with me? I already have a notebook and camera.

HX: No need for a camera. You'll have a **professional** photographer with you to take photographs. You'll find your **colleagues** very eager to **assist** you, so you may be able to concentrate on photography later if you're interested.

ZY: Thank you. Not only am I interested in photography, but I took an **amateur** course at university to **update** my skills.

HX: Good.

ZY: What do I need to remember when I go out to cover a story?

HX: You need to be curious. Only if you ask many different questions will you **acquire** all the information you need to know. We say a good journalist must have a good "nose" for a story. That means you must be able to **assess** when people are not telling the whole truth and then try to discover it. They must use research to **inform** themselves of the missing parts of the story.

ZY: What should I keep in mind?

HX: Here comes my list of dos and don'ts: don't miss your **deadline**, don't be rude, don't talk too much, but make sure you listen to the interviewee carefully.

ZY: Why is listening so important?

HX: Well, you have to listen for detailed facts. Meanwhile you have to prepare the next question depending on what the person says.

ZY: But how can I listen carefully while taking notes?

HX: This is a trick of the trade, If the interviewee agrees, you can use a recorder to get the facts straight. It's also useful if a person wants to challenge you. You have the evidence to support your story.

ZY: I see! Have you ever had a **case** where someone **accused** your journalists of getting the wrong end of the stick?

HX: Yes, but it was a long time ago. This is how the story goes. A footballer **was accused of** taking money for **deliberately** not scoring goals so as to let the other team win. We went to interview him. He denied taking money but we were **sceptical**. So we arranged an interview between the footballer and the man supposed to bribe him. When we saw them together we guessed from the footballer's body language that he was not telling the truth. So we wrote an article suggesting he was guilty. It was a **dilemma** because the footballer could have **demanded** damages if we were wrong. He tried to stop us **publishing** it but later we were proved right.

ZY: Wow! That was a real "scoop". I'm looking forward to my first assignment now. Perhaps I'll get a scoop too!

HX: Perhaps you will. You never know.

四、教学实施与评价

教学情景分析题：根据题目要求进行教学分析，本题用中文作答。

分析以下教学片段：

T: What did you do yesterday, Wang Lin?

S: My friend came and I **shaked** hands with him.

T: Oh, that is nice, you **shook** hands with him, did you?

S: Yes.

T: Where did you shake hands with him?

S: I shaked hands with him in my office.

T: Oh, you shook hands with him in your office. Well, it is very nice.

仿真试题二

一、语言知识与能力

(一)单项选择题

1. When it comes to _____ festivals in the world, Frozen Dead Guy Days may take the cake.
   A. intricate   B. eccentric
   C. gigantic   D. subtle

2. Meanwhile, an overdependence on natural resources—minerals and oil—leaves Africa vulnerable to _____ commodity markets.
   A. cumulative   B. dominant
   C. turbulent   D. prevalent

3. It is estimated that almost half the population in the region are _____ to vote in today's election.
   A. transient   B. edible
   C. feasible   D. eligible

4. While this uncertainty contributes to stock price _____, there is nothing fundamentally new since July 21st.
   A. federations   B. swings
   C. suspensions   D. fluctuations

5. Once my software is loaded, my _____ stays pretty stable for the next few years.
   A. configuration   B. constitution
   C. condemnation   D. contamination

6. The strike by bank employees ended after employers _____ some of their demands.
   A. compromised   B. preceded
   C. slaughtered   D. conceded

7. The country plans to _____ the waters of the powerful rivers for big hydro-electric power projects.
   A. harness   B. handicap   C. converge   D. reserve

8. It's illegal in the country to _____ copyrighted works, even if for discussion or criticism, without the rights-holder's permission.
   A. exile   B. excerpt   C. rally   D. saturate

9. When starting my pond, I was _____ by the generosity of friends and neighbours with all sorts of pond plants.
   A. overwhelmed   B. overthrown
   C. overlapped   D. originated

10. Instead of formulas and charts, the two experienced instructors use games and drawings to _____ their subject.
    A. ignite   B. illuminate
    C. underline   D. terminate

11. As I think of this, a black blanket drops and covers me, almost blocking out the memories of happier times. What actually happened according to the statement?
    A. A black blanket fueled my memories of happier times.
    B. A black blanket appeared in my memories of happier times.
    C. I stopped recalling the happier times.
    D. I began to recall the happier times.

12. When the expedition was announced, I was only twenty and I had always dreamed of adventure. What actually happened according to the statement?
    A. I had experienced an expedition.
    B. I announced the expedition.
    C. I thought the expedition wasn't adventure.
    D. I was eager to join the expedition.

13. Nobody found me until the ship had sailed and I was suffering badly from seasickness. What actually happened according to the statement?
    A. I missed my family.
    B. I didn't miss my family.
    C. I was not used to taking a ship.
    D. I was crazy about sailing in a boat.

14. On January 18th, 1915 the Endurance became stuck in pack ice as we approached Antarctica. What actually happened according to the statement?
    A. The Endurance reached the destination.
    B. The Endurance couldn't move.
    C. We settled on Antarctica.
    D. We slid on the floating ice.

15. I adore you more than anything else in the whole world. What actually happens according to the statement?

    A. My greatest happiness is in loving you.

    B. My greatest happiness is in admiring you.

    C. My greatest happiness is in defeating you.

    D. My greatest happiness is in conquering you.

16. There was nothing like a good dinner of penguin and some dynamic music to make a man feel more cheerful again. What actually happened according to the statement?

    A. Enough food and inspiring music enlightened a man.

    B. A cheerful man enjoyed penguins and music.

    C. Enough food and inspiring music didn't make a happy man.

    D. A cheerful man didn't enjoy penguins and music.

17. An expedition with the great Sir Ernest Shackleton to the South Pole — I was hooked! What actually happened according to the statement?

    A. I was bored with the expedition.

    B. I was interested in the expedition.

    C. I was disappointed with the expedition.

    D. I was proud of the expedition.

18. He was always honest with us and never gave way to disappointment, even when the ship sank. What actually happened according to the statement?

    A. He remained honest and optimistic.

    B. He remained brave.

    C. He got disappointed easily.

    D. He was honest but pessimistic.

19. Soon Shackleton set out the framework for our life here: no differences in rank or in social status; everyone to keep busy; a fair division of food and bedding; and a concern for all. What actually happened according to the statement?

    A. Shackleton focused on team-spirit.

    B. We led a comfortable life.

    C. Shackleton didn't focus on team-spirit.

    D. We didn't leave a comfortable life.

20. Although he is most often associated with the invention of the telephone, he was indeed a continuing searcher after practical solutions to improve the quality of everybody's life. What actually happened according to the statement?

    A. He was longing for improving his life.

B. He was not longing for inventing a telephone.

C. He was the inventor of the telephone.

D. He was not the inventor of the telephone.

21. Some died or returned home, but most remained in California to make a life for themselves despite great hardship. What actually happened according to the statement?

    A. Those who remained in California led a relaxed life.

    B. Those who returned home led a hard life.

    C. Those who died led a hard life.

    D. Those who remained in California led a hard life.

22. In 1911, immigrants from Denmark established a town of their own, which today still keeps up their Danish culture. What actually happened according to the statement?

    A. The immigrants gave up their own customs.

    B. The immigrants observe their own customs.

    C. People tend to emigrate from Denmark.

    D. People tend to immigrate to Denmark.

23. The industry boom attracted Europeans including many Jewish people. What actually happened according to the statement?

    A. Many Jewish people were enthusiastic about Industry.

    B. The increase in industry required more employees.

    C. Many Jewish people were not enthusiastic about Industry.

    D. The increase in industry caused more employees to be laid off.

24. But at last, the determination and patience of the scientists paid off in 1996 with a break through-the cloning of Dolly the sheep. What actually happened according to the statement?

    A. The cloning of Dolly cost the scientists huge amounts of money.

    B. Dolly the sheep was determined and patient.

    C. The scientists succeeded in cloning Dolly the sheep.

    D. All scientist were determined and patient.

(二)阅读理解

"I met this cyclone of a man four years ago in Brazil. He wanted me to help him get into the interior of the rain forest, where the tourists don't go, so I gave him a few of my contacts and we kept in touch. Bobby began his working life scalping tickets to Boston Celtics games and ended up buying the hallowed parquet floor of the Boston Garden, before it was torn down. He made a fortune or three before the age of 40, and now he spends his time roaming the planet looking for projects to support where concrete baby steps matter and can make a very big difference. He's funding the reconstruction of a monastery in Bhutan, helping the Dalai Lama's religious scholars learn science, setting up teacher training programs for Afghan refugees, assisting the people of Rwanda in rebuilding their justice system after the appalling massacres that have all but destroyed their country, and running micro enterprise programs in South Africa, Nepal, and Rwanda."

"Our practical philanthropist spends the rest of the day (in Nepal) photographing children in the village and teaching Jake, my son, some of his secrets. He has a breathtaking series of what he calls "children of conflict" portraits, of children in Afghanistan, in refugee camps in Pakistan and Rwanda, of Tibetan refugees in camps in India, and of Palestinian refugees in camps in Lebanon.

I watch him at work, sitting just outside a group of youngsters; he begins an animated conversation with a mischievous glove puppet, a bright yellow duck. He whispers to it to be quiet and well behaved; the duck nods in obedience and then proceeds to attack Bobby, who only barely manages to control his tiny adversary. The children begin to stare at the strange sight of this big man and his recalcitrant duck, laughing uproariously when the duck gets the better of him. They move closer, and the duck starts to tease the children. Some of them run away giggling; others get closer.

"Never start taking pictures immediately," he tells Jake. "You've got to engage them, make them laugh, get close." Without looking through the lens he casually takes some shots of the children laughing. "The closer you get, the better the pictures, but don't ever lose eye contact."

I watch as my son engage with the children, making them laugh, coaxing the shy ones to break out of their shells, until Bobby starts chasing the entire gaggle of children around the town square like and overgrown kid, whooping and roaring as the children scatter hilariously and hide behind their mother's long skirts.

A young man attempts to give Bobby a can of some soft drink, saying something in Nepalese.

"Pema, what's this kid saying? Why's he trying to give me this can?"

Pema talks to the boy, who is about 12. "He says you saved his grandmother's life last year, Mr. Bobby. She needed an operation in Katmandu, and you put her in the helicopter. He says the family wants to thank you, and this is all they have to give you."

The big brash guy from Boston is suddenly quiet and clearly touched by the gesture. My two abiding memories of this extraordinary and complex man will be of him chasing the village kids like the town fool one minute, and the next reduced almost to tears by this simple gift.

1. In Paragraph 3, "gets the better of him" is similar in meaning to "_____."

   A. gains an advantage over Bobby

   B. eats nice food from Bobby

   C. gives in to Bobby

   D. is brought under control

2. It can be inferred from the passage that Pema is _____.

   A. the author　　　B. Bobby's son　　　C. a doctor　　　D. a local guide

3. What's the purpose of this passage?

   A. To describe Bobby's complex character.

   B. To reflect the importance of presents.

   C. To praise Bobby's acts of kindness.

   D. To indicate charity work is based on wealth.

二、语言教学知识与能力

(一)单项选择题

1. Wordsworth thinks that _____ is the only subject of literary interest.

   A. nation　　　　　　　　　　B. past experience

   C. common life　　　　　　　　D. nature

2. In January _____, Britain became a member of the European Economic Community.

   A. 1957　　　B. 1967　　　C. 1973　　　D. 1979

3. The first "King of the English" was _____.

   A. Alfred　　　B. Egbert　　　C. Bede　　　D. Ethelred

4. Adjectives such as "hardworking", "warm-hearted", and "caring" can be used to describe a teacher's _____, one of the three elements of a good foreign language teacher.

   A. personal style　　　　　　　B. language proficiency

   C. ethic devotion　　　　　　　D. professional quality

5. At beginner level, most new words learned by students usually have immediate practical use and quickly become one's _____ vocabulary.

   A. productive or active　　　　B. receptive or active

   C. productive or passive　　　　D. receptive or passive

6. _____ shaped the world's view of America and made a more extensive combination of American folk humor and serious literature than previous writers had ever done.

   A. Henry James　　　　　　　B. Washington Irving

   C. Theodore Dreiser　　　　　　D. Mark Twain

7. The Great Salt Lake lies in northern _____.
   A. Idaho   B. Arizona   C. Utah   D. Nevada
8. Christmas Day _____, Duke William was crowned in Westminster Abbey.
   A. 1056   B. 1066   C. 1006   D. 1060
9. What's the teacher doing by saying "Who wants to have a try?"
   A. Controlling discipline.   B. Giving prompt.
   C. Evaluating students' work.   D. Directing students' attention.
10. What type of intelligence is cooperative learning best suited for?
    A. Interpersonal intelligence.   B. Intrapersonal intelligence.
    C. Logical intelligence.   D. Linguistic intelligence.

(二)简答题

1. You had an oral examination, didn't you?
   This word is used in spoken language.
2. The train moved slowly south through flat, drab mainline scenery.
   The boats in the harbour make a beautiful scene.
3. The branches of the tree swayed in the wind.
   The pendulum stopped swinging.
4. He takes off his coat to reveal a bright red vest.
   The sleeves of a pale blue waistcoat came only to her elbows.
5. Please notice, it is a vertical line.
   He is an upright citizen.

(三)简要回答下列问题

1. 采用任务驱动型学习的方式对目前教学有什么好处?
2. 教师素质的内容主要有什么?
3. 任何国家进行外语教学的目的是什么?
4. 学习策略中学生因素包括什么?
5. 影响交际策略的因素是什么?

三、教学设计

教学设计题:根据所提供的信息和语言素材进行教学设计,本题用英文作答。

根据所提供的语言素材设计教学活动,要求教学设计目标具体、教学内容分析恰当、教学重点和难点突出、教学过程完整、师生任务明确。

学生概况:本班为中等城市普通学校高中二年级的学生,班级人数为50人。多数学生已具备一定的英语语言能力。学生能够积极参与课堂活动,合作意识较强。

教学时间:25 分钟
语言素材:加粗单词为学生首次接触的词汇

英语必修 5 Unit 3   Life in the future

Spacemail:

liqiang299A@Great Adventure Space Station.com   15/11/3008（Earthtime）

Dear Mum and Dad,

　　I still cannot believe that I am **taking up** this prize that I won last year. I have to remind myself **constantly** that I am really in A.D. 3008. Worried about the journey, I was unsettled for the first few days. As a result, I suffered from "Time lag". This is similar to the "**jet lag**" you get from flying, but it seems you keep getting flashbacks from your **previous** time period. So I was very nervous and **uncertain** at first. However, my friend and **guide**, Wang Ping, was very understanding and gave me some green **tablets** which helped a lot. Well-known for their expertise, his parents' company, called "Future Tours", transported me safely into the future in a time **capsule**.

　　I can still remember the moment when the space **stewardess** called us all to the capsule and we climbed in through a small **opening**. The seats were comfortable and after a calming drink, we felt sleepy and closed our eyes. The capsule began swinging gently **sideways** as we lay relaxed and dreaming. A few minutes later, the journey was completed and we had arrived. I was still on the earth but one thousand years in the future. What would I find?

　　At first my new **surroundings** were difficult to **tolerate**. The air seemed thin, as though its combination of gases had little oxygen left. Hit by a **lack** of fresh air, my head ached. Just as I tried to make the necessary **adjustment** to this new situation, Wang Ping appeared. "Put on this **mask**," he advised. "It'll make you feel much better." He handed it to me and immediately hurried me through to a small room nearby for a rest. I felt better in no time. Soon I **was back on my feet** again and following him to collect a hovering **carriage** driven by computer. These carriages float above the ground and by bending or **pressing** down in your seat, you can move swiftly. Wang Ping **fastened** my **safety belt** and showed me how to use it. Soon I could fly as fast as him. However, I lost sight of Wang Ping when we reached what looked like a large market because of too many carriages flying by in all directions. He was **swept up** into the centre of them. Just at that moment I had a "time lag" flashback and saw the area again as it had been in the year A.D. 2008. I realized that I had been transported into the future of what was still my hometown! Then I caught sight of Wang Ping again and flew after him.

　　Arriving at a strange-looking house, he showed me into a large, bright clean room. It had a green wall, a brown floor and soft lighting. Suddenly the wall moved - it was made of trees! I found later that their leaves provided the room with much-needed oxygen. Then Wang Ping **flashed** a **switch** on a computer screen, and a table and some chairs rose from under the floor as if by magic. "Why not sit down and eat a little?" he said. "You may find this difficult as it is your first time travel trip. Just relax, since there is nothing planned on the **timetable** today. Tomorrow you'll be ready for some visits." Having said this, he spread some food on the table, and produced a bed from the floor. After he left, I had a brief meal and a hot bath. Exhausted, I **slid into** bed and fell fast asleep.

More news later from your loving son,

Li Qiang

四、教学实施与评价

教学情景分析题：根据题目要求进行教学分析，本题用中文作答。

分析以下教学片段：

T: What did you do yesterday, Wang Fei?
S: The floor was dirty and I **sweeped** it.
T: Oh, that is nice, you **swept** the floor, did you?
S: Yes.
T: Where did you **sweep** the floor?
S: I **sweeped** the floor in my yard.
T: Oh, you **swept** the floor in your yard. Well, it is very nice.

参 考 答 案

模块一　英语学科知识与能力

一、单项选择题（一）

1. A 2. D 3. B 4. C 5. C 6. B 7. D 8. A 9. C 10. B
11. D 12. C 13. A 14. B 15. B 16. B 17. A 18. D 19. A 20. D
21. A 22. D 23. C 24. A 25. C 26. C 27. C 28. C 29. D 30. D
31. D 32. A 33. B 34. D 35. A 36. B 37. D 38. A 39. C 40. B
41. C 42. A 43. C 44. C 45. D 46. A 47. A 48. D 49. D 50. B
51. B 52. D 53. A 54. D 55. D 56. D 57. D 58. C 59. B 60. D
61. D 62. C 63. B 64. B 65. D 66. A 67. D 68. D 69. B 70. D
71. D 72. D 73. D 74. D 75. C 76. D 77. D 78. A 79. A 80. D
81. C 82. C 83. A 84. B 85. B 86. D 87. D 88. B 89. D 90. D
91. A 92. C 93. B 94. B 95. A 96. B 97. B 98. C 99. B 100. D

二、单项选择题（二）

1. B 2. C 3. A 4. A 5. B 6. A 7. D 8. B 9. B 10. B
11. A 12. A 13. A 14. B 15. B 16. C 17. C 18. A 19. C 20. A
21. B 22. C 23. C 24. A 25. D 26. C 27. D 28. C 29. A 30. D
31. A 32. A 33. B 34. D 35. D 36. A 37. D 38. D 39. B 40. C
41. A 42. A 43. C 44. B 45. C 46. C 47. A 48. D 49. A 50. A
51. C 52. C 53. C 54. B 55. B 56. D 57. C 58. B 59. B 60. D
61. A 62. B 63. A 64. D 65. D 66. C 67. D 68. D 69. B 70. C
71. B 72. A 73. B 74. A 75. D 76. B 77. D 78. B 79. B 80. C
81. A 82. B 83. D 84. A 85. D 86. D 87. B 88. B 89. D 90. A
91. A 92. C 93. B 94. B 95. A 96. C 97. C 98. B 99. C 100. A

三、阅读理解

1. C 2. A 3. A 4. C 5. A 6. A 7. A 8. D 9. B 10. C 11. A 12. B
13. C 14. D 15. A 16. C 17. A 18. B 19. A 20. B 21. C 22. B
23. C 24. B 25. A 26. D 27. C 28. C 29. B 30. D

模块二 英语学科教学知识与能力

语言教学知识与能力练习题（一）

一、单项选择题

1. A　2. A　3. D　4. A　5. C　6. D　7. B　8. D　9. C　10. D　11. C　12. A
13. C　14. B　15. D

二、简答题

1. 前句是一个含有定语从句的主从复合句。该句主语是 this，表语是 the research center，定语从句修饰的先行词是 the research center，它和定语从句形成了这样的逻辑关系：...visited the research center。或者我们可以理解为：定语从句缺少的是谓语动词 visited 的宾语，这个宾语就是 the research center，所以关系代词 that 引导定语从句且作宾语。

后句是一个含有表语从句的主从复合句。该句主语是 this research center，is 后是一个表语从句，且从句部分缺少宾语，所以连接词必须能作 visited 的宾语。因此，what 在此处相当于 the one (that)，含义是："……的那一个"。

前句：这是你（们）去年参观的那个研究中心吗？

后句：这个研究中心是你（们）去年参观的那个吗？

2. have a big time 意为"尽兴；愉快时刻（指宴会、聚会等）"，其为口语用法，常和 have 搭配使用。be in the big time 意为"地位重要；第一流；最高级（尤指运动、娱乐等）"。例如：

前句：昨晚吉姆在晚会上玩得非常尽兴。

后句：别担心，他现在是一流的。

3. according to 意为"按照；根据；因……而定"。according as 意为"随……而定"。according to 后接名词或从句，according as 后接从句。

前句：据报纸上说，布什明天将来中国。

后句：你们今天做还是明天做这件事，可以根据客观需要而定。

4. add color to 意为"使……有趣；使……增色"，give color to 意为"使……可信；使……看起来有可能"。

前句：他使我的演出增色生辉。

后句：那孩子被撕破的衣服使他说的跟人打架的事显得真实可信。

5. afraid of 意为"害怕；忧虑；担忧"，afraid to 意为"害怕；不敢"。afraid of 后接名词、动名词或从句，它着重强调对可能产生的后果担忧或忧虑。afraid to 后接动词原形，它着重指不敢或害怕去做某事。

前句：她担心会伤了我的感情。

后句：她不敢叫醒她的丈夫。

6. alone 意思是"单独的"，"独自一人"；lonely 意思是："孤独的"，"寂寞的"。

前句:他是独自一个人。

后句:他感到孤独。

7. living 之意是"活着的"、"现存的"、"在使用中的"; alive "逼真的"、"惟妙惟肖的"、"活(着)的"、"活生生的"、"在世的"、"活跃的"、"充满活力的"。

前句:那位老大爷仍然充满活力吗?

后句:那位老大爷还在世吗?

(当然,前句也有后句这个意思,那要由上下文决定。)

8. at the age of 表示"在……岁时",后面接基数词,强调某一时刻的情况或动作,用于一般过去时,作时间状语。by the age of 表示"到……岁的时候"、"在……岁以前",后面接基数词,强调到某一时刻为止的结果,用于过去完成时或将来完成时,作时间状语。

前句:他六岁的时候开始学开小汽车。

后句:到十六岁的时候,他已经学会了开小汽车。

9. add to 意为"增添,增加,增进"; add ... to 意为"把……加到……",是把前一项加到后一项之后或之中。

前句:恶劣的天气增加了我们的困难。

后句:七加二等于九。

10. agree to 表示"同意计划／条件／建议等一类的名词或代词"。 agree with 作"同意某人的意见"解,其后可跟表示人的名词或代词,也可跟表示"意见"或"说的话"的名词或从句。

前句:他们已同意我们的计划。

后句:他们同意我的观点。

11. believe in 是一个动介型短语动词,表示"信奉、信仰"(指对某种思想、主张、观念、行动具有信心)和"信任"(have trust in),表示"信赖(人格)"。

believe 作及物动词时,其后可跟名词,表示"相信某人的话或某事";后接从句或复合宾语时,表示"认为、料想、相信"等。

前句:我信任他(的人格)。

后句:我相信他(的话)。

12. 用于肯定句中时,except ／ but 意为"除……外(不再有)"; besides 意为"除……外(还有),表示(含内)"。

前句:除了吴东外,他们都看过了那部影片。

后句:除了吴东看过那部影片外,他们也都看过了。

13. be known as 意为"作为……而著名",其后的名词表示一个人的身份、职业等。be known for 意为"因……而著名",其后所接内容表示某人或物的特点、特长等。

前句:我们相信你会成为一位著名的画家。

后句：我们相信你会因你对艺术的贡献而闻名。

14. be made of 表示"由……制成"，指从原料到制成品，只发生了形状变化，没有发生本质变化（属物理变化）。be made from 表示"由……制成"，指从原料到制成品，发生了质的变化，已无法复原（属化学变化）。

前句：宫殿的门由金箔做成。

后句：葡萄酒是用葡萄酿成的。

15. wide 表示空间宽度；widely 意思是"广泛地"。

前句：她把门开大。

后句：英语在世界上广泛使用。

三、简要回答下列问题

1. 语法翻译法、直接教学法、听说法、认知法。

语法翻译法是指母语是外语教学的基础，以句子为教学的基本单位，通过讲解、语法规则训练、阅读及翻译的方式，强调语言输出的准确性。

2. 教学策略是指教师在一定教学理念的指导下，根据自己对教学任务以及教学情景的理解和认知，对教学活动起调节作用的系统的行为，以实现最佳的教学效益。

比方教授肯定句和否定句。

句式：I like ... / I don't like ...

技能目标：能听懂别人讲述自己喜欢的东西和不喜欢的东西；能讲述自己喜欢的东西和不喜欢的东西；能用多媒体手段向学生展示一些物品，引导学生谈自己的好恶。

3. 教学是一种活动。对教师来说，教学是指导学习者学习的教育过程；对于学生来说，教学是在教师指导下的学习过程。在这个活动中，学习者在教师指导下掌握知识和技能，同时发展能力，而且身心获得一定的发展，形成相关的思想品德。

4. 能够管理自己的学习行为；能够根据自己的具体情况确立学习目标；自觉制定并及时调整学习计划；选择合理的学习方式；自觉监控学习过程。

5. （1）学科的特性：不同学科由于其特点的差异，要求采用不同的教学方法。（2）学习者的认知水平和年龄特点。对教学方法的选择在一定程度上是对学生原有知识状态和认知特点的合理估计和预测。例如性格外向的学生在课堂活动中容易处于主动地位，而性格内向的学生只能被动地参与。

6. （1）首先要了解学生的思想、情绪；（2）要了解学生的英语水平，学习上的困难以及学生的听、说、读、写能力，语音、语法、词汇水平；（3）要了解学生的学习方法、爱好和对教学的期望；（4）备课时，要考虑如何有意识地结合每次教学，解决一两个学生的问题，以帮助他们进一步提高学习效果。

7. 以词汇意义探究为例，学习者通过搜集图片、听录音、依据上下文猜词义并加以模仿的方式，无需借助教师的讲解和翻译就可以掌握词的意义。

8. 建构主义倡导以学生为中心的教学模式,认为他们是知识意义的主动建构者。同时,教师是整个教学过程的组织者、指导者和协调者,对学习者的意义构建起促进作用,因为以学生为中心的教学设计的每一个环节都离不开教师的有效启发、认真组织和精心指导。

9. 教师应为学生建构一种对知识理解的合理框架,将复杂的学习任务加以分解,引导学生对所学知识进行不断深入的探究。

10. (1)任务的设计;(2)任务的准备;(3)任务的呈现;(4)任务的开展;(5)任务的评价。

11. (1)工具功能:用语言获取他物;(2)调节功能:用语言控制他人的行为;(3)互动功能:用语言与他人交往;(4)人际功能:用语言表达个人感情和意义;(5)启发功能:用语言学习和发现;(6)想象功能:用语言创造一个想象的世界;(7)表达功能:用语言交流信息。

12. 语言能力、社会语言能力、语篇能力和策略能力。

13. 多项选择、判断正误、回答问题、完形填空、信息转换练习等等。

14. 课外学习活动是对学习者课内语言内容的补充、延伸和巩固。主要形式有参加英语角活动、看英语原版电影、收看英语电视节目、阅读英语原版小说、用英语写电子书信等等。

15. 如用英语解释 break 在下句中两种不同的含义。

释义:When a tool breaks or when you break it, it is damaged and no longer works.

语言教学知识与能力练习题(二)

一、单项选择题

1.C 2.A 3.B 4.A 5.C 6.A 7.D 8.C 9.A 10.A 11.C 12.B 13.A 14.C 15.A

二、简答题

1. cause 意为"起因"、"原因",指引起某种结果的必然原因,即主要事实方面的原因,常和 effect 连用,表示因果关系。reason 意为"理由"、"原因",指用以解释某些已发生的事情的理由或借口,这种理由可能是也可能不是真正的理由,强调逻辑推理方面的理由。

前句:告诉我们失火的原因。

后句:告诉我们你改变计划的原因。

2. close, closely 这两个词都可以用作副词,close 表示"靠近"、"紧紧地"。closely 则表示"紧密地"、"严密地"、"密切地"。

前句:警察走近了。

后句:警察紧紧跟上那个陌生人。

3. finish 是普通用语,用得比较广泛,可作及物动词或不及物动词,多用来指"完成"一项任务或活动,不强调其完整性,后面可接名词、代词或-ing,不接不定式。complete 一般用作及物动词,用法较正式,通常用来表示完整性,表示"完成"某个计划、理想、事业、工程、建筑、书籍及作品等,后面可接名词或代词,不接-ing 或不定式。

前句:你的工作完成了吗?

后句:你的计划完成了吗?

4. compare ... with 意为"把……与……相比",侧重指两者间的区别。compare ... to ... 意为"把……比作……",着重注意两者间的相似点。

前句:把这辆汽车与那辆汽车相比较,你就会发现它们之间的区别。

后句:这首歌把我们的国家比作一个大家庭。

5. 两者都可用作动词,意为"采访",cover 的宾语是事情;interview 的宾语是人。

前句:然后记者们就被派去采访这些事件。

后句:他上午采访了五个人。

6. congratulate 作"祝贺"解时,其宾语是人,常与介词 on 搭配。celebrate 作"庆祝"、"庆贺"解时是及物动词,它的宾语往往是表示"事物"的词,如节日、生日、胜利、成功等,不可以是人。

前句:今天是她的生日,所以我们要庆祝一番。

后句:他热烈祝贺我考试取得了好成绩。

7. damage 意为"损坏、破坏"。它可用于表示损坏或破坏具体的物品,一般暗示损坏后价值或效益会降低,这种损坏是部分性的,通常指损坏的程度不那么严重,还可以修复再用。也可用于表示损坏抽象的东西,有时该词也用于借喻。destroy 意为"破坏;摧毁;消灭;毁灭",通常指程度非常严重的"毁坏",一般情况下不可以修复再用。另外,它既可表示毁坏具体的物品,也可表示毁坏抽象的东西。

前句:这场大火把整座房子烧毁了。

后句:这场大火把整座房子损坏了。

8. day by day 意为"一天一天地"、"逐日",表示事情的逐渐变化过程。该短语只能作状语。day after day 意为"日复一日"、"一天又一天",表示一个重复(周而复始或循环重复)的动作或事件。该短语可作主语和状语。

前句:那孩子一天天好了起来。

后句:我得日复一日地做这项工作。

9. deal with 和 do with 侧重"处理"的手段、方法或方式。do with 常与 what 连用,deal with 常与 how 连用。

前句:你打算怎样处理这个旧手机?

后句:你打算怎样处理这个旧手机?

10. invent 意为"发明",指通过劳动,运用聪明才智"发明／创造"出以前从未存在过的新事物。discover 意为"发现",表示"偶然"或"经过努力"发现客观存在的事物、真理或错误,即指发现原来客观存在但不为人所知的事物,也可表示发现已为人所知的事物的新的性质或用途。

前句:是谁发明电话的?

后句:哥伦布 1492 年发现了美洲。

11. fit 用作及物动词,意为"与……相符、符合";"合……身";用作不及物动词,意为"适合"、"合身"。多指衣物等尺寸大小合身、合脚。suit 意为"适合"。多指衣物等的颜色、款式、质地等适合,穿起来协调、好看;合乎需要、口味、性格、条件和地位等。

前句:这件外套不适合你。

后句:这件外套不合你的身。

12. for the first time 意为"首次"、"第一次"。表示有生以来或一段时间内第一次做某事,在句中一般单独作状语。the first time 首次;第一次。常引导时间状语从句,其重点不是讲第一次做什么,而是说明另一动作或情况;也可以作表语,强调到说话为止某一情况或动作的次数。

前句:两位女生开学初首次交谈。

后句:第一次见到她,我就知道我们会成为好朋友。

13. stare 意为"凝视",它也是一个不及物动词,其后通常接介词 at 才能接宾语。glare 意为"怒视",也是不及物动词,其后要接介词 at 后才能接宾语。

前句:他们盯着他看。

后句:他们瞪着他。

14. go on to do sth. 表示"接着做另一件事",即接下去做与原来不同的一件事;go on doing sth…表示"继续不停地做某事或间断后继续做原来没有做完的事"。

前句:读完课文后,学生们继续做练习。

后句:一路上学生们一直有说有笑。

15. habit 指个人的"习惯",通常用于表示做事、思考问题或行为举止的不自觉的方式方法;custom 指长期而广泛采用的行为或方法,即风俗习惯,按照某地区人们共同生活及其行为的准则或规范,它不仅有指导意义,而且具有必须遵循的意义;

前句:这证明是我的失败,因为我不久就回到在电视屏幕前打瞌睡的坏习惯去了。

后句:一个人从诞生的那一时刻起,他降生后所处的风俗习惯便给他的阅历和行为定了型。

三、简要回答下列问题

1.在一节课中教师自始至终眼观四面,耳听八方,尽力保证每个学生都进入自己的学习状态,像乐队演奏中的不同乐师一样。

2. 制订任务的评价阶段目的是为了引导学习者重新审视任务过程,包括任务的准备和展开阶段,尤其关注任务过程中语言使用的正确性、得体性、流利性和复杂程度。例如:任务的评价可以通过真实学习任务形式完成,教师设计真实的学习任务,引导学习者对任务过程中出现的一些语言形式问题加以反思,以达到完全正确掌握这些语言形式的目的。

3. 首先,教学策略来自教师对教学理论的分析和判断;其次,教学策略还产生于对具体教学方法和技巧的深入分析和思考;最后,对教学经验的总结和反思也有利于教学策略的产生。借助于教学经验的反思,如记教学日记或教学观摩,教师会加深对个人经验的认识。

4. "做中学"的教学方法,即通过口头表达、交际活动,使学习延伸为一种技能,使其与现实生活相链接。

5. (1)以学习者为中心,发挥教师的主导作用;(2)开展策略教学,培养策略者的策略意识;(3)从外部监督逐渐发展成为自主控制;(4)构建自助学习中心,提供自主学习资源。

6. 教师鼓励学生就所学材料的标题展开讨论,允许学生自主发挥,根据自己的理解,提出不同的看法和意见。学生根据所得到的相关信息预测将要学习的内容。学生在参与类似活动的过程中,逐渐具备了选择注意的能力,选择注意力强的学生善于发现所学习内容中的关键词、短语、主题句以及相关信息等。

7. 可以根据教师提供的一系列关键词和短语预测学习材料的内容。由于学生已经建立了一定程度的图式知识,因此,这些关键词和短语对学生已有的图式知识起到了激活的作用。例如,Benz是一种名牌汽车的商标,车主具有相当的经济地位;而 Mini 则是一种价格较低的小型汽车,车主可能是属于收入较底层的人等。

8. 词义猜测是一种有意识使用元认知知识的技巧,学生通过交际语境、阅读材料的上下文、构词法等信息猜测不熟悉的词语意义,提高自己逻辑推理能力。学生能够将自己原先的预测或猜测与获得的信息加以对比,确认或修改已有的假设。

9. 合作。例如学生进行小组活动,阅读篇章后进行讨论并交换意见,通过合作填充图标内容。

角色扮演。例如某个学生扮演某种社会角色,如记者,通过阅读文章获得相关知识,并利用这些知识采访所阅读文章的作者。

10. (1)检测学生对某一学习任务理解能力;(2)选择适应学生发展水平的学习任务;(3)提供教学支持,即让讲解和组织能力较强的学生来支持和帮助其他学生的学习。

11. (1)语言训练;(2)技能培养;(3)策略培养。以语言知识训练中的语音训练为例,节奏常常是学习的难点。节奏包括重音、长短、连读,其中重音起决定性作用,即节奏与句子重音和词的重音关系密切。

12.口语表达的流利性强调意义的完整表达,而准确性强调语言形式的正确使用,过于重视流利而忽视准确,很可能使语言难于理解;过于重视准确而忽视流利,则可能使意义表达缺乏连贯性。以纠错为例,过分重视流利性而很少纠错可能导致学生形成错误的语言表达方式,影响听者的理解,影响交际的顺利进行。过分强调准确性而经常纠错可能导致学生情绪焦虑,或对英语学习产生抵触情绪。

13.交际教学法认为,交际的形式既包括言语交际,也包括书面语交际。因而,交际教学法既重视口语,也不忽视书面语。

14.语言知识通常指语音、词汇、语法规则等方面的知识,学生对这些知识的掌握程度关系到语言表达的准确性。正确的语音、语调不仅是口语交际的声音符号,更是交际者有效传递信息的重要手段。词汇是句子的组成成分,学生必须掌握丰富的词汇,才能准确恰当地表明思想。语法规则知识是学生组织词汇、句子进行言语表达的基础。

15.促进者、监控者和参与者。

语言教学知识与能力练习题(三)

一、单项选择题

1.C 2.A 3.D 4.C 5.A 6.B 7.B 8.C 9.D 10.D 11.A 12.B 13.C 14.D 15.A

二、简答题

1.have sb.do sth.为"使(让、请)某人做某事"之意,其中作宾补的不带to的不定式只表示发生过某事。have sb./sth.doing sth.为"让某人(某事)一直做某事"之意,其中作宾补的现在分词表示保持或一直存在的状态。

前句:士兵们让男孩背对着父亲站着。

后句:士兵们让男孩背对着父亲整夜站着。

2.hear from 表示"收到……的来信"、"收到……的来电",后面接指人的名词或代词;hear of 表示"听人说起"、"听说过",侧重于间接听说;

前句:我每个月收到两封哥哥的信。

后句:我听说她上周死了。

3.hurt 为普通用语,既可指肉体上的伤害(可被 badly, slightly, seriously 等修饰),也可指精神上、感情上的伤害(被 very much, rather, deeply 修饰),多指伤痛。injure 比 hurt 正式,主要指意外事故中损害健康、容貌等,强调功能的损失,也可指"损害(名誉等)、伤害(感情等)"。

前句:在那场足球赛中,我的腿受了重伤。

后句:一颗子弹伤了他的左眼。

4.illness 指"生病(的状况或时期)",与 health 相对;sickness 指"(生)病、患病",也可

指"恶心、呕吐感"。mountain sickness 高山病与 morning sickness 孕妇晨吐、sleeping sickness 昏睡病(非洲采采蝇 Tsetse Fly 引起的)一样,都是常见的固定词组。

前句:他患有高山病。

后句:这孩子已经病了两年了。

5. increase...by 表示数量增加的幅度,即在原有的基础上"增加了多少";increase to 则表示"增加到多少"。

前句:与去年相比,这些卡车的生产成本降低了三分之一。

后句:印度的人口已经增加到了十亿。

6. in all 意为"总共",既可放在句首,也可放在句末。after all 意为"毕竟",表示"和预期相反"常放在句末,用来提醒不要忘记某个重要的结论或理由,一般放在句首还可译为"要记住,别忘了"。

前句:总共有 25,000 因纽特人。

后句:我以为他会帮助我们的,但他终究没有帮我们。

7. in the way 意为"挡道"、"妨碍(某人)"。in a way 单独使用,way 前不加任何修饰语,意为"在某种程度上"、"在某些方面(某一点上)"。

前句:叫那个男孩别挡道碍事。

后句:从某种程度上来说,这篇文章写得不错。

8. knock into = bump into 意为"撞在……上",后接宾语。knock down 意为"撞倒、打倒"。down 为副词,宾语是名词时,down 可位于名词前或后,宾语是人称代词时,down 必须位于宾语后。

前句:小心!别撞到别人身上。

后句:小心!别撞倒别人。

9. late 可作形容词或副词,意为"迟(的)"、"晚(的)"。lately 是副词,意为"最近"、"近来"相当于 recently,常与现在完成时连用。

前句:他上学常迟到。

后句:我最近没收到他的来信。

10. possible 指"由于有适当的条件和方法,某事可能发生或做到",强调"客观上有可能",但常含有"实际希望很小"的意思。probable 系常用词,指"从表面迹象来看很可能"。

前句:现在有可能登上月球。

后句:现在很有可能登上月球。

11. 两者都表示"行李",均是不可数名词。luggage 属英式英语,是随身携带行李的总称;baggage 属美式英语,是各种行李的总称。two pieces of luggage / baggage 两件行李。

前句:她有多少行李?

后句:她有多少行李?

12. manage to do sth. 暗含 succeed in doing sth. 之意,指"(经过努力和克服困难之后)将某事做成",即经过努力达到了目的,重点在于结果,后接动词不定式,不接 v-ing。try to do sth. 指"设法或试图"做某事,强调要做某事或尽力做某事(但不一定成功)。

前句:他总算按时完成了任务。

后句:他设法按时完成任务。

13. meet 可作"遇见"、"迎接"解。 meet with 表示"遇见"、"碰到"时,常含有"偶尔"的意思(= come across,come upon)。此外,meet with 还可表示"遭遇"或"经历"的意思。在美国英语中,meet with 还可以表示"会见"。

前句:系主任在街上遇见她。

后句:系主任在办公室会见她。

14. meeting 可以用于两人或多人,表示偶然的或拟定的,短暂的或持续的聚会。它的用途很广,可用于日常普通场合,也可用于特殊的或官方的正式场合。conference 指专门性的正式会议,常用于就某个重大问题进行专门研究或交换意见的讨论会、协商会等。

前句:学生们上周五举办了班会。

后句:很多记者来参加了新闻发布会。

15. happen to sb./sth. 指不好的事情发生在某人(物)身上;occur to sb./sth. 指"某种思想等呈现于某人的知觉中"。

前句:他碰巧知道那个地方。

句子:你难道就没想过给他们打个电话?

三、简要回答下列问题

1.对各类语言技能的评价就是考查学生听、说、读、写、语篇构成等方面的能力。以阅读测试为例,测试学生阅读能力的方法有很多,如选择填空、回答问题、完成句子、判断正误、排序、匹配等。

2.有活动观察、学习日记、项目作业、学习文件夹、有声思维、访谈,及调查问卷等等。比方,教师提供给学生一个学习任务,与学生讨论如何制订计划并解决问题,教师观察、记录并评价其策略的有效性。

3.(1)母语的影响;(2)年龄;(3)语音输入;(4)语音能力;(5)学习态度;(6)学习动机;(7)性格。

4.词汇展示应采用直观性、情景性和趣味性策略。直观性指利用实物、手势、图片等来展示词汇的意义,如教室里的各种实物和用品。

5.素质教育原则:教师要以素质教育作为中学英语教学的指导思想和教学原则,以培养学生听说能力为目的教学，在对学生传授基础知识和进行基本训练的过程中形成学生的英语语言素质。

交际性原则：语言是表达意义的体系；语言的主要功能是交际；语言的主要单位不仅是语法的结构特征，还应包括功能范畴。

6. 任务型教学是一种以具体的学习任务为目的或动机，以完成任务的过程为学习过程，以展示任务成果的方式来体现的教学效果的教学方式。任务型教学的特点：(1)任务型教学强调学习过程。(2)任务型教学不仅重视培养学生的交际能力，更强调培养学生综合运用语言的能力。(3)倡导以语言运用能力为目的语言教学。

7. 阅读整体教学就是把一篇课文作为整体来教。它注重理解课文的思想内容。它把传授语言知识和利用课文进行技能训练这两方面放在同等重要的地位，即它利用技能训练的各种方式增加语言知识的复现率；同时，在逐步掌握语言知识的过程中，提高技能训练的熟练程度和水平，从而做到"词不离句，句不离篇"，保证课文的连贯性、趣味性和逻辑性。整体教学的方法容易引起学生的兴趣，便于教师采用从视、听、说入手的教学方法和情景教学法，有利于提高课文教学的质量。

8. 英语水平测试的目的在于检查应试者的英语熟练程度是否达到进行某种活动应有的要求，如出国留学、专业培训等。美国的 TOEFL 考试就属于这一类型。

9. (1)加强目的性教育；(2)教学内容应该适合学生的实际水平；(3)总结要点；(4)鼓励为主；(5)适当开展竞赛活动；(6)讲授或训练内容要有启发性；(7)从已知到未知；(8)练习和作业的难度要适中，不要过难或过易；(9)鼓励学生多参加课堂的语言实践活动，大胆地使用英语表达思想；(10)让学生了解英语国家的文化背景知识。

10. (1)注意教态；(2)课堂操练不为成绩检查；(3)谨慎对待纠正错误。

11. 综合语言运用能力的形成是建立在学生语言技能、语言知识、情感态度、学习策略和文化意识等素养整体发展的基础上。语言技能、语言知识是综合语言运用能力的基础，文化意识是得体运用语言的保证。情感态度是影响学生学习和发展的重要因素，学习策略是提高学习效率、发展自主学习能力的保证。

12. 模拟交际性操练是有意义操练的发展和提高。在操练的过程中，学生的能动性更大，目的在于培养学生灵活运用的能力。它与有意义操练的显著差别在于：第一，不仅语言形式要正确，而且内容要符合真实情景；第二，学生叙述的内容有较大的灵活性，可因交际的需要围绕新句进行。例如在形容词比较等级的模拟交际性操练活动中，可让学生以小组为单位互相问年龄，比大小或问身高，比高矮等。

13. 从英语教学整个过程来看，听、说、读、写四项技能必须得以综合训练，不可偏废。

14. 能力倾向测试的目的不是检查应试者的现有英语水平，而是判断应试者学习语言的禀赋或潜在能力，因而又称为"语言禀赋测试"。测试的内容不应是应试者所学的知识，而是应试者的智能，如学习英语所需要的敏感性、模仿力、记忆力、观察力以及逻辑推理、分析比较、综合归纳等思维能力。

15.动机是一种驱策力量,是愿望改变行动的动力。动机指向目标、需求,它反映个体的某种需求;动机也指向行动,它为获得需求的满足而产生行动。动机越强烈,发起行动就越坚决,维持行动就越长久。所以,动机对英语学习是至关重要的。没有个体的学习愿望和毅力,就不可能产生真正的学习。

语言教学知识与能力练习题(四)

一、单项选择题

1. D 2. A 3. C 4. C 5. C 6. B 7. A 8. B 9. A 10. B 11. C 12. A 13. B 14. C 15. B

二、简答题

1. officer 常指穿着特别制服的"官员、军官、武官"等。official 常指"政府官员、行政官员、高级职员"。

前句:他父亲是军官。

后句:他父亲是政府官员。

2. on earth 作"到底"或"究竟"解,置于 what,when 等疑问词之后,以加强问句的语气。on the earth 作"在地球上"。

前句:你究竟为什么要说谎?

后句:我们生活在地球上。

3.两者均表示"互相、彼此",为代词,仅作动词或介词的宾语,不作其他成分。两者虽可换用,但 each other 多用于两者之间的关系,one another 多用于三者或三者以上之间的情况。

前句:我们俩每天在办公室碰面。

后句:这六个盲人不同意彼此的看法。

4. persuade sb. to do sth. 意为"说服某人干某事",其结果是成功的(即成功地说服某人干某事)。advise sb. to do sth. 意为"劝说某人干某事",其结果可能是劳而无功(即"说"而未"服")。

前句:汤姆终于说服他父亲戒烟了。

后句:汤姆劝说他父亲戒烟,他就是不听。

5. prepare for 意为"为……作准备",for 后面的宾语是准备的目的,即所要应付的情况。be prepared for 意为"准备好,有所准备",强调已准备好的状态。

前句:我们在为期中考试做准备。

后句:我们为期中考试做好了准备。

6. prize 是表示"奖品"或"奖(彩)金"之意。而 medal 是指"奖牌(章)"或"勋章"。

前句:1921 年,爱因斯坦获得了诺贝尔物理奖。

后句:卡尔·刘易斯夺得四块金牌。

7. put 意为"放、安置"。常指把某物弄到某个地方,并把它留在那里。Place 意为"(小心或有意)放置、安放",主要指把东西放在一定的位置上。

前句:请把伞放在门后。

后句:她把桌子放在房间的中央。

8. lie(vi.) lied—lied—lying"撒谎"。lie(vi.) lay—lain—lying"躺、位于"。

前句:他从小就一直撒谎。

后句:他躺在地板上看书。

9. quiet 意为"安静的、寂静的"。用于自然环境,指没有活动、喧闹的寂静状态;指人时,表示生性安静、不易激动。silent 意为"寂静的、沉默的",表示不说话、不弄出声响,但不一定指没有活动。

前句:简是个天性好静的女孩。

后句:简是个寡言少语的女孩。

10. 本题依据 is,are 来理解 all 的意义。前句中的 all 指"一切、宇宙、万物",属于不可数;后句中的 all 指"全体、大家",具有复数性质。

前句:万籁俱寂。

后句:大家都保持沉默。

11. raise 意为"抚养(指人);饲养(指动物或禽畜)"之意。support 意为"养活",不用于饲养动物。

前句:那些羊从小羊羔时就是他喂养的。

后句:她赡养老母亲。

12. refer to 意为(1)"谈及","提到";(2)"查阅","参考"。refer...to 意为(1)"把……提交给","把……归功于";(2)"让……处理/查找",可用于被动语态。

前句:当第一次在这儿驾驶时,他参看市政地图。

后句:当第一次在这儿驾驶时,他建议我参看一下地图。

13. road 意为"路","道路",指供车辆或人通过的广阔平坦的大道,常指"公路"、"马路"等。street 指城镇、乡村两旁有建筑物的"街道"。

前句:汽车沿着这条路行驶。

后句:沿着大街走,在第三个路口往右拐。

14. place 指人们从事各种活动的"地方、场所、位置",是可数名词。space 意为"空间",是不可数名词,表示万物存在之处;作"空隙、空白"解时,是可数名词。

前句:教室放不下30张桌子。

后句:武汉夏天很热。

15. run after 意为"追赶;追逐;寻找;搜寻"等。run away 意为"逃走;逃跑;溜掉"等。

前句:狗在追野兔。

后句:警察到的时候,小偷逃跑了。

三、简要回答下列问题

1. 直接法(Direct Method)就是直接教外语的方法。"直接"包含三个方面的意思:直接学习、直接理解、直接应用。它通过外语本身进行的会话、交谈和阅读来教外语,而不用(学生的)母语,不用翻译和形式语法。重视使用实物、图画或演示动作等各种直观教具进行外语教学。这个方法的最终目的,是要培养学生在交谈、阅读或写作时都用外语思维。

2. 认知法(Cognitive Approach)是在以 Chomsky 为代表的转换生成语法、Caroll 的认知心理学的理论基础上产生的。这种方法从学生已知的知识出发,通过学习和分析,对语音、词汇和语法 的形式获得有意识的控制,并在有意识的情景中培养语言的交际能力。这种教学方法的理论重视人的思维作用,把语言学习看作是智力活动,重视对语言现象的理解,着眼于培养实际运用语言的能力。

3. 原因是多方面的,主要原因:一是教师缺乏反思意识;二是缺乏提供反思资料的手段。

4. (1)阅读记忆策略训练;(2)兴趣记忆策略训练;(3)最佳时期记忆策略训练;(4)猜测记忆策略训练;(5)拆词记忆策略训练;(6)词汇图记忆策略训练。

5. 研究性学习法是指学生基于自身兴趣,在教师指导下,从自然、社会和学生自身生活中选择和确定研究专题,主动地获取知识、应用知识、解决问题的学习活动。

6. 教师说话时间太多是不合适的,因为老师说得越多,学生练习说话的机会就会越少,需要练习说话的是学生,而不是老师。

7. (1)互动观;(2)目标观;(3)师生观;(4)形式观;(5)情境观;(6)评价观。

8. (1)语言障碍:词汇方面的障碍、句法方面的障碍、语篇和问题方面的障碍。(2)非语言障碍:智力方面的障碍、非智力方面的障碍、语感、背景知识方面的障碍,阅读技巧方面的障碍,阅读策略方面的障碍。

9. (1)重视共同基础,构建发展平台;(2)提供多种选择,适应个性需求;(3)优化学习方式,提高自主学习能力;(4)关注学生情感,提高人文素养;(5)完善评价体系,促进学生不断发展。

10. (1)使学生学到一定数量的单词和习语。现行《大纲》要求学会的词汇,学生应会读会拼,能听懂,知道基本的词义,并能正确运用于口头表达中。(2)使学生掌握学习词汇的方法,培养学生学习词汇的能力。

11. 学习策略是指学生为了有效地学习和发展而采取的各种行动和步骤。英语学习的策略包括认知策略、调控策略、交际策略和资源策略以及内省策略、情意策略等。

12. 通常,结对活动和小组活动常见于大班,它们可以给学生更多的互动机会。而在一对一的教学背景下,教师可以根据个人的特别需求修改教学方案,而在大班教学中就要平衡全班与个人的之间的需求。

13.年龄的差别、学习风格的差异、水平的差异、教育与文化背景的差异等等。

14.(1)教师要为学生自主学习创造有利的条件;(2)在教学过程中做到"教"与"学"并重;(3)在自主学习中渗透和指导学习方法;(4)鼓励学生自主学习的同时,培养学生的创新意识和实践能力。

15.(1)兴趣是最好的老师;(2)做好课堂设计,创造一个轻松愉快的英语学习环境;(3)注重双向交流;创设学习情境;(4)安排丰富多彩的课外活动。

语言教学知识与能力练习题(五)

一、单项选择题

1.C 2.B 3.C 4.A 5.C 6.B 7.C 8.C 9.A 10.B 11.C 12.B 13.C 14.A 15.B

二、简答题

1. run out of 表示"某人用完某物",相当于及物动词。run out 指"某物用完了",为不及物动词,不能用于被动语态。

前句:我们的燃料快用完了。

后句:燃料很快就要用完了。

2. satisfied 指"达到希望时所感觉到的较强的满足感";content 指"满足",为普通用语,语气较弱,其要求值不高,一般的事情只要过得去或没有什么不满就算 content。

前句:我对你的成功感到满意。

后句:我对你的成功感到满足。

3. search sb. "搜某人的身";search for sb. / sth. "搜寻、寻找某人、某物"。

前句:那警察正在搜小偷的身。

后句:那警察正在搜寻那个小偷。

4. such 和 so 这两者都可以表示"如此"、"这样"。such 是形容词,用来修饰名词,如果修饰单数可数名词(名词前常有形容词修饰),常用"such+a 或 an+*adj.*+*n.*(单数)"的结构形式。so 是副词,用来修饰形容词+单数名词时,常用"so+*adj.*+a 或 an+*n.*(单数)"的结构形式。

前句:他给我们讲了一个很有趣的故事。

后句:他给我们讲了一个很有趣的故事。

5. sometime 是个副词,意为"某时",指时间上不确定的某一点,常用于过去时或将来时。some time 是个名词短语,意思是"一段时间",在句中常与 for,take 等词连用。

前句:七月有一天我曾见到过他。

后句:我将在这儿待一段时间。

6. plant 意为"栽、插、移植",其后跟作物(多为苗状的);grow 作及物动词时,意为"种植、培植",后接宾语(不表明种状还是苗状,强调种植后的栽培及管理过程)。

前句:在那个村子里他插秧的速度最快。

后句:他们只能在地里种土豆。

7. spend "花费"常用于 sb. spend(s)some money(time)on sth. 或 sb. spend(s)some money(time)(in)doing sth. 其主语一般是人。take 常用于占用或花费"时间",其句型为:sth. takes sb. time 或 It takes sb. time to do sth.

前句:他花了20元钱买了这支钢笔。

后句:这项工作将花费我们两小时。

8. 这两个词都与"走、步行"有关,它们都可以作动词或名词。step 多用来指"走一步","走一小段路",而 walk 多用来表示"漫步,散步或走(路),步行"。

前句:那位年轻人走进房子里。

后句:那位年轻人走进房子里。

9. firm 常译为"坚固的","坚决的",表示具体的事物地位"牢固"不易动摇;也可表示意志、信仰的"坚定"。steady 则意为"稳固的","扎实的",强调保持平衡不动摇,如指有形物,则指根基的稳固;也可用于指运动中的平稳。

前句:我们的友谊坚如磐石。

后句:他正取得稳定的进步。

10. fight 意为"打仗,战斗,和……作斗争"。常构成词组:fight for "为……而战";fight against "为反对……而斗争";fight with "和……一起战斗"。struggle 意为"挣扎",也可指"斗争",与 fight 相比,斗争更为费力,处境更难。struggle against:和(同)……斗争;struggle for:为……斗争。

前句:林肯为全民的自由而奋斗。

后句:那些加拿大人那些年一直和我们一起同日本人斗争。

11. supply, provide 两者均可表示"供应;供给",指对于缺乏或不足的事物进行补充或供给,用法如下:supply 常与 to / for 或 with 连用,其结构是:supply sth. to / for sb. 或 supply sb. with sth.;provide 常与 for 或 with 连用,其结构是:provide sth. for sb. 或 provide sb. with sth.

前句:他们供应食物给幸存者。

后句:他给家人提供衣食。

12. think of 多用来指"想起,认为";think about 多用来指"考虑某事情或对某事进行思考"。

前句:昨晚我睡觉前,想起了我的父母。

后句：想想你所做的这一切吧！

13. through 意为"通过；穿过"，侧重于指从物体的中间穿过；across 意为"横过；穿过"，一般指从房间、原野、海洋等一端横越到另一端或两个动作方向成十字交叉状。

前句：学生们和怀特先生通过大门。

后句：学生们和怀特先生穿过街道。

14. trip 是非正式用语，指短时间内往返的商业旅行或观光旅行；journey 常指由某一地点到另一地点的旅行，也指旅行的路程，尤指长途旅行，是比较正式的用语。

前句：在假期里我们到最近的海滨作了一次愉快的旅行。

后句：他从北京到伦敦做了一次长途旅行。

15. try on 指"试穿（衣服、鞋子）"及"试戴（帽子）"等，其中的 on 为副词，当宾语是代词时，该宾语要放在 on 之前；如果宾语是名词，该宾语放在 on 之前或之后均可；try out 指"试验或试用"某种机器、理论或方法，其中的 out 为副词，当宾语是代词时，常用于 try out 之间。

前句：这新帽子是给你的，请试试看。

后句：我来试试看能否行得通。

三、简要回答下列问题

1. 黑板、粉笔、录音机、语言实验室、录像机、投影仪、计算机、数字投影仪、交互式电子白板。学习使用各种类型的设备，是现代教师培训的主要内容之一。然而，我们应该尽力避免热衷于设备本身，只有当其他设备或教学方法不可替代时，才值得使用。好的教学关键，即师生关系、职业精神、好的活动，远比实际的传播方式更重要。

2. 任何学问都是科学与艺术的结合，教学也不例外。教学既有理性，也有感性，它是一门科学，这自不待言。之所以它又是一门艺术，这是因为：(1)教学具有艺术的内涵，它既要求教师具备高超精湛的教书育人的技艺、技能，又要极富创意地工作，不拘一格并恰到好处地表达所教内容和随之产生的情感；(2)教学与艺术有相似的对象，既反映客观世界，又反映人的主观世界。教学和艺术一样，对象是人，同时都受对象的制约；艺术的终极目标是培养知、情、意和谐发展的人，而教学的终极目标是培养德、智、体、美全面发展的人；(3)教学中有艺术性的内容，教学内容都是真善美的统一，它含有丰富的审美因素，具有明显或潜在的艺术性，这决定了师生在教学过程中进行审美和艺术交流的必然性；(4)教学最讲究语言的艺术性和其他辅助手段的艺术性；(5)教学与艺术具有相同的功能：认识功能、教育功能、审美功能；(6)教学体现着艺术的三大特点：形象性、情感性和创造性。

3. 文化是指所学语言国家的历史地理、风土人情、传统习惯、生活方式、文学艺术、行为规范、价值观念等。

4. 教学要符合学生生理和心理特点，遵循语言学习规律，力求满足不同类型和不同学生的需求,使每个学生得到健康的发展。

5.形成性评价常用于对学习过程的评价,评价标准可根据需要进行评定;终结性评价常用于对学业成绩的评价,评价标准主要基于学习目标。

6.顺利进行口头交流并不需要大量的词汇,通过操练来熟练运用一小部分具体词汇即可。一般而言,2000个高频词可以作为口语的目标词汇。

7.(1)创设学习条件的方法指导;(2)心理调节的方法指导;(3)掌握知识的方法指导;(4)学习各环节的方法指导;(5)学习各具体学科的方法指导。

8.在教学中要把握好英语和母语的关系,二者相辅相成。一方面,在英语课堂中应尽量使用英语,让学生大量接触英语,并沉浸在使用英语的氛围中,才能有效地排除母语的干扰,培养运用英语的能力。另一方面,需要指出的是,英语教学中要尽量使用英语,但不排斥适当利用母语,不要把英语和母语对立起来。母语对学习英语有干扰的一面,但也有可以被利用的一面。实践证明,适当地,即恰当地、有目的地、有控制地利用母语,对于英语教学是有利的。

9.(1)人与自然关系领域;(2)人与社会关系领域;(3)人与文化关系领域;(4)人与自我关系领域。

10.调控策略、资源策略、认知策略、记忆策略、活动策略。活动策略:词汇学习不限于理解和记忆,还必须能够使用。因此,学生应该能够利用真实语境或创造语境使用词汇,如造句、叙述故事、写信及与他人进行交流等。

11.习得的意思是在人们没有真正意识的努力下获得语言的方式,换句话说,就是不考虑语法或词汇,或是为了语言的各个部分如何摆放而操心。习得是无意识的、没有焦虑的,是通过语言渗透而产生的,往往直接渗入长期记忆,且产生语感。而学习是有意识、有目的的过程。往往先储存在短期记忆,再经过长期反复练习,最终才进入长期记忆,因此有过程痛苦和效果不佳的特点。

12.学生能大致明白的、水平稍高于他们实际能力的语言的输入。

13.先给学生一些小的语法规则和词汇清单,然后让学生用这些语法规则和词汇做翻译练习。

14.它的意思是教师先呈现语言项目(Presentation),然后教师讲解。练习(Practice)和学生用该语言项目进行表达(Production)。在PPP课堂的各项活动均是教师事先设计规定好的某个语言项目的练习。(如 going to 和 He's going to visit his teacher.)

15.就是利用前缀、后缀和词根来理解词汇意义,这项策略尤其适用于语言水平较高的学生。

语言教学知识与能力练习题（六）

一、单项选择题

1. A 2. B 3. C 4. D 5. D 6. D 7. D 8. B 9. A 10. B 11. D 12. C 13. A 14. B 15. A

二、简答题

1. used to 意为"过去常常（做某事）"，后接动词原形。常用来表示今昔对比，含"（现在）已不那样做了"之意；be used to 有两个含义：（1）"被用来做某事"，后接动词原形。（2）"习惯于；适应"，后接名词、代词或 v-ing，表示一种状态。

前句：他过去工作很努力。（暗指现在工作不努力了。）

后句：他现在习惯于艰苦的工作。

2. vast，huge 两者都是形容词，意思是"巨大的、庞大的"。在强调面积和范围的宽广或博大时，用 vast；指体积或容量等方面"巨大、超过一般标准"时，用 huge。

前句：这个地区被一片广袤的森林覆盖。

后句：那艘船好大。

3. broad，wide 这两个词均含"宽，宽阔的"之意。broad：普通用词，指向两边延伸的宽度，强调两边之间面积的广阔，也可指向四方伸展开去；wide：常用词，侧重指两边或两点之间的距离。着重距离的远近。

前句：这些小山碧绿陡峭，矗立在这条宽阔的河流之上。

后句：所有的厨房操作台都应该足够宽大，为制作食物提供足够的空间。

4. very，just 二者都含有"正好，就是"之意。very 是形容词，用来修饰名词，位于 the，this，my 等限定词后；just 作副词，用来修饰谓语（常为动词 be）或作状语的介词短语等，须放在 the，this，my 等限定词之前。

前句：就在学期开始的时候，他们举行了一次考试。

后句：他正是我所想要的演员。

5. have on 作"穿（戴）着"解，同 wear 一样，表状态，但不用于进行时态；put on 着重强调"穿（戴）上"的动作。

前句：小王今天穿着一件白衬衫。

后句：冬天，我喜欢外出时戴上帽子。

6. work on 表示"从事"、"创作"、"进行"，后面接名词、代词或 v-ing，强调做具体的事；还可表示"继续工作"、"努力说服"，既可作及物动词用，又可作不及物动词用；work at 表示"致力于"、"从事于"、"研究"、"学习"，后接名词、代词或 v-ing，强调把时间和精力等用在某一方面的事情上，侧重于说明所从事的工作性质。

前句：刘老师正在写一部新书。

后句:张先生正从事于一项新的发明。

7. would do sth., used to do sth.这两个短语都可以表示"过去经常做某事",但区别是:would do sth.表示过去某一段时间内习惯性的,但不规则的行为、活动,不与表状态的动词连用;used to do sth.在时间上主要是同现在对比,暗含"现在已不这样了"的意思;其后既可接表示动作的动词,也可接表示认知或状态的动词。

前句:他过去常常在河边一坐就是几个小时。

后句:他以前起床晚。

8. hit 表示"有目标地打",着重"打击"某一点;beat 表示"连续地打或拍",有"殴打、击败"之意。

前句:他打了他的脸。

后句:那个人被打得青一块、紫一块。

9. but, however 这两个连词都有"但是,可是,然而"之意。but 连接两个分句或有关部分,表示转折或逻辑上的对比关系,使用最广,口语中更为常见。however 转折意味比 but 弱,连接的两个分句或有关部分的关系较为松弛,后一部分常起附带说明或衬托作用。however 常以插入语形式出现在句子中间,前后用逗号隔开,也可置于句首或句末。

前句:我们热爱和平,但我们并不害怕战争。

后句:可是后来他决定去了。

10. by sea 意为"走海路,坐轮船",其中 by 表示乘坐交通工具或行走方式,by 与名词间不可用冠词;by the sea 意为"在海边",其中 by 表示"在……旁边",by 与后面的名词间常有冠词修饰。

前句:他们将坐轮船去美国。

后句:海边有个小村庄。

11. care about"关心,计较,在乎",指由于某事重要,或因责任所在而关心计较,一般用于否定句;care for"关心,照料,喜欢,愿意",作"关心,照料"讲,一般用于肯定句或疑问句。

前句:他不讲究衣着。

后句:你离开期间谁照顾你的孩子?

12. carry off 或 carry away 均可。但二者也有不同之处:carry off 可表示"夺去(某物)"、"带走……"、"运走……"、"夺得"某种奖赏;carry away 可表示"吸引住(某人)"。

前句:在毁掉村子之后,敌人把牲畜都掠走了。

后句:她的歌声令我们浑然忘我。

13. cheer 意为"欢呼",侧重表示高声呼叫以示欢迎,强调气氛的活跃,常含鼓励之意;greet 表示用语言、行动等"迎接",常含"友好、热情、亲切"之意。

前句:孩子们为他们的足球队喝彩。

后句：我们在大门口迎接客人。

14. clear away 表示"清除掉"、"收拾掉"、"散掉"、"消散"；clear up 表示"露出（喜色）"、"（天气）放晴"、"清理"、"整理"。

前句：我们必须清除掉我们当中的这些思想。

后句：她整理好书桌，然后向另一所学校走去。

15. come up 常表示位置"上升"；从水中或土中"冒出"；芽苗等"长出"；"引起注意、被提出"等；come out 常表秘密等"传出、被获悉"，书籍等的"出版"，"结果是"。

前句：你的问题在会上被提出来讨论。

后句：她的新书什么时候出版？

三、简要回答下列问题

1. 词汇图记忆策略训练是利用词汇的话题归属、范畴类别、词性等制作词汇图，帮助学生记忆词汇。

2.（1）既要力求使全班学生都投入活动，又要防止有的学生在活动中不懂装懂的现象。（2）既要合作学习，又要以个人学习作为合作学习的基础。（3）既要活跃，又要沉静，以适应外向和内向学生的需要。

3. 内容的教学组织策略，确定教学信息传播形式和媒体、教学内容传递顺序的教学传递策略；组织教学过程、安排教学秩序、呈现特定教学等等。

4. 专家进课堂听课，并进行诊断性反馈；教导处、教研室成员进课堂听课，并进行针对性的课堂指导；同事相互听课，借助录像等反馈技术进行反馈；通过观摩名师讲课对比自省。

5. 这是肯定的。词汇教学是语言教学中重要的组成部分，要提高学生的语言运用能力，无论是听、读还是说、写的技能，足够的词汇量都是基本的保证。

6. 教学设计不应该是一成不变的僵化的预设，而应该是根据教学过程中反馈的各种教学信息，不断地调整教学策略，甚至对教学过程中可能出现的问题，预设一些预案，从而在教学过程中根据教学反馈不断修正教学策略，促进教学有效性的提高。

7. 首先，语言不仅仅是把词汇植入语法句型中，而是还具有如邀请、同意或不同意、建议等的语言功能。交际教学法不仅是与语言有关，换句话说，它是有关如何使用语言的。交际教学法的第二个原则是如何让学生得到足够的语言接触，以及语言使用的机会。

8. 教学设计是一种理性化的教学准备活动，可以促进青年教师教学实践从经历到经验的提升，帮助教学经验不多的教师在短时间内成长为经验丰富的教师，达到可以根据教学信息反馈随时调整教学策略的目的。

9.（1）通过创意的导入激发兴趣和求知欲达到新课标的"情感态度目标"；（2）注重非感知输入，介绍文化背景清除阅读障碍；语言素质和课文结构分析并重，培养阅读策略，逐步增强语言素质；阅读教学应遵循整体性教学原则；在阅读教学中体现思想、情

感教育 思想情感教育;落实"培养阅读策略"贯彻课内外阅读相结合结果。

10.(1)组员一个一个地说,说出自己的见解;(2)别人说过的尽可能不重复;(3)轻轻地说,只要组内成员能听清楚;(4)注意听,听不懂的马上问;(5)整理小组研究成果,准备大组交流。

11. 主要有两种:一是表格式;二是流程图式。

12. 接受型学习、体验型学习、自主学习、合作学习和探究式学习等。

13. 这是最常见的教学模式,体现了通用的教学程序。阅读和听力中 PWP 是指 pre-reading, while-reading 和 post-reading。

14. 教师参与并没有错,但不能喧宾夺主。但当活动进展不顺利的时候,教师就不得不进行干预。比如说角色扮演的一方不知道该说什么了,或者讨论就要冷场了,那么教师就要采取行动。

15. 一是鼓励学生尽可能经常和不断地听,帮助学生做好听的准备。一次可能不够。鼓励学生对听的内容进行反应,而不是仅仅关注语言。不同听力阶段任务不同。

语言教学知识与能力练习题(七)

一、单项选择题

1. B 2. D 3. B 4. D 5. C 6. C 7. C 8. B 9. A 10. A 11. C 12. B 13. B 14. A 15. B

二、简答题

1. common 强调"常见的"、"普遍的"; ordinary 强调"平常的"、"平淡无奇的"。

前句:感冒在冬天很常见。

后句:他通常的晚餐不过是面包和牛奶。

2. general 意为"普遍的"、"一般的"; normal 指"正常的"、"正规的"、"常态的"。

前句:这本书是为一般读者写的,不是为专家写的。

后句:人的正常体温是多少?

3. country 意为"国家,国土",侧重指版图、疆域;nation 意为"民族,国家",侧重指人民、国民、民族。

前句:中国是一个历史悠久的伟大国家。

后句:听到这一噩耗,全国人民悲痛万分。

4. state 意为"国家、政府",侧重指政权、政体;land 意为"国土,国家",带有感情色彩,多用于文学作品中。

前句:在我国铁路为国家所有。

后句:这是我的祖国,我要用自己的生命保卫她!

5. cut off 表示"隔绝"、"断绝"、"(电路)切断"、"剪下"、"砍掉"; cut up 表示"切割开来"、"切碎"、"使难过"。

前句：大楼挡住了我们的视线。

后句：把蛋糕切开分给我们每人一块。

6. damp 指"潮湿的，使人感觉不舒服的"，相当于 rather wet；wet=covered with liquid or in a liquid state；not dry；rainy 指"含水分或其他液体的"、"湿的"、"下雨的，多雨的"。

前句：我不喜欢潮湿的天气。

后句：他浑身湿透。

7. demonstrate 意为"证明，论证"，以科学严谨的态度，通过推理、辩论或提供证据来证明事物的正谬。illustrate 指用实物、图片等进行"说明"，illustrate 后常用介词 by，with。

前句：演讲者用黑板阐明了他的观点。

后句：这些数字清晰地论证了国家所面临的经济问题的大致情况。

8. disgrace 指"失去别人的尊敬"、"因自己或别人的行为所产生的耻辱感"；dishonor 指"因自己的言行而丧失自尊或玷辱名誉"。

前句：他因为粗鄙的行为而为人所不齿。

后句：他的投敌行为对他的家庭是耻辱。

9. shame 指"由于失去自尊心而感到羞愧或羞耻"；scandal 指"引起公愤的行为"、"丑事"、"丑闻"。

前句：我认为那样浪费太可耻了。

后句：政府官员接受贿赂是可耻的事。

10. finally 用来表示某一动作发生的顺序是在"最后"；at last 表示经过一番曲折或努力之后某事才发生，强调其结果，其语气和感情色彩较强。

前句：最后关上灯锁好门。

后句：这项工程终于竣工了，我们可以休息了。

11. wear 主要用于穿衣服、戴眼镜（手套、首饰、帽）等，以强调"穿（戴）着"的状态；dress 既可作及物动词，又可作不及物动词，所接宾语是人而不是衣、帽等物。

前句：吴先生冬天总是穿着一件蓝色大衣。

后句：她母亲正在给她穿衣服。

12. 前句：他像侍者那样工作。（本身不是侍者）

后句：他做侍者工作。（本身是侍者）

13. live on 意为"以……为主食"，"靠……过活"，后接表示"食物"、"人"、"收入"等的词；live by 意为"靠……（手段）谋生"，后常接表示"获得经济手段"的名词或-ing 形式。

前句：那些士兵靠吃野菜为生。

后句：作家靠笔谋生，而渔夫以捕鱼为生。

14. once；as soon as 二者均为从属连词，引导时间状语从句，都表示主句的动作紧跟在从句的动作之后发生。主要区别在于：once 除含时间之意外，还表示"条件"，一般译作"一旦……就……";而 as soon as 强调的只是时间,译作"刚……就……"或"一……就……"。

前句:他一旦下定决心,就决不会放弃(本句不可用 as soon as)。

后句:我一到北京就写信给你。

15. get away from 表示"逃"的动作或行为,含有动作快速而敏捷之意,多用于口语中;get away with 表示"侥幸逃脱"。

前句:他从火灾中逃出来了。

后句:我不会让他用那种借口蒙混过关。

三、简要回答下列问题

1. 教学过程中遇生词的时候作解释;词汇的教学与其他语言活动相联系;课内或课外的专门词汇学习活动。

2. 教学目的有偏差,教学模式极端化;忽视非语言因素的教学;片面追求阅读材料教学,不追求质量;强调权威性,缺乏自主性。

3. 通常分为直接式和间接式。直接学习是直接的词汇练习和活动,如词形拼写练习、词汇游戏等。间接式学习则是学生的注意力并不在词汇学习上所进行。即:教师可以在教材内容的选择上考虑到词汇产生的原因是什么。

4. 任务呈现、任务准备、语言输入、任务完成、语言巩固。语言输入是教师呈现所学语言,让学生学习的环节。语言吸收是学生经过练习内化所学语言项目的环节。吸收是影响学生效果的最为关键的环节,没有吸收就不可能有语言学习的结果,这就不可能形成语言运用的能力。

5. 我们应基于学习目标、学习内容、学生特点和教学策略与教学过程的设计,依据各种教学媒体所具有的教学功能和特征,选择教学媒体和教学设计媒体辅助活动,而没有适用于所有教学内容和教学情境的媒体。

6. 一是要有自我意识,即自身对学习目的、学习动机等方面的认识;二是要有语言意识,学生要意识到语言是一个有组织的学习系统;三是要有自我评估能力,即学生能够监视和评价自己在学习过程中取得的进步。

7. 语言最基本的功能就是作为人类的交际工具,具体表现为听、说、读、写四个方面的技能。听、读是理解技能,说、写是表达技能。听、读是输入,说、写是输出,四项技能互相联系,互相依存,密不可分,一强俱强,一废俱废。因此必须全面发展,不可偏废。

8. 基于"互动性反思"的课堂教学研究是教师学科知识构建的主要途径之一,通常包括三种相互交织的过程。(1)描述有效教学具体过程和特点的"微观研究";(2)发现有效教学本质的"宏观研究";(3)提出教师专业发展原则的"理论归纳"。

9. (1)整体性原则;(2)细节理解和整体理解相结合的原则;(3)精读与泛读相结合的原则;(4)听说读写统筹兼顾的原则。

10. 在平时的教学过程中,尽管教师课前会预测学生的信息走向,并预备几种不同的教学方案,但在实际教学中,由师生互动、生生互动生成的资源是师生心智活动的产物,生动鲜活而又充满灵性,它稍纵即逝,可遇不可求;教师应该把握机会,引导学生对生成的资源进行进一步的挖掘,实现教学资源的优化与重组。

11. 分析、设计、评价、修正模式。其中有学习目标的分析、教学过程的设计、评价目的的确定,依据反馈不断修正教学策略,是至为关键的要素。

12. 自主学习是指学生在分析自我需求的前提下制订自己的学习计划、安排自己的学习活动、监控自己的学习行为、评价自己的学习效果、调整自己学习方式的一种学习行为。

13. 学生运用语言的时候常犯的错误有三种:一是疏忽,一旦老师指出,学生自己能矫正的错误;二是差错,是学生不能自己改正的错误,因此需要讲解;三是尝试,是当他们想表达却不知道怎样去表达的时候犯的错误,可以由老师或同学帮助纠错。

14. 读物是分级的,即不同级别的人使用适合于本级别的语言材料,才能使学生更有效地使用阅读材料,这样学生才能在阅读中得到乐趣,尽量不要让他们读太难的文章,否则他们会把阅读材料丢到一边去。

15. 可分为消遣性阅读和理解性阅读。

语言教学知识与能力练习题(八)

一、单项选择题

1. A 2. B 3. D 4. B 5. A 6. B 7. D 8. B 9. C 10. D 11. D 12. A 13. C 14. D 15. D

二、简答题

1. give up 指因行为或努力受挫或别的原因而主动放弃,可用作及物动词,跟名词或 v-ing 作宾语;也可作不及物动词。give in 指不再坚持自己的行为或观点等,而按别人的要求去做,一般作不及物动词。

前句:除有两个中途放弃外,其他的姑娘都跑完了比赛的全程。

后句:由于双方都不肯让步,所以没能达成协议。

2. hand down 作"把……传下来"解;hand over 作"转交"或"移送"解。

前句:这个故事世代相传。

后句:请将这笔钱转交小周。

3. like, as 二者用作介词时,as 强调同类属或完全像,往往指本身就是;like 侧重于比较,本身不是。

前句:她像老师那样工作。(本身不是老师)

后句:她做老师的工作。(本身是老师)

4. like, as 二者都可以用作连词,作"像……一样"解,但 like 多用于非正式的美国英语里,as 用于较为正式的场合。此外 as 从句中的谓语部分可以省略,而 like 从句中则不能省略谓语。

前句:请像李先生那样做实验。(does 可以省略)

后句:那鱼的味道不应该是那样的。

5. genuine 多用来指不是伪造的;real 可以指与现实相符。

前句:有一幅毕加索的真画。

后句:南京大屠杀是一些确凿的事实之一。

6. everyday 作形容词,表示每天的,或日常的;every day,表示每一天,作状语。

前句:这只是一件日常小事。

后句:她天天上学。

7. elder, eldest 用于长幼之长;older, oldest 用于实际年龄之大。注意:英、美用法不同:(英)He was the eldest of four childen.(美)He was the oldest of four childen.

前句:他是我的哥哥。

后句:我有一个哥哥。(实际上却表示这个哥哥比此前提到过的另一个哥哥年长。)

8. 两者都可表示"借",但是 borrow 指"借入",而 lend 则指"借出"。

前句:她借给他一些钱。

后句:他向她借了一些钱。

9. little 通常指小和可爱,往往带有感情色彩,它的反义词是 great,big;small 是中性词,不带感情色彩,主要用来强调形体、年龄、大小,它的反义词是 great,large。

前句:她是一个可爱的小女孩。

后句:她是一个年龄不大的女孩。

10. for example 和 such as 都可当作"例如"解。但 such as 用来列举事物,插在被列举事物与前面的名词之间;for example 意为用来举例说明,有时可作为独立语,插在句中,不影响句子其他部分的语法关系。

前句:这个农场种植各种各样的庄稼,例如麦子、玉米、棉花和稻米。

后句:这儿的许多人,例如约翰先生,宁愿喝咖啡。

11. astonish 语气比 surprise 要强,含有令人难以置信的意思;surprise 最普通用词,意为"使惊讶,使吃惊",含有"意想不到"之意。

前句:在西藏见到他,我真感到惊异。

后句:看到家乡的巨大变化我惊讶不已。

12. shake 用作不及物动词时,可指人或物"摇动,发抖"。指人时常用于因感情激动、寒冷、惧怕引起的身体颤动。在表示"因……而颤抖"时,多用 with;在表示"使……受震撼,使(信念等)动摇",常用于 be shaken by/with/at 中;tremble 用作及物动词时,意指"使……战栗,使……震颤,使……发抖(因恐惧、愤怒、寒冷、体弱等)",常常与 shake

相互替换,但指握手、摇头或捧腹大笑时用 shake;tremble 常用作不及物动词。

前句:这个可怜的男孩正冻得发抖。

后句:她气得声音发抖。

13. rise 指自然"上升",常用于日、月、云、霞、烟、水蒸气、物价、温度、河水、潮水及人的职位等;raise 指用外部的力量,"举起、提高"。

前句:他已经升职了。

后句:人民的生活水平已大大地提高了。

14. burst into + sth.; burst out + doing.

前句:她突然哭起来了。

后句:她突然哭起来了。

15. suppose 常指根据一些证据而得出的推断,强调暂时性,可接不定式(特别是 to be)、介词短语、形容词等的复合结构,接从句等,作"假定、猜想"等解;guess 表达说话人在缺乏了解和证据时所陈述的见解,其后可接名词、复合宾语、从句。

前句:让我们假定他是对的。

后句:猜猜看这东西值多少钱。

三、简要回答下列问题

1. 形成性评价是指在教学过程中为了获得有关学习的反馈信息,对学生所学知识的掌握程度所进行的系统性评价,是日常教学过程中由学生和教师共同参与的评价活动,其目的是对学生的学习行为、学习结果以及学习过程中的情感、态度、策略等方面的而发展进行评价。

2. 首先,语言不仅仅是把词汇植入语法句型中,而是还具有如邀请、同意或不同意、建议等的语言功能。交际教学法不仅是与语言有关,换句话说,它是有关如何使用语言的。

交际教学法的第二个原则是如何让学生得到足够的语言接触,以及语言使用的机会。它还能提醒教师,人们学习语言是为了运用语言,指点他们注意使用时的风格和得体。

3. 一是以学生为中心,发挥教师的主导作用;二是开展策略学习,培养学生的策略意识;三是从外部监督逐渐发展成为内部监督;四是构建自主学习中心,提供自助学习资源。

4. 这种情况下,即时插入的纠错是不合适的。因为它会干扰活动的流程,并在学生应该尽最大努力要激活他们语言知识的时候,却抑制了他们。

5. 先行组织者教学策略:先行组织者是指在学习任务之前教师呈现学生的引导性材料,目的是以旧知识来导入、整合和联系当前学习任务中的新知识。

探究教学策略:英语教学过程是学生的探究过程。探究教学策略认为,一切知识都是尝试性的,学生从自身的兴趣出发,通过自身的体验主动获取知识。

6.(1)教学理论:理论的指导是教学设计由经验层次上升到理性、科学层次的一个基本前提。(2)学生特点:教学设计的基本特征之一是它既关心"教"又关心"学"。(3)教学实际需要:教学设计从根本上讲是为了满足教学活动的实际需要,是为教学活动的实际展开提供行动方案。(4)教师经验。

7. 教师应为学生建构对知识的理解提供一种理论框架,将复杂的学习任务加以分解,引导学生对所学知识不断深入。

8.(1)设计课堂教学的整体思路和环节,一般包括复习、引入、新课讲解、知识应用、反馈练习。(2)处理教材教法和学生实际之间联系的方法。(3)表述每一环节,每个层次、每个步骤的设想安排,以及这样的依据和预期效果。(4)科学分配和利用课堂教学时间。(5)设计习题。

9. 教学目标是教学活动预期达到的结果,是由一系列有递进关系的目标组成的系统,它是教学活动的出发点和归宿,是课堂教学的灵魂。教学目标是教师组织教学内容、运用教学方法、教学策略、教学媒体以及调控教学环境的基本依据,也是评价教学活动效果的基本依据;同时,明确具体的教学目标也是学生自我激励、自我评估、自我调控的重要手段。所以,在教学设计中,科学合理地确定好具体的教学目标,对于保证教学活动的顺利进行具有十分重要的作用。

10.(1)在编写形式上;(2)在编写内容上;(3)对于教学目标的理解和陈述上;(4)在出发点上。

11. 一般而言,在教学活动实施前要有"准备性评价";在教学活动实施中,要设计并实施"形成性评价";在教学活动告一段落后,要设计并实施"终结性评价"。教学评价采用的具体方法是多种多样的,有课堂提问、讨论、练习,有各种测验、考试、情境测试,还有实验、实践、任务完成等等。

12.(1)教学目标设计;(2)教学内容设计;(3)教学方法设计;(4)教学时间设计;(5)教学评价设计。

13. 促进者、监控者和参与者。

14. 引导注意、告诉学生目标、刺激对先前学习的回忆、呈示刺激材料、提供学习指导、诱导行为、提供反馈、评定行为、增强记忆与促进迁移。

15. 英语"四位一体"复习法将高考英语总复习分为:阶段训练、专项训练、综合训练和模拟训练四个阶段。

语言教学知识与能力练习题(九)

一、单项选择题

1. D 2. D 3. B 4. A 5. B 6. D 7. C 8. C 9. A 10. B 11. D 12. D 13. C 14. B 15. A

二、简答题

1. between 常用于两者之间；among 一般指三者或三者以上之间。若指三者以上的每两个部分之间时，仍然要用 between。

    前句：这个女孩走在她父亲和母亲之间。

    后句：她在她同学当中是最高的。

2. above all 意为"尤其是"、"首先"、"最重要的是"，常位于句首或句中，作插入语，起强调作用；after all 意为"毕竟"、"终究"、"终归"、"到底"，在句中位置较灵活。可位于句首、句中或句末。

    前句：但首先快些告诉我该做什么。

    后句：毕竟，两周后就是你的生日。

3. thing 意为"事情、事物"，不管大事小事、好事坏事均称为 thing，一般不能专指事务；复数 things 还可作"形势"解。matter 侧重指须留心的要事或问题、难题。

    前句：这可能是一件有积极意义的事情。

    后句：这是一件不愉快的事。

4. a great deal 用作名词，意为"大量"，"许多"，作主语、宾语；用作副词，意为"很"或"非常"；作状语，修饰动词或用来强调比较级。a great deal of 意为"大量的"，"非常多的"，相当于 much，作定语，后接不可数名词。

    前句：经过大量研究后，这（被认为）是最好的办法。

    后句：大量的金钱花在那个工程上了。

5. agree on 作"就……取得一致意见"解。agree to 意为"同意……"，其后跟表示"计划/条件/建议"等一类的名词或代词。

    前句：上月，就建一座新汽车厂之事达成了协议。

    后句：他们已同意我们的计划。

6. allow 与 permit 用法的区别是：permit 通常指上级、规则或法令等表示的准许，其语气较重；而 allow 通常指不加反对，有时含有听任或默许之意，语气较轻。

    前句：参观者不准拍照。

    后句：他的父母不允许他在外待得很晚。

7. though 用作连词意为"虽然"引导状语从句。though 用作副词，可以放在句末，表示"但是"。

    前句：他虽然相信它，但却不肯有所行动。

    后句：他们说他们会来，可是他们并没有来。

8. argue 着重就自己的看法或观点，提出论证，同他人"争论"或"辩论"。argue 同 with 搭配，其后接人；与 about 连用，其后接事物。quarrel 是指对某事不喜欢或强烈不满而发生的"争吵"或"吵架"。同 with 搭配，其后接某人；和 about 连用，其后接某事。

    前句：这个问题我们同他们辩论了很长时间。

后句:他常为家务事同妻子争吵。

9. asleep / sleeping 二者都是形容词。asleep 仅用作表语,不能作定语,表示"睡着,熟睡"的意思;而 sleeping 一般只能用作定语,放在名词前,表示"睡眠中的,休止的"意思。

前句:这里有一个熟睡的婴儿。

后句:他头枕着手臂在熟睡。

10. even though,意为"即使",引导让步状语从句。though 也引导让步状语从句,意为"虽然";even though 有退一步设想的意味,与 though 不同。though 引导的句子所说的是事实,even though 引导的句子所说的则不一定是事实。

前句:即使他知道这个秘密,他也不肯说出来。

后句:他虽然知道这个秘密,但他不会说出来。

11. attack 是常用词,指"攻击敌人"或"用言论攻击他人";charge 指"猛攻"、"猛冲"、"冲锋"。

前句:德国在1941年开始进攻苏联。

后句:骑兵向前线猛冲。

12. at the time 通常用于过去时句子中,指某件事情发生的"当时"、"那时";at a time 意为"一次",表示一个时间单位。它常与表示数量的词语连用,表示频率。

前句:当时,许多人都看到了这件奇怪的事情发生。

后句:这些药每天服三次,每次服三粒。

13. as 与 since 引导的从句多置于句首,不过 as 表示十分明显的原因,只说明一般的因果关系,可译为"因为,由于";而 since 则表示稍加分析、大家已知的原因,一般可译为"既然"。

前句:由于他身体欠佳,我决定独自去那里。

后句:既然大家都到了,咱们就开始吧。

14. 用于肯定句中时,except 意为"除……外(不再有)";besides 意为"除……外(还有)"。

前句:除了汤姆外,他们都去看过那里。

后句:除了汤姆去过那里外,他们也都去过了。

15. be to do sth. 表示按计划或安排即将发生的动作,后可跟时间状语;be about to do sth. 表示打算或安排即将发生的动作,它通常不与时间状语连用。

前句:十点钟以前你得交上试卷。

后句:我正要出去,这时有人敲门。

三、简要回答下列问题

1.(1)交际原则;(2)任务原则;(3)意义原则。

2. 没有语言能力就不可能有基础坚实的语言交际能力,语言能力和语言交际两者不可分割。交际能力在语言运用中体现。语言能力是交际能力的重要组成部分,是交际能力的基础，而语言交际能力也包含着语言能力，是检验语言能力的基础。离开了语言能力，语言交际便成了无源之水；离开了语言交际，语言能力又成了空中楼阁。交际能力是一种综合能力，它是诸多分项能力的合力。两者相辅相成，互为因果。

3. 就是语义的演变。语义可以扩大（Extension），也可以缩小（Reduction）；可以变为褒义（Amelioration），也可以变为贬义（Deterioration）；或作为隐喻（Metaphor）使词义有所变化。（可替换术语：semantic shift 语义演变，shift of meaning 语义演变，vocabulary change 词汇变化。）

4. 所谓教学设计，简单地说，就是指教师为达成一定的教学目标，对教学活动进行的系统规划、安排与决策。具体说来，教学设计是教师以现代教学理论为基础，依据教学对象的特点和自己的教学观念、经验、风格，运用系统的理论与方法，分析教学中的问题和需要，确定教学目标，建立解决问题的步骤，合理组合和安排各种教学要素，为优化教学效果而制定实施方案的系统计划过程。

5. 以词汇意义探究为例，学生通过搜集图片、听录音、猜词义并加以模仿的方式，无需借助教师的讲解和翻译就可以掌握词的意义。

6. 构建主义倡导以学生为中心，认为他们是知识意义的主动建构者。同时，教师是整个教学过程的组织者、指导者和协调者，对学生的意义构建起促进作用，因为以学为中心的教学设计的每一个环节都离不开教师的有效启发、认真组织和精心指导。

7. 教师应为学生构建知识的理解提供一种理论框架，将复杂的学习任务加以分解，引导学生对所学知识不断深入。

8. 即了解学生的初始状态，包括他们的原有知识水平、技能和学习动机、学习准备、状态等；分析学生从初始状态到教学目标要求之间的距离，其间学生应掌握的知识技能或应形成的态度和行为习惯。

9. 交际教学法是以社会语言学理论、心理语言学理论为基础，以交际功能为大纲，以交际能力培养为目标的教学法体系。

10. 语言能力、社会语言能力、语篇能力和策略能力。

11. （1）听并重复；（2）填空；（3）造句；（4）使用有意义的上下文；（5）使用图片；（6）使用绕口令。

12. 课外学习活动是对学生课内语言内容的补充和巩固。主要形式有参加英语角活动、看英语原版电影、收看英语电视节目、阅读英语原版小说、用英语写电子书信等等。

13. 促进者、监控者和参与者。

14. 可以根据需要删掉某一课，但需要用合适的材料把教材上的东西换掉。第二个选择就是给教材加东西，最后一个选择是教师自己改变教材内容。简言之，就是根据学生的需求和教师的知识和经验把"教材内容"变为"教学内容"。

15. 写作给学生提供更多的思考空间，这就让他们有更多的机会进行语言加工；另一方面,为写作而写作是为了培养他们的写作技能,写作关注的是全文,也包括文章的结构、格式、风格和效果。

语言教学知识与能力练习题(十)

一、单项选择题

1. A 2. A 3. C 4. A 5. D 6. D 7. B 8. A 9. C 10. D 11. B 12. A 13. D 14. B 15. C

二、简答题

1. beat 强调连续或反复地"打",因此像心脏跳动、打鼓、打拍子等之类具有连续性或反复性的动作,一般要用 beat。hit 表示有意或无意地打或撞等,往往含有重重一击或用力敲打等之意。

前句:谁在击鼓?

后句:他重重地打了她一耳光。

2. break into 表示"强行进入"、"闯入"、"破门而入"、"打断(谈话、讨论)"、"突然……起来";break in 表示"闯入"、"打断"、"插嘴",其中 in 是副词。

前句:昨晚小偷到布朗先生家行窃,偷走很多东西。

后句:我们外出度假时,小偷闯入屋内行窃,偷走很多东西。

3. bring on 表示使发生、引起。端上(饭菜)。bring in 为引来、引进、吸收。

前句:天气突然变冷,使他再次感冒。

后句:我们也从英语中吸收了一些词汇。

4. destroy 意为"破坏、摧毁、消灭、毁灭",通常指程度非常严重的"毁坏",一般情况下不可以修复再用。另外,它既可表示毁坏具体的物品,也可表示毁坏抽象的东西。ruin 多用于借喻之中,有时泛指一般性的破坏,指把某物损坏到了不能再使用的程度。

前句:这场大火把整座房子都烧毁了。

后句:我被那场官司毁了,我破产了。

5. moist 指"微湿的"、"湿润的",常含"不十分干,此湿度是令人愉快的"意思;humid 为正式用语,常表示"空气中湿度大的"。

前句:草被露水润湿了。

后句:在东方,夏季空气潮湿。

6. get rid of 表示"处理",侧重"消灭、摆脱或清除";deal with 侧重"处理"的手段、方法或方式。

前句:我们要除掉田里的草。

后句:他们怎样处理这类事件?

7. find 意为"找到、发现",指找到或发现自己所需要的东西或丢失的东西,着重指找到的结果;find out 指经过研究或询问查明某事的真相。

前句：我们已在南海发现了石油。

后句：你能查出火车几点发出？

8. disgrace 指"失去别人的尊敬"、"因自己或别人的行为所产生的耻辱感"。shame 指"由于失去自尊心而感到羞愧或羞耻"。

前句：他因为行为不检而为人所不齿。

后句：我认为那样浪费太可耻了。

9. ever since 意为"从……之后一直"，其中的 since 既可作副词，也可作连词，该短语与完成时连用，有时 ever 可以省略。ever before 意为"比以往任何时候"，其中的 before 为副词，常与比较级连用并放在 than 之后。ever 用来加强 before 的语气，before 有时可以省略。

前句：他 1969 年去了西藏，自此一直住在那里。

后句：花儿比以往更漂亮了。

10. glance 意为"匆匆一瞥"，是不及物动词，其后必须接介词 at, over 等才可以接宾语；stare 意为"凝视"，它也是一个不及物动词，其后通常接介词 at 才能接宾语。

前句：他匆匆看了一下手表。

后句：她惊讶地瞪着他看。

11. escape 指安全地"逃走或跑掉"，强调结果；flee 强调"逃"这一动作急促或迅速，不强调结果。选用时根据上下文的含义来定。

前句：他从火灾中逃出来了。

后句：他从燃烧的房子中逃出。

12. give up 指行为或努力受挫或别的原因而主动放弃，可用作及物动词，跟名词或 v-ing 作宾语；也可作不及物动词；give out 意为"用完，耗尽，体力不支"，是不及物动词。

前句：除有两个中途放弃外，其他的姑娘都跑完了比赛的全程。

后句：走了很长的路，我已筋疲力尽，再也走不动了。

13. have sb./ sth. do 为"使(让、请)某人做某事"之意，其中作宾补的不带 to 的不定式只表示发生过某事；have sb./ sth. doing 为"让某人(某事)一直做某事"之意，其中作宾补的现在分词表示保持或一直存在的状态。

前句：士兵们让男孩站着。

后句：两个骗子让灯整夜地亮着。

14. have sth. done 意为"(主语)让(别人)做某事"。有两层含义和用法：其一，作"(有意地)让他人为自己做某事"解，其二，作"(无意识地)让某人(物)被做(遭受不幸)"解。即过去分词所表示的动作由别人完成，而宾语是过去分词所表示动作的承受者或动作对象。

前句：我要用这种布料做一套新衣服。

后句:他的手提包被人偷了。

15. knock...into...意为"把……插／撞／敲／打入……中";knock at / on 意为轻轻而有节奏地"敲"。它常用来表示"敲门／窗"等。

前句:然后他们把木棒插入泥土中。

后句:谁在敲门?

三、简要回答下列问题

1. 最好的处理办法是照常推进教学活动。

2. Make somebody known by name to one another. eg. "Mum, this is my teacher, Miss Yang." "That's TangLin. Come on. I'll introduce you."

3. 研究性学习法是指学生基于自身兴趣,在教师指导下,从自然、社会和学生自身生活中选择和确定研究专题,主动地获取知识、应用知识、解决问题的学习活动。

4. (1)创设学习条件的方法指导;(2)心理调节的方法指导;(3)掌握知识的方法指导;(4)学习各环节的方法指导;(5)学习各具体学科的方法指导。

5. (1)互动观;(2)目标观;(3)师生观;(4)形式观;(5)情感观。

6. (1)人与自然关系领域;(2)人与社会关系领域;(3)人与文化关系领域;(4)人与自我关系领域。

7. 英语教学内容是英语教师根据自己的教学目标对英语课堂活动中可能涉及的知识、技能、策略、情感等语言学习内容及其结构关系的一种个人选择。因此,"教学内容"不能等同于"教材内容",英语教师选择教学内容,也不像从教材上选择"可以教的语言点"那么简单,它是教师利用自己的教师知识和经验所进行的一种创造,即对课堂上学生所需英语学习活动(包括学生的学习行为、条件和结果)的综合策划。

8. 首先,教学策略来自教师对教学理论的分析和判断;其次,教学策略还产生于对具体教学方法和技巧的深入分析和思考;最后,对教学经验的总结和反思也有利于教学策略的产生。借助于教学经验的反思,如记教学日记或教学观摩,教师会加深对个人经验的认识。

9. 本着"做中学"的教学方法,通过口头表达、交际活动,使学习延伸为一种技能,使其与现实生活相链接。

10. 学科的特性:不同学科由于其特点的差异,要求采用不同的教学方法,例如:小学教育作为终身学习的基础阶段,既要重视语言素质,又要重视综合素质。

学生的认知水平和年龄特点:对教学方法的选择在一定程度上是对学生原有知识状态和认知特点的合理估计和预测。例如:性格外向的学生在课堂活动中容易处于主动地位,而性格内向的学生只能被动地参与。

11. 先行组织者教学策略,先行组织者是指在学习任务之前教师呈现给学生的引导性材料,目的是以旧知识来导入、整合和联系当前学习任务重的新知识。

探究教学策略,英语教学过程是学生的探究过程。探究教学策略认为,一切知识都是尝试性的,学生从自身的兴趣出发,通过自身的体验主动获取知识。

12. 学情是指学生在某一个单位时间内或在某一个学习活动中的学习状况。它包括学习兴趣、学习习惯、学习方式、学习思路、学习进程、学习效果等诸多要素。学情具有多样性,这是由学习主体的多元性决定的。而学情的多样性就是个体差异存在的根本原因,忽视学情就会忽视个体差异。

13. 建构主义倡导以学生为中心,认为他们是知识意义的主动建构者。同时,教师是整个教学过程的组织者、指导者和协调者,对学生的意义构建起促进作用,因为以学为中心的教学设计的每一个环节都离不开教师的有效启发、认真组织和精心指导。

14. 教师应为学生建构对知识的理解提供一种理论框架,将复杂的学习任务加以分解,引导学生多所学知识不断深入。

15.(1)反映所学英语材料的语用特征;(2)学生易于接受且易于设置。

模块三 英语学科教学设计能力

一、教学设计题(一)

Ⅰ. Teaching aim

1. Students will be able to know the development of English and feel the role that culture plays in the change of language.

2. Comprehend the whole passage.

3. Students will be able to know how to get the key sentence of a paragraph.

Ⅱ. Teaching procedures

Step 1　Lead-in

Ask students several questions in the form of brain storming.

1. Do you know the countries where people speak English? List them on a piece of paper.

2. What are the two main groups of English?

3. Do you know the differences between British English and American English?

4. Do you know the history of English?

Step 2　Fast reading

1. Prediction

English is not only different from country to country, but also different from what it was before. Read the title "the road to modern English" and predict what the passage is mainly about?

2. Filling in the form

Ask the students to scan the text to find or make out a key sentence for each paragraph, and let them find out key sentence of each paragraph or ask them to summarize the main point for each paragraph in their own words.

Paragraph 1: The spread of the English language in the world

Paragraph 2: Native speaker can understand each other but they may not be able to understand everything.

Paragraph 3-4: All languages change when cultures communicate with one another.

Paragraph 5: English is spoken as a foreign language or second language in Africa and Asia.

Step 3 Intensive reading

1. Comprehending

Enjoy the whole passage paragraph by paragraph again. Pay special attention to the following questions:

(1) How did old English develop into modern English?

(2) Why does English change all the way?

(3) What other Englishes developed from the old English?

(4) Give the three major periods of the development of English.

(5) Who promoted the spread of English?

(6) Although the native speakers speak English, yet sometimes they can not understand each other well, why?

Because there exist differences between different Englishes, not only in vocabulary, but also in pronunciation and spelling. (hot/mum/honour/ honor/neighbour/neighor...)

(7) How do these differences come about? (Why does English change over time?)

Because of cultural communication.

(8) Besides the countries where English is used as a native language, where else is English used as a foreign language?

South Asia, India, South Africa, Singapore, Malaysia and China.

2. Filling in the chart

A.D.450—1150	English was based on _____
_____	English was more like French.
At the end of the 16th century	How many people speak English? _____
_____	Shakespeare made use of a wider vocabulary.
_____	American English gained its own identity.
Later	_____ English had its identity.

3. Answer the following questions

(1) What is the clue of the passage?

(2) Why does India have a very number of English speakers?

(3) When did people from England begin to move to other parts of the world?

Step 4 Post-Reading

T: From the passage we can see English is widely accepted as a native, second or third language. No wonder the number of people learning English in China is increasing rapidly. Will Chinese English become one of the world Englishes? ——"Only time will tell."

T: How do you understand this sentence?

— It means that something can only be known in the future.

T: What can you infer from this sentence about the development of English in China?

— It indicates that it remains to be seen just how much the Chinese culture will influence the English language in the present country.

Step 5 Language focus

(1) **even if** = even though: in spite of the fact; no matter whether: He likes to help us even if he is very busy.

(2) **communicate with** = exchange information or conversation with other people: He learnt to use body language to communicate with deaf customers.

(3) **actually** = in fact: used when you are adding new information to what you have just said: We've known for years. Actually, since we were babies.

(4) **be based on**...= in a way that depends on differences in situations

(5) **make use of** = use sth. available

(6) **Only time will tell** = to say that something can only be known in the future: Will China's national football team enter for the next finals of the World Cup? Only time will tell.

Step 6 Discussion

Work in groups. Discuss the question and then ask two groups to report their answers to the class.

1. Why do you think people all over the world want to learn English?

Possible answer:

The reasons why people all over the world want to learn English:

★ With economy globalization, English has become the best bridge to serve the purpose of people all over the world communicating with one another.

★ However, like all major languages in the world, English is always changing. In order to adjust to native speakers from different parts of the world, it is a must for people all over the world to learn English, whether in English speaking countries or in non-English speaking countries.

★ Also, people from different parts of the world speak English with various accent and dialects, and people have to learn about the difference between different kinds of English in order to avoid misunderstanding while communicating.(All persuasive reasons can be accepted.)

Step 7 Homework

1. Read the passage as fluently as you can.

2. Find out some words and sentences you think are beautiful and recite them.

3. p.11, Exx. 2.3.4

二、教学设计题（二）

Unit 5　Music
THE BAND THAT WASN'T

I. Aims

1. To learn to talk about kinds of music.

2. To learn to read about bands.

II. Procedures

Step 1　Warming up

Thinking and saying:

Have you heard about any of the famous bands in the world? List some if you can.

Step 2　Pre-reading

1. Listening, talking and sharing

Let's listen to some pieces of music from different bands. Work in groups of four. Tell your group mates which band you like best. Why? Then the group leader is to stand up and share the group idea with the class.

2. Do you know anything about "The Monkees"?

Step 3　Reading

1. Reading aloud to the recording

Now please listen and read aloud to the recording of the text THE BAND THAT WASN'T. Pay attention to the pronunciation of each word and the pauses within each sentence. I will play the tape twice and you shall read aloud twice, too.

2. Reading and underlining

Next you are to read and underline all the useful expressions or collocations in the passage. Copy them to your notebook after class as homework.

Collocations from THE BAND THAT WASN'T

Dream of doing, at a concert, with sb. clapping and enjoying..., sing karaoke, be honest with oneself, get to form a band, high school students, practice one's music, play to passers-by, in the subway, earn some extra money, begin as a TV show, play jokes on..., be based loosely on..., the TV organizers, make good music, put an advertisement in a newspaper, look for rock musicians, pretend to do sth., the attractive performances, be copied by..., support them fiercely, become more serious about..., play their own instruments, produce one's own records, start touring, break up, in the mid-1980s, a celebration of one's time as a real band.

---

3. Reading to identify the topic sentence of each paragraph

Skim the text and identify the topic sentence of each paragraph. You may find it either at the beginning, the middle or the end of the paragraph.

4. Find out the main idea of each paragraph

> 1st paragraph: How do people get to form a band?
> 2nd paragraph: Most musicians meet and form a band.
> 3rd paragraph: One band started as a TV show.
> 4th paragraph: "The Monkees" became even more popular than "The Beatles".

5. Reading and transferring information

Read the text again to complete the tables, which list how people formed a band and how The Monkees was formed by the TV organizers and became a real band.

(1) How do people get to form a band?

Members	High school students.
Reasons	They like to write and play music.
Places	They practice their music in someone's home.
Forms	They may play to passers-by in the street or subway.
Results	They can earn some extra money. They may also have a chance to dream of becoming famous.

(2) How was The Monkees formed and became a real band?

The Monkees in 1968 (left to right): Micky Dolenz, Peter Tork, Mike Nesmith & Davy Jones.

beginning of the band	It began as a TV show.
style of the performance	They played jokes on each other as well as played music.
first music and jokes	Most of them were based loosely on the band called "The Beatles".
development of the band	They became more serious about their work and started to play their own instruments and write their own songs like a real band. They produced their own records and started touring and playing their own music.
changes of the band	The band broke up in about 1970, but reunited in the mid-1980s. They produced a new record in 1996, which was a celebration of their time as a real band.

6. Reading and understanding difficult sentences

As you have read the text times, you can surely tell which sentences are difficult to understand. Now put your questions concerning the difficult points to me.

Step 4　Consolidation

1. Do the comprehending exercises No. 1, 2, 3 and 4.

2. Do you think the TV organizers were right to call "The Monkees" a band when they did not sing or write their own songs? Why?

3. Do you agree that the jokes were more important than the music for this band? Give a reason.

4. A tree diagram

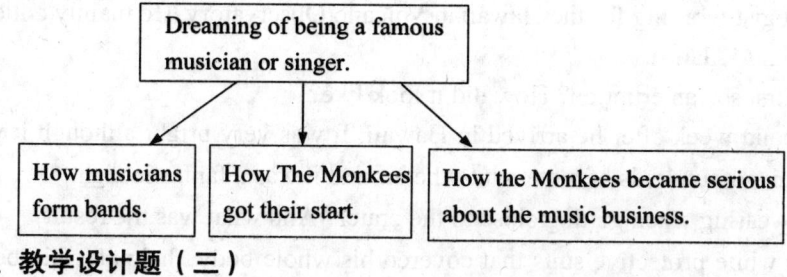

三、教学设计题（三）

Unit 5　The power of nature

Ⅰ. Teaching aims

1. Enable the students to grasp and remember the detailed information of the reading material.

2. Let students understand the general idea of the passage.

Ⅱ. Teaching important & Difficult points

Help the students to grasp and remember the detailed information of the reading material.

Ⅲ. Teaching aids

a tape recorder, a projector, slides and pictures

Ⅳ. Teaching method

Group or pair disscussion, individual task.

Ⅴ. Teaching procedure

Step 1　Pre-reading

1. Can you imagine climbing into an active volcano to take the temperature of the boiling rock inside?

2. To be a volcanologist, what qualities are needed?

Step 2　A quiz

Are you suitable for being a volcanologist?

Question	Yes	No
1. Do you like working outside as well as inside?		
2. Do you enjoy travelling to unusual places?		
3. Do you enjoy taking risks?		
4. Do you dislike doing the same thing every day?		
5. Do you like adventure in your life?		
6. Are you interested in studying rocks and other things that make up the surface of the earth?		

What kind of work do you think a volcanologist do?

Step 3　Skimming

Skim the text and answer the following questions.

1. What is the writer?

He is a volcanologist working for the Hawaiian Volcano Observatory. He mainly collects information about Mount Kilauea.

2. When did he first see an eruption? How did it look like?

It was in the second week after he arrived in Hawaii. It was very bright although it was night. Red lava fountained hundreds of meters into the air and it was a fantastic sight.

3. What was he wearing when getting close to the crater? And what was the result?

He was wearing white protective suits that covered his whole body, helmets, big boots and special gloves, just like a spaceman. As a result, it made him difficult to walk.

Step 4　Scanning

Scan the text and answer the following questions.

1. Why is a volcanologist's job important?

Volcanologists study volcanoes so that they can warn people when the volcano is going to erupt and so save many lives.

2. Why is the lava that flows on Mount Kilauea more dangerous than the actual eruption?

The lava flows down the mountain and can cover up or burn villages in its path. The rocks that erupt from the volcano usually don't damage anything because no one lives near the crater.

3. Why did the scientists have to get close to the volcano after it began erupting?

The scientists needed to get samples of the lava so they could study them.

4. What does the writer find impressive about volcanoes even after studying them for 20 years?

The author is impressed by the beauty of the eruption and also by its potential to cause great destruction.

Step 5　Detailed reading

Read the text more carefully and answer the following questions.

1. What made the author realize that an eruption occurred?

my bed began shaking/a strange sound/My bedroom became as bright as day./an absolutely fantastic sight/red hot lava was fountaining hundreds of meters into the air.

2. What did the scientists do after the eruption?

(1) Put on white protective suits, helmets, big boots.

(2) Dropped as closed as possible to the crater.

(3) Slowly make our way to the edge of the crater.

(4) Looked down into the red boiling center.

Step 6　Homework

1. Find out words, expressions and sentences which you think are useful, important or difficult to understand.

2. Finish exercises in Learning about Language. (Exx. 1, 2)

四、教学设计题（四）

Unit 1　Festivals around the World

Ⅰ. Teaching goals

1. To get the students to talk about festivals.

2. To learn about how festivals begin and how to celebrate festivals so as to enable them to learn more about different cultures while learning different language.

3. To develop the students' reading skills: skimming, scanning, summarizing, and finding out details.

4. To arouse the students' interest in festivals, cultures, especially those in China, thus promote their culture awareness.

Ⅱ. Important points

1. Comprehension of the reading part.

2. Knowledge accumulation of festivals and cultures.

3. Useful words and expressions concerning festivals.

Ⅲ. Teaching aids

A computer, a projector, courseware, a tape-recorder

Ⅳ. Teaching procedures

Step 1　Revision

Revise the festivals

Festivals	Time
The Spring Festival	Lunar January 1
The Lantern Festival	Lunar January 15
The Tree-planting Day	March 12
The Qingming Festival	April 4—6
The Dragon Boat Festival	Lunar May 5
The Double Seventh Festival	Lunar July 7
Teachers' Day	September 10
The Double Ninth Festival	Lunar September 9
The National Day	October 1
New Year's Day	January 1
Valentine's Day	February 14
Fool's Day	April 1
Labour's Day	May 1
Children's Day	June 1
Halloween	October 31
Thanksgiving Day	The fourth Thursday in November
Christmas Day	December 25

Step 2　Pre-reading

What is your favourite holiday of the year? Why?

Step 3　Fast reading

1. How many kinds of festivals are mentioned in the text? What are they?

2. Let's get to know more about these festivals and fill in the form on p.3.Ex.1.

Step 4　Careful reading

Paragraph 1：When did ancient people celebrate?

At the end of winter; When good weather returned; a good harvest; animals caught

Paragraph 2：Festivals of the dead

1. What are festivals of the dead for?

2. How do Japanese honour their ancestors?

3. What do the people in Mexico do in memory of the dead?

4. Are there any similar festivals in China? What to do? What to eat?

The Qingming Festival

Paragraph 3：Festivals to honour people

Festivals	Country	People honoured
The Dragon Boat Festival	China	Qu Yuan, the famous ancient poet
Columbus Day	The USA	Christopher Columbus
National Festival	India	Mahatma Gandhi

Paragraph 4：Harvest Festivals

(1) Why are autumn festivals happy events?

Because people are grateful and happy and a season of agricultural work is over.

(2) What do people do to celebrate it?

In European countries, it is the custom to decorate churches and town halls with flowers and fruit; get together to have meals; win awards for their animals, flowers, fruit and vegetables; admire the moon.

Paragraph 5：Spring Festivals

Festivals	Country	What to do
The Lunar Chinese New Year	China	Eat dumplings, fish and meat; Give lucky money; Dragon dances
Carnivals	Christian countries	Parades, dancing, loud music, colourful clothing
The Cherry Blossom Festival	Japan	Enjoy the cherry tree flowers

Paragraph 6：What are the purposes of festivals?

Festivals: To have fun with each other / To let us enjoy life / To be proud of our customs/ To forget our daily life for a little while / To honour the dead / To honour famous people / To celebrate harvest/To welcome a new year and look forward to the future/To ask people to pay attention to something.

Step 5   Post reading

Do T or F

(1) The ancient people needn't worry about their food. (F)

(2) Halloween used to be a festival intended to honor the dead. (T)

(3) Qu Yuan was a great poet whom people honor a lot in China. (T)

(4) Mid-autumn Festival is held to celebrate the end of autumn. (F)

(5) Easter celebrates the birth of Jesus. (F)

(6) There is pink snow in spring in Japan. (F)

Step 6   Group work

1. Making a plan

Festivals are created. Now you've got the chance to create a new festival. Discuss in groups to make a plan, including four key points:

(1) When the festival takes place?

(2) What the festival is for?

(3) What people do at the festival?

(4) What people eat at the festival?

2. A sample

Peace Day

It takes place every year on January 2, the day after the New Year's Day. At the beginning of a new year, we create such a festival in order to call for peace, to make the world a better place for everyone. People have to learn about foreign countries on that day. The TVs and newspapers will be all about foreign countries. And people are asked to eat foreign food on that day. And they are asked to talk about peace with their families, friends, and so on.

Step 7   Homework

Write an introduction of the festival your group have created.

五、教学设计题（五）

Unit 4   Global Warming

Period 2: Pre-reading, Reading, Comprehending

Ⅰ. Teaching Goals

1. To read about global warming.

2. To get some idea about the effect of global warming.

3. To develop some basic reading skills.

II. Teaching Procedures

Step 1　Warming Up

Purpose: To arouse students' interest in learning about global warming.

1. Team work

Answer the questions below:

(1) Have you ever seen a greenhouse?

(2) How does a greenhouse work?

(3) What do you think greenhouse gases do?

2. Group work

Look at the picture, and ask students some questions.

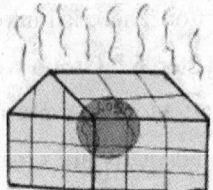

T: What is this building made of?

S1: It's made of plastic.

T: What's its purpose?

S2: Plants can grow in it when it's cold outside.

T: How does it work?

S3: The glass traps the heat from the sun, making the air warm so that plants grow better.

Step 2　Pre-reading

Purpose: To get students to learn about greenhouse gases.

1. Group work

Now look at the word "GREENHOUSE GASES". What does it mean?

Greenhouse gases (GHG) are gaseous components of the atmosphere that contribute to the greenhouse effect. The major natural greenhouse gases are water vapor, which causes about 36%~70% of the greenhouse effect on Earth (not including clouds): carbon dioxide, which causes between 9%~26%; and ozone, which causes between 3%~7%(note that it is not really possible to assert that such—and—such a gas causes a certain percentage of the GHE, because the influences of the various gases are not additive. The higher ends of the ranges quoted are for the gas alone; the lower end, for the gas counting overlaps).

Naturally occurring greenhouse gases include water vapor, carbon dioxide, methane, nitrous oxide, and ozone. Certain human activities, however, add to the levels of most of these naturally occurring gases.

Very powerful greenhouse gases that are not naturally occurring include hydrofluorocarbons (HFCs), perfluorocarbons (PFCs), and sulfur hexafluoride (SF6), which are generated in a variety of industrial processes.

Each greenhouse gas differs in its ability to absorb heat in the atmosphere. HFCs and PFCs are the most heat-absorbent.

2. Individual work

Get students to answer these questions individually. Then let them discuss the answers.

(1) Who wrote the magazine article? What is the name of the magazine?

(2) What are the names of the three scientists mentioned in the article?

(3) What do they think about global warming? Do they agree with one another?

(4) What are the two graphs about?

(5) What is the main topic of the article?

Step 3　Reading

1. Skimming

Purpose：To get a brief understanding of the text.

Read through the text, preferably the first and the last sentences of each paragraph and write the key sentence of each paragraph.

Key sentences of each paragraph:

(1) A debate over whether it is human activity that has caused the global warming or whether it is just a natural phenomenon.

(2) Many scientists believe people have caused the increase in the earth's temperature.

(3) The increased extra amount of carbon dioxide traps more heat energy causing the global temperature to go up.

(4) The levels of carbon dioxide have increased greatly over the last 100 to 150 years.

(5) There are some different attitudes towards the causes of this increase in carbon dioxide.

(6) Over the next 100 years, the amount of warming could be as low as 1 to 1.5 degrees Celsius but it could be as much as 5 degrees Celsius.

(7) An increase of five degrees would be a catastrophe.

(8) Future warming would cause the sea level to rise by several meters.

(9) Some predict any warming will be mild with few bad environmental consequences.

(10) More carbon dioxide is a positive thing.

(11) No one knows what the effects of global warming will be.

2. Scanning

Purpose：To get students to have some details in the text.

Read the article carefully. Are these statements true or false? Write a T for each true sentence and an F for each false sentence.

(1) The temperature last century didn't increase much. (　)
(2) Everyone believes that global warming is caused by the activities of humans. (　)
(3) Janice Foster believes that burning fossil fuels causes global warming. (　)
(4) Natural gas is a greenhouse gas. (　)
(5) Carbon dioxide is a byproduct of burning fossil fuels. (　)
(6) People accept Charles Keeling's data because he took accurate measurements. (　)
(7) Flooding could be one of the effects of future global warming. (　)
(8) George Hambley believes scientists are just guessing about the effects of global warming. (　)
(9) Geroge Hambley is worried about the effects of carbon dioxide on plant growth. (　)
(10) It is clear what the effects of global warming will be. (　)

Suggested Answers：
(1) F (2) F (3) T (4) F (5) T (6) T (7) T (8) T (9) F (10) F

3. Listening
Purpose： To train students listening ability.
Listen to the tape and follow it in a low voice.

4. Group work
Students are divided into four groups. Each group is supposed to read through each part and then discuss them.

Part 1 (Paragraph 1)
(1) compare 比较
● 常见用法：
① compare...with... 把……和……比较
Compared with him, I am fast.
② compare...to... 把……比作……
Life is often compared to voyage.
(2) come about 发生
How did it come about? 那事是怎么发生的？
● 常见词组：
come across 偶遇；碰到　　　　　come round 恢复知觉
come along 进展；进行　　　　　come to 涉及；到达；共计
come out 公开；问世；出版　　　come to oneself 恢复知觉
come up with 想出
(3) phenomenon *n.* 现象
It is only a social phenomenon, but not a phenomenon of nature.

Part 2（Paragraph 2,3,4）

(1) fuel *n.* 燃料

Don't leave the engine switched on. It wastes fuel.

● 拓展：fuel *v.* 加油；补给燃料

The car is being fuelled ready to try to beat the speed record.

(2) quantities of 大量

Large quantities of money have been spent on the bridge.

● 拓展：a large quantity of 大量的

He ate a large quantity of nice.

(3) per *prep.* 每；每一

The fruit costs 30 pence per kilo.

How much do you earn per week?

Part 3（Paragraph 5,6,7,8,9）

(1) data *n.* 资料；数据

We haven't got enough data.

(2) result in 导致

The accident resulted in the death of two passengers.

It resulted in success.

● 拓展：result from 由于

His illness resulted from eating bad food.

(3) catastrophe *n.* 突如其来的大灾难；大灾祸

The war was a terrible catastrophe in which many people died.

(4) climate *n.* 气候

We have a mild climate here.

(5) consequence *n.* 结果；后果；影响

As a consequence of being in hospital, Shelly decided that she wanted to become a nurse.

● 常见词组：in consequence 因此，由此

in consequence of... 由于……的缘故

(6) state *vt.* 陈述；说明

The busmen have stated that the strike will continue until general agreement is reached about pay and working conditions.

(7) range *n.* & *v.*

① 种类；范围；幅度

There is a wide range of temperature. 气温变化很大。

② *vi.* (在一定范围内)变化

The number ranges between 5 and 15.

③ *vt.* 排列,整理

Please range the goods neatly in the shop window.

Part 4（Paragraph 10）

（1）build up 逐步建立；增加；增进

We need to build up our reputation.

Traffic is building up on roads into the city.

（2）keep on 继续

Price kept on increasing.

He didn't stop running; he just kept on.

● 拓展：

keep on doing 与 keep doing 的区别：

keep on doing 表示动作反复发生；keep doing 表示状态或动作的持续。

He kept on standing up in class. 他在课堂上一再地站起来。

He kept standing there for half an hour without moving. 他一动不动地在那里站了半个小时。

Step 4　Post-reading

Purpose：To have a deep understanding of the text.

1. Group work

Now you are going to discuss the statement：We should do nothing about global warming. Follow these instructions：

（1）Get into groups of six. Decide which three in your group are going to agree with the statement.

（Group A）and which three are going to disagree with the statement（Group B）.

（2）Group A students discuss why they agree with the statement；Group B students discuss why they disagree.

（3）Groups A and B get together. They tell each other the reasons for agreeing or disagreeing with the statement.

2. Individual work

Ask students to answer the following questions. Present their opinions to other classmates.

（1）What do you think of global warming?

（2）Do you think it serious?

3. Discussion

（1）Global warming refers to an average increase in the earth's temperature, which in turn causes changes in climate.

(2) Earth's climate has been changing constantly over its 5-billion-year history.

(3) The earth could be getting warmer on its own.

(4) Scientists are sure about the greenhouse effect. They know that greenhouse gases make the Earth warmer by trapping energy in the atmosphere.

(5) Without the greenhouse effect, the earth would not be warm enough for humans to live.

(6) A warmer earth may lead to changes in rainfall patterns, a rise in sea level, and a wide range of impacts on plants, wildlife, and humans.

(7) Scientists don't know exactly what will happen in the future. But they can use special computer programs to find out how the climate may change in the years ahead.

(8) Global warming may be a big problem, but there are many little things we can do to make a difference.

Step 5　Reflective thinking

First show the following questions to students and then ask students to discuss them in groups.

1. What do you think cause global warming?

2. How does global warming affect you and others?

3. How does global warming affect the nature?

4. When do you send gases into the air, which affect the earth? (Use the air conditioner, ride in a car, and use a fridge...)

Step 6　Homework

1. Use the new words and expressions to make some sentences.

2. Try to write a short composition. The title is "How to slow climate change", beginning with "Global warming does not have to occur. It is possible for the human race to slow down global warming and maybe even remove all of the effect that people have on the climate."

六、教学设计题（六）

Unit 5　Theme Parks

Ⅰ. Aims

To help students develop their reading ability.

To help students learn about Theme parks.

Ⅱ. Procedures

Step 1　Warming up

1. Warming up by discussing

Good morning, class. Today we are going to visit theme parks. But first what do you think a theme park is? With a classmate discuss what you might do in a theme park.

(For reference: A large Christmas party is being prepared at our Theme park. Visitors will find a dancing carnival, a European wedding, military band performances, classical Christmas plays and Christmas parades in the theme park. The 108-meter-tall Eiffel Tower will be lit up during the holidays with four types of lights.)

2. Warming up by watching and listening

Hi, every one. Today we are going to visit Theme parks. Look at the screen and listen to me telling you about them.

This is the Universal's Islands of Adventure which was opened in 1999, making Universal Orlando the nation's second multi-gate theme park resort (after Walt Disney World). IOA was Universal's first non-studio theme park, and was intended to pay tribute to characters from books, comics, cartoons and legend, rather than movies.

Of course, that hasn't stopped Universal and other studios from making films about almost every character represented in IOA over the past few years, rendering the park thematically indistinguishable from its sister, Universal Studios Florida.

3. Warming up by telling experiences

Nice to see you again, boys and girls. As you all have travelled somewhere before I shall ask two of you at random to tell the class about your travel experiences.

(For reference: Visiting Disney World was a childhood dream of mine, and I was able to realise it last year. I plan to keep going back, even given the overt commercialism. It is not a place I could live in, but it definitely has magic.

One of the best parts was that I was able to interact with most of the Disney characters, even though their appearance and mannerisms varied from the Disney comic books I read. A few select pictures are included here, but my recommendation if you're taking a kid is to make sure they get some time with the characters. I can't think of anything cooler.)

Step 2　Pre-reading

1. Looking and saying

Work in pairs. Look at the photos and theme parks and predict the contents of the text. When you are ready, join another pair and compare your predictions and the clues that helped you to make the predictions.

(For reference: From the photos and title I guess that the text tells about Theme parks where you can joy yourselves and have fun with various activities...)

2. Talking and sharing

Work in groups of four. Tell your group mates what you know about theme parks. Then the group leader is to stand up and share your group idea with the class.

Boating Lake

Pedalo boats on our boating lake with views of Megafobia. Suitable for up to five people.

(For reference: As you wander down Mainstreet USA in the Magic Kingdom Park of Walt Disney World, you might stop and take a peek in the Mainstreet Theatre. Here, Steamboat Willie shows how it all began depicting the first appearance of Mickey Mouse. At this point, people usually stop for a bit, perhaps to rest from the hot Florida summer, laugh at Mickey's antics as he uses various animals as musical instruments (long before Beavis and Butthead were throwing cats in drying machines), and walk away amused and entertained. That was Walt Disney's primary goal. Today, people might consider the first cartoon featuring Mickey as art, along with a host of other creative works produced by people who work at Disney. Notable among them are Carl Barks and Don Rosa, whose works sell in the thousands. However, Walt Disney himself never thought that what he, and his employees, did was art: "I don't pretend to know anything about art. I make pictures for entertainment, and then the professors tell me what they mean.")

Step 3 Reading

1. Reading aloud to the recording

Now please listen and read aloud to the recording of the text THEME PARKS—FUN AND MORE THAN FUN. Pay attention to the pronunciation of each word and the pauses within each sentence. I will play the tape twice and you shall read aloud twice, too.

2. Reading and underlining

Next you are to read and underline all the useful expressions or collocations in the passage. Copy them to your notebook after class as homework.

Collocations from THEME PARKS—FUN AND MORE THAN FUN

> provide sb. with sth., amuse oneself, escape one's busy life for a while, share a purpose, find ways to do sth., meet one's need, sit chatting, play games, listen to birds' singing, relax a bit, have picnics, have fun, it costs some money to do sth., in recent decades, provide entertainment, use shuttles to get around, have a variety of things to see and do, charge money for doing sth., make a profit, sell souvenirs, advertisie sth. on television, have a certain idea, base sth. on sth., a sports theme park, involve sb. inphysical exercise, buy a brand of sports equipment, come to life, go for rides on animals, cook cultural foods, have pictures taken, chare admission, name sb. after sb./sth., a place of fantasy, get close to sth. /sb., take an active park in experiments, go on trips to space, use computer techniques to do sth.

3. Reading to identify the topic sentence of each paragraph

Skim the text and identify the topic sentence of each paragraph. You may find it either at the beginning, the middle or the end of the paragraph.

Waterfall

A steep shoot sends you skipping across a shallow pool of water on a single sledge. Beware, you might get wet on this ride.

(For reference:

1st paragraph: Parks provide people with a place to amuse themselves and to escape their busy lives for a while.

2nd paragraph: Many parks have been designed to provide entertainment.

3rd paragraph: Theme parks have a certain idea—a certain theme—that the whole park is based on.

4th paragraph: Some are history or culture theme parks.

5th paragraph: The oldest theme park in the world is Disneyland, built near Los Angeles, California in 1955.

6th paragraph: There are also science theme parks.)

4. Reading and transferring information

Read the text again to complete the table.

THEME PARKS —FUN AND MORE THAN FUN

1. What is a park?	2.
3. What is a theme park?	4.
5. What is a sports theme park?	6.
7. What are history or cultural theme parks?	8.
9. Facts about Disneyland.	10.
11. Facts about marine, ocean, and science theme parks.	12.

5. Reading and understanding difficult sentences

As you have read the text several times, you can surely tell which sentences are difficult to understand. Now raise your questions concerning the difficult points.

Step 4　Consolidation

1. Comprehending exercises

To end the lesson you are to do the comprehending exercises No. 1, 2 and 3 on page 34.

Do you lake a theme park? Why or why not?

(For reference: All over the world people seek stimulating experiences to take their mind away from everyday troubles, and the United States is definitely no exception to this rule. Most of its residents have the money and time to entertain themselves as it pleases them —— and visiting amusement parks certainly does please them.)

2. Defining a theme park

What is a theme park? Define it in your own words.

(For reference: How do theme parks differ from ordinary amusement parks? National Amusement Park History Association defines a theme park as "an amusement park, in which the rides, attractions, shows and buildings revolve around a central theme or group of themes. Examples include the Disney parks, the Six Flags Parks and the Paramount parks." An amusement park, according to NAPHA, is "an entertainment facility featuring rides, games, food and sometimes shows." The World of Coasters' glossary defines a theme park as "an amusement park which has one or more "themed "areas, with rides and attractions keyed to the theme of their location within the park. Disneyland, Knotts Berry Farm, and Busch Gardens Williamsburg are examples of theme parks.")

七、教学设计题（七）

Unit 2 A Pioneer For All People

Step 1   Lead-in

Listen to the tape carefully and then answer these questions.

(1) When and who did become the first agricultural pioneer in the world to grow rice that has a high output?

(2) What did Yuan Longping invent?

Step 2   Reading for details

Read the passage once again, and then decide if these sentences are true or false.

(1) Dr. Yuan is more a farmer than a scientist.

(2) Dr. Yuan's kind of rice is the most suitable for China's farmland.

(3) Dr. Yuan would rather work than relax.

(4) Dr. Yuan has dreams when he is asleep and also when he is awake.

(5) Dr. Yuan enjoys a simpler life than most rich and famous people.

Step 3   Topic sentences

Find out the topic sentences of each paragraph

Para.1: He became the first agricultural pioneer in the world to grow rice that has a high output.

Para.2: He has devoted his life to finding ways to grow more and more rice.

Para.3: He cares little about spending the money on himself and would rather keep time for his hobbies.

Para.4: Dr. Yuan's dreams.

Step 4 Yuan Longping's personal information

In pairs, read the text, find information to complete the following form.

Facts about Yuan Longping		Facts about Yuan's super hybrid rice	
age		capacity	
education		application	
major		contribution	
hobby		overseas	
ideal		future	

Step 5 Language points

1. struggle for... 为争取……而斗争; struggle against... 为反对……而斗争; struggle with... 与……争斗。

(1) The swimmer struggled against the tide.

(2) We had to struggle with/against all kinds of difficulties.

(3) The slaves struggled for the freedom.

2. search (sb. / sth.) for ... 搜查,搜索。

He searched all the rooms for the missing person.

They searched the man all over for money.

3. thanks to 由于,多亏,相当于 because of。

4. twice as large as before 是从前两倍那么多,相当于 once larger than before。

5. be satisfied with...对……感到满意,相当于 be pleased with。

adj. satisfactory/satisfying *n.* satisfaction

6. care about 在乎,在意; care for 照顾,关心。

My aunt cared for me when my parents were away last week.

Dr. Yuan never cares about money and fame.

7. Indeed, his sunburnt face and arms and his slim, strong body are like those of millions of other Chinese farmers.

e.g: The streets in Beijing are wider than those in my hometown.

The number of students in our school is larger than that in their school.

8. Dr Yuan grows what is called super hybrid rice.

e.g: He came to what is called America.

9. This special strain of rice makes it possible to produce one-third more of the crop in the same fields.

make +it +*adj./n.* +to do 使做……成为……

The fine weather makes it possible (for us) to swim.

He makes it a rule to run every morning.

其他可用这种结构的词：feel，find，think，consider...

10. Dr. Yuan awoke from his dream with the hope of producing a kind of rice（that could feed more people）.

e.g：He went to the U.S with the hope of finding a better job there.

Step 6　Dictation

To end the period you will take a dictation. It is about Yuan Longping,"Father of Super hybrid rice".

八、教学设计题（八）

Unit 1 A Student of African wildlife

Ⅰ. Teaching goals

1. Target language

（1）重点词汇

achieve, achievement, condition, welfare, institute, connection, campaign, organization, specialist, behave, behavior, worthwhile, nest, observe, observation, respect, argue, entertainment, inspire, support, devote ... to ...

（2）重点句子

Watching a family of chimps wake up is our first activity of the day. p.2

Everybody sits and waits while the animals in the group begin to wake up and move. p.2

But the evening makes it all worthwhile. p.2

... we see them go to sleep together in their nest for the night. p.2

Only after her mother came to help her for the first few months was she allowed to begin her project. p.2

For forty years Jane Goodall has been helping the rest of the world understand and respect the life of these animals. p.2

2. Ability goals

（1）Learn Warming Up, and know how to talk about the great women and the famous women.

（2）Learn the way to describe a person from what the person did, what she/he looks like and so on.

3. Learning ability goals

Teach students how to describe a person.

Ⅱ. Teaching important points

（1）By reading *A Student of African wildlife*, students can learn from Jane Goodall in at least two aspects: one is what is the humane way to study animals; the other is that it was her great personality — universal love and mercy that made her successful. If everyone had such kind of heart, they would give everything benefit for all living things. Then our world will be full of love and peace, without any war and starvation.

(2) Ask students to answer these questions:

① What made her a great success?

② What should we learn from Jane Goodall?

III. Teaching difficult points

Let everyone believe that all of us can become Jane Goodall.

IV. Teaching methods

Inspiration, Questioning and Discussion.

V. Teaching aids

A computer, a projector and a recorder.

VI. Teaching procedures

Step 1　Lead-in

T: Good morning, everyone! Haven't seen you for a long time. Did you have a good time in your holidays? What did you do during the holidays?

S1: Yes, I had a good time. You know I enjoy movies, sports and other types of entertainment. I saw several favorite films and every afternoon, I would play basketball with my friends.

S2: I would die of boredom. I didn't know what to do but read. I didn't know how to relax myself. I just hoped that the new term began. The sooner, the better.

T: That sounds interesting. In fact, boredom is a kind of feeling. There is a good way to be away from it. Believe it or not, that is to help others, no matter who they are, human being or animals. Have a try, Ok? Today we'll learn Unit 1. It introduces several women to us and tells us how they live and work. Now let's turn to Page 1. Look at these pictures and the brief introductions, then work in pairs to discuss which of these women you think is a great woman. You need to give your reasons for your choice.

Give students 3 minutes to do this task, and then ask some of them to speak out their choices. Teacher should give them some guide. For example, what is her ambition? What were the problems she met? And what are her sacrifices? After that the teacher can refer to the chart on Page 11 in the reference book. And then give them a brief summary about their discussion. A sample summary:

As great women, they don't care for themselves at all, and at some point or rather, they must give some sacrifices, just like Lin Qiaozhi, who devoted all her life to medical work for Chinese women and children and had chosen not to have a family of her own. Instead, she made sure that about 50,000 babies were safely delivered to their mothers. Not all people can do this.

Once they have chosen their careers, they would carry on with them without any withdrawal. What they did is encouraging thousands of people to continue their careers. Those who are only famous but not great can't be matched.

Step 2　Reading

There are four tasks in this step:

(1) Pre-reading to find the main idea of each paragraph

(2) Making a chart of the text structure

(3) Language points

(4) Comprehending

Task 1　Pre-reading

There are three paragraphs in the text, and each one has its main idea. These main ideas support the title A Student of African wildlife. Teacher can give students some time to read the text quickly and find these main ideas to form an overview of the text.

T: How many paragraphs are there in the text?

Ss: Three.

T: What are the main ideas of theirs?

S1: The first paragraph is about a day in Combe National Park.

S2: The second one tells us how Jane Goodall did her research and the achievement she has made in her research.

S3: The third one tells us her influence to the world.

T: OK. Can we divide the text in this way? There are four parts in the text. The first one is about a day in the park. The second one is her way of doing her research and some achievement. The third one is her attitude and feeling to the animals. And the last one is a short summary to her.

Ss: That's right.

T: Thanks. Well, let's draw a chart of the text together according to the main ideas we've found.

Task 2　Making a chart

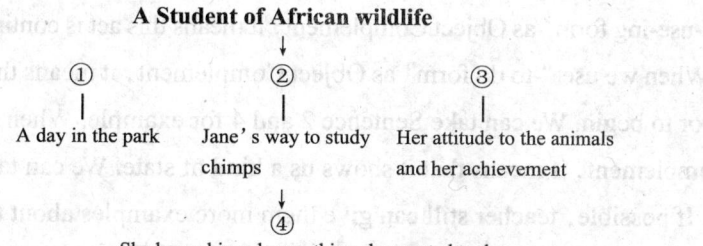

Task 3　Language Points

T: By now, we have mastered the main idea and the details. Do you have some difficulties in the language?

S1: Yes. What does this sentence mean: "Watching a family of chimps wake up is our first activity of the day"?

T: Who'd like to help her?

S2: The subject of the sentence is a "v-ing form", and the Predicate is "is" not "wake up". So the meaning of the sentence is: 今天我们的第一件事是观察一个猩猩家庭的早起。

T: That's right. Sometimes we should depend on the structure of the sentences to help us understand the meaning.

S3: Miss Wu, the sentence: "This means going back to a place where we left the chimp family sleeping in a tree the night before." is beyond me.

T: This sentence is a little difficult. First, it includes an Attributive Clause. The clause is: where we left the chimp family sleeping in a tree the night before. Second, there are two structures in the sentence. One is "to mean doing"; the other is "leave ... doing". For the first one, we can refer to the Appendices in Page 76. Now let's look at the second one. In fact, there are several same structures in this text. Please look at these sentences.

Show the sentences on the screen:

1. ... where we left the chimp family sleeping in a tree the night before.
2. ... we see them go to sleep together in their nest for the night.
3. But the evening makes it all worthwhile.
4. ... was she allowed to begin her project.
5. ... Jane Goodall has been helping the rest of the world understand and respect the life of these animals.

T: Now look at the boldface(黑体字). All the structures of the Predicates are Verb + Object + Object Complement. Let's translate these sentences to taste the meaning and usage of Object Complement.

Ask some of the students to translate these sentences. Give them some explanations: When we "V-use-ing form" as Object Complement, it means this act is continuing. For example, Sentence 1. When we use "-to do form" as Object Complement, it means this process of the act has finished or to begin. We can take Sentence 2 and 4 for example. When we use an objective as Object Complement, it means that it shows us a kind of state. We can take sentence 3 and 5 for example. If possible, teacher still can give them more examples about this structure.

(*I heard the teacher call my name.*)

(*I will let you know the result of the voting as soon as possible.*)

(*We watch the children diving into the water from the top diving board.*)

(*Let's go; let him alone.*)

S4: Miss Wu, I find this sentence a bit strange: Only after her mother came to help her for the first few months was she allowed to begin her project.

T: Yeah, this sentence uses the structure of inversion. The sign is that only phrase is placed at the beginning of the sentence. We will learn it later. Now it is ok that you know the meaning of the sentence. Any questions?

Ss: No.

Task 4   Comprehending

T: Do you still have any questions? No? Ok, let's finish next task. Read the text again and try to finish Exercise 1&2 in page 3 as quickly as you can.

Give students some time to do this. After that, check the answers with the whole class.

Step 3   Discussion

When we are guiding students to read something, besides hoping that they can learn some basic knowledge the material shows, we still hope they can learn something that can reflect the spirit of human being. This is the most important thing a teacher should show to students.

Ask students to work in groups of four and discuss the following questions:

1. What made her a great success?
2. What should we learn from Jane Goodall?

T: I think, there is not a single person who doesn't admire success. But what is the way to succeed? Now we have read Jane Goodall, can you make sure what made her a great success, and what we should learn from her? Please discuss these two questions, and then some of you will report your opinions to all the class.

Give students some time to discuss.

T: Boys and girls, have you finished your discussion? How about your group?

G1: We think that there are two points that made her successful. One is her way to study chimps, and the other is her true love to the animals. The first one is easy, because it is only a way. Everyone can do it. But for the second one, it is more easily said than done. As a woman, she gave up everything, went to the forest to study the chimps and devoted all her love to these animals. It is really not easy. What we cannot understand is that how she has such great personality.

T: These are very interesting questions. As far as I know, it is her relief that raised her personality. Everything is equal, no matter what they are. It isn't because we are human being that we are superior to the other living thing. We don't have any right to control other living thing. We all live on the same planet; they are our brothers or sisters. The only difference is that we have different shapes and have different wisdom. If you have the same love to the things around you, you can turn to be her. OK, how about the second question?

G2: At first, we admire her for her wisdom and courage to give up her chance to go to university and went to Africa to begin her own research. This makes us think over what we should think when we are choosing our majors or a university. Secondly, most of us think that man is the master of the world, because he is the most intelligent animal on the earth. So he can decide every thing he thinks right, including doing some experiments on animals, in spite of their pains. Jane not only saw this, but also tried her best to help them and argued for them to be left in the wild and not used for entertainment or advertisements. What she said in the text is very moving. It shows her deeply love to the animals. We should learn this from her. In fact, there is so much we should learn from her, her consideration, her hard work and so on.

Step 4　Listening

Let students listen to the reading material, follow and repeat it, paying attention to the new words and expressions, as well as the sentence structures they have learned just now.

Step 5　Homework

T: I'm very glad to hear what you said. You have learned what you should learn from Jane Goodall. And I believe you will be Jane Goodall, if you treat everything around you equally and show your love to them. Now time is up. Today's homework is to finish the exercises on Page 4 and 5. Make some preparations for the next class. See you next time.

Ss: See you.

九、教学设计题（九）

Unit 2　Healthy eating
Reading: Come and Eat Here (1)

I. Teaching aims

1. Students will be able to develop their reading ability and use some reading strategies such as guessing, skimming and so on.

2. Students will be able to realize the importance of having a healthy diet.

3. Students will be able to grasp some useful words and expressions in this passage.

II. Teaching important and difficult points

1. Understand the text well.

2. Master the useful new words & expressions in this period.

III. Teaching procedures

Step 1　Revision

1. What kind of food do we eat?

| meat   vegetable   seafood   fruit   snacks   staple food (主食) |

2. Give the names of Chinese fast food & Western food to students.

3. What substance do we get from each kind of food?

(sugar, protein, fat, fibre, vitamin, minerals, etc.)

Step 2   Discussion

Discuss and finish the exercise: which food contains more...?

Which food contains more...?	Examples of foods	Answer
sugar	chocolate or grapes	
	cakes or bananas	
fat	cream or rice	
	chocolate or chicken	
fiber	peas or nuts	
	pork or cabbage	
protein	potato crisp or ham	
	eggs or cream	

Step 3   Lead in

Show a pyramid of food to the students.

T: As we know, a healthy diet is very important to us. If we don't have the right diet in our daily life, there will be something wrong with us sooner or later. Now, let's read a story related to the diet.

Come & eat here

Where? What?

Step 4   Skimming

1. Reading strategies

(1) Make a guess according to the title "Come and eat here" before reading.

①Where are you invited to go?

②What foods are you offered there?

(Collect some ideas from the class and put some of them on the Bb.)

(2) Read fast to prove your guess. Get the students to read the whole story fast to prove whether their guess is right. Then ask the following questions to finish the table:

Qs: Where are you invited to go?

Whose restaurant?

What foods are offered there?

Do these foods make a healthy diet? Why not?

What problems may these foods cause to customers?

Restaurants	Foods offered	Problems with these foods
Wang Peng's	mutton kebabs, roast, pork, fried rice, cola, ice cream	not enough fibre food
Yong Hui's	fruit, water, raw vegetables	not enough energy food

2. Give the students 2 minutes to summarize the main idea of the story with the help of the above table, using 2 or 3 sentences.

(Wang Peng found out why he had lost his customer and decided to win them back.)

Step 5 Careful reading

1. Divide the whole passage into three parts, and give the general idea of each part.

Part 1	Part 2	Part 3
Wang Peng felt frustrated because he found his customers had come to other places to eat.	Wang Peng found the reason why YongHui's restaurant was more attractive.	Wang Peng thought out a good idea to have a competition with YongHui's restaurant.

2. Read for details.

T: The story is mainly about two persons, that is, Wang Peng and Yong Hui.

Q: Who is the main character in the story? (Wang Peng) Now let's read the story again to get more about him.

(1) Get the students to read the story carefully to make a list of places where he stayed & went and his feelings in these places.

(2) Ask some questions to help the students have a better understanding of the story.

Qs: What did Wang Peng feel when he was in his own restaurant? Why did he do so? Did his friend enter his restaurant as usual? Where did he go instead? Did Peng go there too? What made him do so? What did he feel in Yong Hui's restaurant? Why? Where did he go after he left Yong Hui's restaurant? Why did he go there? What did he feel after doing the research? Why? In this way, the competition between them was on!

Step 6 Post reading

T: Now, it's the time for us to read the text carefully and decide which sentences are true. Then correct the false ones. First, read the sentences.

1. Usually Wang Peng's restaurant was full of people.

2. He provided a balanced diet in his menu.

3. Yong Hui served a balanced diet.

4. Yong Hui could make people thin in two weeks by giving them a good diet.

5. Wang Peng's customers often became fat after eating in his restaurant.

6. Yong Hui's menu gave them energy foods.

7. Wang Peng's menu gave them foods containing fiber.

8. Wang Peng admired Yong Hui's restaurant when he saw the menu.

9. Wang Peng decided to copy Yong Hui's menu.

Step 7　Discussion

1. Get the students to discuss in pairs.

Who will win the competition at last? Give your reasons.

(Neither will, because neither of them provide their customers with a healthy diet. Foods in Wang Peng's makes people fat while foods in Yong Hui's makes people tired easily.)

2. Please think of a way to help them put an end to their competition. (cooperation)

3. Work in groups of four to design a sign for the cooperatedly—opened restaurant.

Step 8　Summary

Wang Peng felt __1__ in an empty restaurant because no eaters have came to his restaurant __2__ since he got up early in the morning. He wanted to find out why. He hurried out and __3__ Lichang into a newly—opened restaurant. He found that the owner __4__ Yong Hui was serving slimming foods to make people thin. Driven by __5__, Wang Peng came __6__ to take a close look at the menu. He could not even __7__ his eyes. He was __8__ at what he saw. He hurried outside and got __9__ to do some __10__. After a lot of reading, he __11__ that Yong Hui's food made people become __12__ quickly because it was no __13__ food. Arriving home Wang Peng rewrote his own sign. To his joy, people began coming to his restaurant again. He was able to __14__ his living now. He looked __15__ to being rich and he wouldn't be in __16__ any longer. Then all of a sudden Yong Hui walked in with anger. Wang Peng asked her to try a meal of his. Although enjoying the dumplings served there, Yong Hui looked ill and felt sick with the fatty pork and all those heavy food. They __17__ about offering a __18__ diet and providing a balanced menu to cut down the fat and increase the __19__ in the meal. They learned from each other. In the end they decided to turn the two restaurants into a big one. They got __20__ and lived happily ever after!

Key: 1.frustrated　2.ever　3.followed　4.named　5.curiosity　6.forward　7.believe

8.amazed　9.online　10.research　11.realized　12.tired　13.energy-giving

14.earn　15.forward　16.debt　17.chatted　18.balanced　19.fibre　20.married

Homework:

Read the story aloud and find out some beautiful sentences.

Comprehension questions

1. Why did Wang Peng go to Yong Hui's restaurant? He wanted to _____.

   A. know where his customers had gone   B. spy on the slim lady Yong Hui

   C. have lunch with Li chang   D. have something special

2. Wang Peng found the following EXCEPT _____ in Yong Hui's restaurant.

   A. There were only raw vegetables, meat and water

   B. There were a lot of customers

   C. The prices here were higher

   D. The only drink here is water

3. What's wrong with Yong Hui's menu? The following statements are right EXCEPT _____.

   A. The food here was too limited   B. It didn't give enough energy—giving food

   C. The food on the menu was more delicious   D. It offered slimming food only

4. Which of the following is TRUE according to the passage?

   A. Wang Peng's customers often became fat after eating in his restaurant.

   B. Wang Peng provided a balanced diet.

   C. Yong Hui could make people thin in 2 weeks by giving them a good diet.

   D. Wang Peng's menu gave people food containing enough fibre.

   （Key：1. A　2. A　3. C　4. A）

十、教学设计题（十）

Unit 3　A Taste of English humor

Ⅰ. Teaching aims

Knowledge aim：

1. Learn something about Charlie Chaplin.

2. Useful words and phrases.

Ability aim：

1. Develop the ability of finding information through different reading skills.

2. Enable students to retell the text, or at least write a summary.

Emotion aim：

Enjoy humor to be relaxed and happy.

Ⅱ. Teaching key points

Read the passage to learn about Charlie Chaplin and to finish the reading tasks by using different reading skills.

Ⅲ. Teaching difficult points

Develop reading ability to gather useful information.

IV. Teaching procedure

Step 1　Lead-in

Present the following sentences on the screen. Ask students to read and translate them.

(1) He was born in Hong Kong, known as an outstanding actor and director.

(2) He is full of sense of humor, and his performance makes people laugh.

(3) He creates many classic roles, like Wei Xiaobao, Sun Wukong, etc.

(4) You may be familiar with his movie called "A Chinese Odyssey"(大话西游之月光宝盒).

　　Questions: 1. Do you know this man? Who is he?

　　　　　　　2. What do you think of his performance? Is it humorous?

Step 2　Pre-reading

Prepare a short video about Charlie Chaplin's film, which lasts about 2-3 minutes. And discuss:

1. What is the type of his performance? Do you think it is interesting?

2. What do you know about Charlie Chaplin?

Step 3　Reading

1. Fast reading

Ask students to skim the passage silently for 3-4 minutes and then finish the reading exercises. Complete the basic information about Charlie Chaplin on page 19.

Suggested answers

Born	1889
Job	actor
Famous character	Little tramp
Costume	large trousers; worn—out shoes; small round black hat and a walking stick
Type of acting	mime
Died	1977

2. Intensive reading

Encourage students to read the passage carefully to get further understanding.

(1) True or False

A. Charlie had a happy childhood. (　)

B. Charlie's most famous character, a little tramp was a social success and very popular. (　)

C. Charlie usually made a sad situation entertaining. (　)

D. Nobody has been able to do this better than Charlie Chaplin. (　　)

Suggested answers: F, F, T, T.

(2) Match the main idea with each paragraph.

Paragraph 1 (　　) Paragraph 2 (　　) Paragraph3 (　　) Paragraph 4 (　　) Paragraph 5 (　　)

A. What Charlie's childhood was like?

B. An example of a sad situation that he made funny.

C. Why people needed cheering up?

D. His achievements.

E. What his most famous character was like?

Suggested answers: C, A, E, B, D.

3. Post-reading

Have students work in pairs to complete the summary of this passage, using the words from the text.

Chaplin made people laugh at a time when they felt depressed, so they could feel more content with their lives. He was popular with all over the world for his particular form of humorous acting. The little tramp became known throughout the world. He played the main character who was poor and homeless, and wore large trousers, worn-out shoes and a small round black hat, and carried a walking stick.

The character was a social failure, but he won the love of audience for his determination in overcoming difficulties and being kind to others.

In his films *The Gold Rush*, Chaplin successfully made a sad situation entertaining by eating a boiled shoe.

As an everlasting(永远的) humor master, Charlie Chaplin will always be remembered by us.

Step 4　Consolidation

1. Close books to recall the typical image of Charlie Chaplin.

2. Work in groups and try to retell the text to each other, according to the written summary.

Step 5　Discussion

Please discuss what you can learn from his words.

"To truly laugh, you must be able to take your pain, and play with it."

Step 6　Homework

1. Review the words and phrases, and prepare for the dictation.

2. Surf the internet to find more information about Chaplin.

模块四　英语学科教学实施能力

参考答案(略)

仿真试题一

一、语言知识与能力

(一)单项选择题

1. B　2. D　3. C　4. B　5. A　6. B　7. B　8. A　9. A　10. C　11. A　12. B
13. A　14. D　15. A　16. C　17. A　18. C　19. B　20. A　21. A　22. B
23. C　24. D

(二)阅读理解

1. D　2. D　3. B

二、语言教学知识与能力

(一)单项选择题

1. C　2. C　3. A　4. A　5. C　6. C　7. C　8. A　9. D　10. A

(二)简答题

1. wait (v.)"等候","等待"。指某事发生之前停留在原地,不采取行动。通常此词作为不及物动词而和 for 连用。await (v.)"等候","期待"。书面语。特指对于断定必来的人或事的不断的期待。

　前句:你等我多久了?

　后句:我们正焦急地等候你的回复。

2. wither (v.)"枯萎","凋谢"。指因无活力而失去生气。fade (v.)"凋谢","褪色"。多指颜色的逐渐消失,有时也作"暗淡"讲。

　前句:花凋谢了。

　后句:那块小蓝地毯经过多年已褪色了。

3. fierce (adj.)"凶暴的"。指易怒的和有凶暴脾气的人或动物。savage (adj.)"野蛮的","残酷的"。表示不开化,或缺乏感情的控制力。

　前句:凶恶的匪徒从山上下来。

　后句:我从未见过如此粗暴无礼的举止。

4. waste (n.)"废物"。普通用语。指任何被遗弃的东西。rubbish (n.)"垃圾,废物"。指体积较小、破碎的、没有用的废物,和可收集起来进行处理的弃物,间或指愚蠢无用的话语和思想。

　前句:必须阻止工业废物污染河流。

　后句:这些垃圾必须扔掉。

5. stride (v.)"走"。指大步行走,并且步伐均匀。stroll (v.)"走"。指为了消遣而慢慢地步行。

前句：士兵们正昂然阔步而行。

后句：一大群人在复活节游行时走过第五街。

（三）简要回答下列问题

1.（1）学生疲倦了，需要来点儿唱歌之类的活动振奋一下；（2）学生都遇到困难，需要改变教学内容或活动方法；（3）学生缺乏活动的语言材料，需要帮助解决。

2.（1）音标、字母和音节教学；（2）重音教学；（3）语调教学；（4）节奏教学；（5）连读。

3.（1）面谈；（2）学习周记；（3）学习档案；（4）测试；（5）节目汇演。

4.（1）教一种语言项目，同时介绍学习该项目的方法；（2）随着教学的进展介绍英语学习的特殊方法，如记词方法，听音方法；（3）介绍同班优生的学习方法。

5.课程资源划分为校内资源、校外资源和网络化资源。校内资源，主要包括本校教师、学生、学校图书馆、实验室、专用教室、动植物标本、矿物标本、教学挂图、模型、录像片、投影片、幻灯片、电影片、录音带、VCD、电脑软件、教科书、参考书、练习册，以及其他各类教学设施和实践基地等；校外资源，主要指公共图书馆、博物馆、展览馆、科技馆、家长、校外学科专家、上级教研部门、大学设施、研究机构、有关政府部门、其他学校的设施、学术团体、野外、工厂、农村、商场、企业、公司、科技活动中心、少年宫、社区组织、电视、广播、报纸杂志等广泛的社会资源及丰富的自然资源；网络化资源主要指多媒体化、网络化、交互化的以网络技术为载体开发的校内外资源。

三、教学设计

Reading　　　　　　　My First Work Assignment

—"unforgettable", says new journalist

Ⅰ. Teaching aims

To improve the students' reading ability.

Ⅱ. Teaching important points

Know what is needed to become a journalist and how to conduct an interview

Ⅲ. Teaching procedure

Step 1　Leading in

1. Where can we get information?

2. Who make the news?

Step 2　Fast reading

1. Read the text in 2 minutes, and find out how many questions Zhou Yang asked.

2. Divide the text into three sections according to the duties of a journalist.

Section 1: what you should do when covering a story

Section 2: a case where journalists were accused

Section 3: to work with colleagues

3. What does the reading passage mainly talk about?

　　A. The qualities needed to become a good reporter.

　　B. The skills to become a professional photographer.

　　C. How to have a good interview.

　　D. Being carefully in the new environment.

Step 3　Detailed reading

A. Choose the best answer

1. When can a new journalist cover a story by himself?

　　A. Never can a new journalist cover a story by himself.

　　B. Only after he has seen what an experienced reporter does.

　　C. Not until he is old enough.

　　D. Only when he takes a camera with him.

2. The footballer was thought to be guilty because _____.

　　A. he usually told lies

　　B. he stopped the reporter publishing an article

　　C. he took money for deliberately not scoring in order to let the other team win

　　D. he bribed another football team

B. True or False

1. Zhou took a course of photography at mid-school. (　　)

2. While interviewing, the journalist would just ask the questions prepared before hand. (　　)

3. The footballer admitted he took the money. (　　)

4. Zhou Yang is very eager to cover a story. (　　)

C. Fill in the blanks with proper words

1. What a new journalist should do on the first day?

　(1) The first time he will be sent with an _____.

　(2) There is no need for him to take a _____ with him. He will have a professional _____ with him to take photographs.

2. What does a journalist need to remember when going out to cover a story?

　(1) He needs to be _____.

　(2) A good journalist must have a "_____" for a story.

　(3) He has to listen for the _____.

　(4) If necessary, he can prepare a _____ to make sure that he gets all the facts straight.

D. Translate the following sentences

1. What do I need to remember when I go out to cover a story? (to report on an important event)

2. A good journalist must have a good "nose" for a story. (be able to tell whether is a true story)

3. This is a trick of the trade. (clever ways known to experts)

4. We sometimes use small recorders to make sure that we get all your facts straight. (to present ideas fairly)

5. Have you ever had a case where someone accused your journalists of getting the wrong end of the stick? (not to understand properly)

Step 4 Consolidation

Summary of the text

To the journalists, it's _____ for them to take a camera because they have _____ with them. The journalists should be _____ and they must have a _____ for a story. They know how to _____ the information they need. While interviewing, they won't _____, they won't talk too much, and they listen to the interviewee carefully. They will listen to the _____ facts and ask new questions. There is a trick of the _____, that is, with the permission of the interviewer, they would use _____ which could keep the evidence to help _____ their story.

Step 5 Group discussion

What qualities does a good news journalist or a photographer need to have?

1. Adjectives to describe a journalist

2. Adjectives to describe a photographer

Step 6 Homework

Please write a short passage after class: What is the main difference between a journalist and a photographer?

四、教学实施与评价

教学情景分析题（答案略）

仿真试题二

一、语言知识与能力

(一)单项选择题

1. B 2. C 3. D 4. D 5. A 6. D 7. A 8. B 9. A 10. B 11. C 12. D 13. C 14. B 15. A 16. A 17. B 18. A 19. A 20. C 21. D 22. B 23. B 24. C

(二)阅读理解

1. A 2. D 3. C

二、语言教学知识与能力

(一)单项选择题

1. C 2. C 3. B 4. A 5. A 6. D 7. C 8. B 9. B 10. A

(二)简答题

1. oral (*adj.*) "口语的"。指口头表达和交流。spoken (*adj.*) "口语的"。指口语表达和交流,此时与 oral 一词无区别,但 spoken 可以构成复合形容词,表示以一种特定方式讲话。

前句:你考了口试,是吗?

后句:这个词用于口语。

2. scenery (*n.*) "景色","外景"。指一个地方乃至一个国家的整个外景或外貌。scene (*n.*) "景色"。可与 view 通用,但都包括了其中的人及其活动。

前句:火车穿过干线两侧风景单调乏味的地区,缓缓地向南驶去。

后句:港中的船只构成美丽的景色。

3. sway (*v.*) "摇动","摆动"。指有弹力的东西被压弯后又恢复原位的摆动。swing (*v.*) "摇动","摆动"。指任何一头固定而另一头活动的动作,也泛指不正规的动作。

前句:树枝迎风摇晃。

后句:钟摆停止了摆动。

4. vest (*n.*) "背心","马甲"。美国用语。waistcoat (*n.*) "背心","马甲"。英国用语。也用于英国的商业。

前句:他脱下上衣,露出一件鲜红的马甲。

后句:一件淡蓝色马甲的袖子只垂到了她的臂弯处。

5. vertical (*adj.*) "直立的"。指与水平面垂直或大致垂直。upright (*adj.*) "直立的"。指与一平面大致垂直,强调非倾斜性。可用于比喻。

前句:请注意,这是一条垂直线。

后句:他是一位品格端正的公民。

(三)简要回答下列问题

1. 可以改变目前教学中仍然存在的知识传授比重较大、语言实践不足甚至单纯讲授语言知识的现状,有利于新课程标准的实施。

2. 教师素质的内容主要有职业道德、学科知识、文化素养、教学能力、协同共事能力、元认知能力。

3. 任何国家进行外语教学的目的都是为了通过与外国、外民族互相沟通和相互交流而促进本国的发展,其出发点自然是本国的需要;而满足发展的基本力量又是本国文化。

4. 学习策略中学生因素包括年龄因素、性别因素、外语水平、学生观念和情感因素。

5.影响交际策略的因素是什么？

影响交际策略的因素是语言水平、个性、学习环境和任务的难易度。

三、教学设计

Unit 3 Life in the future
The First Period-Reading

Content：

Students' Book：Warming up and Reading.

Ⅰ. **Teaching aims**

1. Ability aim

（1）Enable students to talk about their life at present.

　　Look back to the life in the past.

　　Predict the life in the future.

（2）Understand the text and try to find out what life in the future is like.

（3）Understand the details about the text and make a comparison among life in the past, life at present and life in the future.

2. Language aim

Important words and phrases: take up; constantly; remind; lack of; lost sight of; sweep up; catch sight of

Ⅱ. **Teaching important points**

1. Compare life in the past, life at present and life in the future.

2. What is life in the future like? What changes will take place?

Ⅲ. **Teaching method**

1. Fast and careful reading.

2. Asking-and-answering activity to check students' understanding.

3. Individual, pair or group work to finish each task.

4. Discussion.

Ⅳ. **Teaching aids**

A computer, a projector

Ⅴ. **Teaching procedures**

Step 1 Warming up

1. Lead in the topic

Start the lesson by listening to a song "whatever will be will be". Ask students about their predictions about future.

2. Set a scene for the students

Imagine you are working for a tour firm. Your company organize a special trip to transport people to the past and transport people in the past to your city. Ask students to organize the trip, and think of something which are representative of that age to introduce to those travelers.

3. Do a life style investigation

Compare life in the past and life at present, let students have some impression about the changes.

Step 2　Pre-reading

1. Get the students to discuss about the problems that human beings are facing today. (such as pollution, all kinds of shortages.)

2. Make a prediction about the future. Which problems may be solved, and which will still be there. This part will prepare the students for the text.

Step 3　Reading

1. Get the students to read the text quickly and get the general idea. Give students a few minutes and then ask them to rearrange the correct order of some of the sentences picked out from the text.

2. Ask students to scan the first two paragraphs quickly to get some basic knowledge of the travel, and then check their understanding by asking some comprehending questions.

3. Give students a few minutes to go through the third paragraph and to think over the questions. Get some details on the environment in the future. Encourage them to find out the reasons for the terrible environment.

4. Get students to read the forth and fifth paragraphs and find out something about both transportation and daily life in the future. Try to retell the daily life in Wang Ping's house.

5. Get students to close their books and try to review what they had read by judging some true or false questions.

Step 4　Follow up activity

Get students to compare life at present and life in the future. Find out the changes on several items. Try to distinguish which changes are good and which are not good.

四、教学实施与评价

教学情景分析题(答案略)

参考文献

1. 全日制义务教育普通高级中学英语课程标准(实验稿),中华人民共和国教育部制订.
2. 王德春.现代语言学研究.福建人民出版社,1983.
3. 文秋芳.英语学习策略论.上海外语教育出版社,1999.
4. 韩刚.英语教师学科教学知识的建构.上海外语教育出版社,2011.
5. 黎奇主编.新课程背景下的有效课堂教学策略.首都师范大学出版社,2006.